COMMODORE VANDERBILT:
AN EPIC OF AMERICAN ACHIEVEMENT

ARTHUR D. HOWDEN SMITH

COSIMO CLASSICS
NEW YORK

Commodore Vanderbilt: An Epic of American Achievement
© 2005 Cosimo, Inc.

All rights reserved. No part of this book may be used or reproduced in any manner whatsoever without prior written permission except in the case of brief quotations embodied in critical articles or reviews.
For information, address:

Cosimo, P.O. Box 416
Old Chelsea Station
New York, NY 10113-0416

or visit our website at:
www.cosimobooks.com

Commodore Vanderbilt: An Epic of American Achievement originally published by Robert M. McBride & Company in 1927.

Library of Congress Cataloging-in-Publication Data
A catalog record for this book is available from the Library of Congress

Cover design by www.wiselephant.com

ISBN: 1-59605-642-8

Cornelius Vanderbilt

CONTENTS

ILLUSTRATIONS

COMMODORE VANDERBILT

Commodore Vanderbilt

—————— ❧ ——————

BOOK ONE

PHEBE HAND'S BOY

I

SOMETIME after the year 1650 a family of poor Dutch farmers named van der Bilt emigrated from Holland to the colony of New Netherlands. They were so obscure, so unimportant, that in the annals of the little settlements clinging precariously to the banks of the Hudson there is no record of their individual names or of how many of them embarked upon the bluff-bowed trading-ship of the Dutch West India Company. They — perhaps it should be he — are figures misty and visionary, as lacking in authenticity as the remote ancestors who bred us in those dim centuries when a welter of races were groping toward a civilization which should supplant stone with bronze. Why did they come? What complex of social or economic forces tore them from surroundings which must have been familiar for generations? Was it hunger for new scenes, for a freer life? Or a failure so drastic as to demand a fresh start in the wilderness beyond the Atlantic?

Certainly, Dutchmen who left their native land in the period when William II was Stadtholder could not complain of hard times or lack of opportunity. The specter of war was seldom absent, it is true, war with England, war with Spain, war with France, war with Sweden; but the United Provinces were at the height of their power. Throughout the Thirty Years' War they had prospered as *entrepreneurs* to the combatants, and by the Peace of Westphalia in 1648 their independence was finally and definitely recognized by the leading nations of Europe. Their navy conquered Spain's, humbled Sweden's, swept the flag of France from the Narrow Seas and held its own against England's. The Dutch merchant marine of 10,000 sail, manned by 168,000 seamen, transported cargoes annually valued at a billion francs, and were become, in the words of a contemporary French author, "wagoners of all the seas." The Dutch East India Company reigned supreme at the Cape of Good Hope, in Ceylon, upon the coasts of Malabar and Coromandel, in Java, in the Moluccas; it controlled the trade with China and Japan. And in North and South America the companion West India Company was competing not unfavorably with Spain and Portugal, France and Britain. A ceaseless flow of commerce enriched the Dutch cities, stimulating a national prosperity which reached all classes, so that the people lived upon a scale of comfort beyond any other's. They had, for the times, a remarkably democratic government, with liberty of conscience and political tolerance.

Nowhere in the world was life kinder to the masses. But apparently the van der Bilts were dissatisfied with their lot, sufficiently so to accept the terms of emigration the Dutch West India Company proffered with scant success to a population that has never readily adapted itself to alien conditions. Perhaps they were a family whose farm was ruined when the sluices in the dykes were opened to defeat the French invasion, and who lacked the patience to reclaim their wasted fields. Perhaps they were intelligent enough to perceive the limited term of their country's greatness, for soon, all too soon, the prey of civil confusion and ground between the ponderous bulks of France and Britain, the United Provinces should lapse into a mere pawn on the chessboard of Continental politics.

At any rate, and whatever the cause, these first shadowy van der Bilts had the courage to dare the unknown. We catch the earliest glimpse of them in 1685, when one Aert Jansen van der Bilt was recorded as holding a large part of the village of Flatbush on Long Island under a patent from Governor Dongan. It is possible that Aert was the original settler, although more likely that his father, Jan, or an uncle had preceded him. Aris van der Bilt, a relative of Aert, perhaps a brother, also was settled in Flatbush by this date, and had married a woman named Hilitje — patronymic unknown. So far, it is evident, the van der Bilts had prospered in the new world. They were of some consequence in the forest-bound community on Long Island, and in addition to their Flatbush holdings Aris owned a considerable tract of land on "Staaten" Island, which he seems to have traded from the Indians. It is reported that one of them was an elder in the church, and that the other presented the edifice with "a fine bell imported from Holland."

If they and their children were gifted with imagination, which they almost certainly were not, they may have dreamed of rising in time to a parity with the patroon families that lorded it over vast estates, proudly aloof behind a barrier of manorial rights and feudal privileges. There was no reason why they should not have done so had they possessed the requisite ability and ambition; New Netherlands had become New York, and economic freedom had supplanted the hard, narrow policy of the Dutch West India Company. With English rule, too, had come a broadening of men's outlook, a restless vigor in place of the stolidity of the Dutch régime. But the van der Bilts were peasants, honest, sturdy, hard-working peasants, who, after a first flash of energy, lapsed into the plodding pace their stock had kept from time immemorial. Not for a century and a half — and then only after an admixture of more volatile blood — would they be able to break the invisible bonds that yoked them to the earth that was at once their mainstay and their mistress.

Of course, they may have been satisfied with their lot, those earlier generations. It is more likely than not. Farmers, and occasionally fishermen, they lived always on the edge of want, yet they reared tremendous families, paid their bills, avoided quarrels and wrought their just share in the task of wrenching a homeland from the wilderness. Wholly uninspired, scarcely intelligent, they seem to have possessed a dour continuity of purpose, a steadfastness, which gave promise of what their strain might achieve when vision was grafted upon its tenacity. A strange study in heredity.

It is with Aris and Hilitje and their progeny that we are concerned. They had numerous children, one of them Jacob, born January 25, 1692. This Jacob married, in 1715, a woman named Neilje (Eleanor) — again the bride's family name is missing. To start the young couple off Aris deeded to Jacob his land on Staten Island in the neighborhood of New Dorp; and in the course of the next thirty years Jacob and Neilje had eleven children, and cleared a good farm in the forest's midst. They were almost alone when they first moved to their new home, but a number of Moravian refugees presently settled in the vicinity, and the van der Bilts became converts to the beliefs of this sect. In 1741 the celebrated Count Zinzendorf, recently banished from Saxony, visited the New Dorp community, and kindled such a flame of enthusiasm that this handful of struggling farmers and fishermen resolved to build a ship in which members of the United Brethren might emigrate from Germany. It was built, too, Jacob and his sons doing their full share on the ways, and launched May 29, 1748. During the next nine years it crossed the Atlantic to Amsterdam and back twelve times, ceasing its ferry service only when it was wrecked by a French privateer in 1757. But so many emigrants had been added to the New Dorp community that in 1762 Jacob's seventh son, Cornelius — the first appearance of this name in the family — joined with others in petitioning the central authority of the Brethren at Bethlehem, in Pennsylvania, for permission to erect a meeting-house. The cornerstone was laid on July 7, 1763, and again the van der Bilts contributed the labor of their hands to enhance the glory of their faith.

Jacob's fourth son, born January 6, 1723, bore the same name. Jacob II married Mary Sprague, an event which is interesting chiefly because it represents the first introduction of alien blood, English, probably. However, the Sprague strain added nothing to the dominant van der Bilt qualities, which leads one to suspect that the Spragues were much the same sort of people as the van der Bilts, stolid, industrious tillers of the soil. The only thing to be remarked about Mary is that she produced the smallest number of children, seven, of any of the Vanderbilt wives, from the time of Aris to the Commodore, a period which covers parts of three centuries and more than two hundred years. They were a prolific race.

Of the children of Jacob II and Mary, the youngest, born August 28, 1764, was named Cornelius, undoubtedly after his uncle, mentioned previously, who was also a seventh son. Poor, young Cornelius grew to manhood in the drear, pinched days of the Revolution, which is possibly an explanation of the character he developed. To tell the truth, the family were due for hard times. In the century that had elapsed since Jacob I and Neilje moved to Staten Island to clear a farm in the forest, generation after generation had been bred upon its scanty acres; lot after lot had been whittled away for one son or daughter after another. What had been a fine miniature estate was now a patchwork of odds and ends, no unit of it sufficient to support a family comfortably.

Once in a while a daughter married herself into better circumstances, and every now and then a son struck off for himself. An uncle of Cornelius II kept the Rose and Crown Tavern at Stapleton, Staten Island, which was a great hangout for British officers

THE NARROWS FROM STATEN ISLAND IN 1837. NOTE THE SOLITARY STEAM VESSEL PUTTING OUT FROM THE QUAY IN THE RIGHT NEAR DISTANCE

during the Revolution. There may have been a petty tradesman here and there among the family's offshoots. But taken as a whole, the Vander Bilts — for so they began to spell their name, now — were a miserable set of farmers, fishermen and laborers, noses close to the grindstone and the clods never shaken off their boots — when they could afford boots. I cannot find that they played any part in the Revolutionary struggle, and as a family, I suspect they were rather Royalist than Patriot, which is not surprising, considering that they were always under British control, and that their poverty must have compelled them to trim their course in order to live.

Certainly, young Cornelius, who was sixteen years old in 1780, mature as many a lad in the ranks of Washington's Continentals, was not inspired to slip by the British patrols at South Amboy, and "'list for a sojer." He began earning his living, instead, by running market produce from his father's and other farms across the Bay to New York for the Royal garrison. There was in him, as in all his family, including his famous son, a marked lack of that spirit of impersonal adventure which leads men to sacrifice comfort and safety for an ideal. They were not interested in what they could not understand.

II

ONE DAY in November, 1783, New York harbor was white with the sails of British transports, winging toward the Narrows. The next morning the waters stretched empty from shore to shore; only a handful of periaugers, as the local craft were called, were beating up to the little town on the tip of Manhattan Island. Probably Cornelius II was at the tiller of one of these vessels, intent, like the other boatmen, on discovering the effect of evacuation upon their traffic in foodstuffs. If he was, he must have returned home sorely disheartened. New York was stagnant, its commerce at a standstill. For seven years it had lived on the British Army; its shipping, necessarily, had been under the British flag; twice in the interval it had been ravaged by disastrous fires. Now, it was dead, gutted economically; thousands of Royalists had fled with Sir Henry Clinton; the few hundred soldiers of the garrison Washington introduced were a poor market compared to the luxurious messes of the British officers.

But the spirit of the citizens was undaunted. Gradually, through that dreary winter, exiled patriot families returned to their old homes. Business revived; American shipping reappeared; and with the growth of trade came a demand for transportation. Cornelius, put to it for a means of support, commenced to operate a sporadic ferry service with his periauger between Stapleton, on the Staten Island shore, and Whitehall Landing, alongside the Battery, the first regular service of this kind the harbor had known. But he was not a youth of any self-reliance or initiative. It made him uneasy to be dependent upon the ferry traffic, which was dormant during the winter months when the harbor was choked with ice, often completely frozen over. So he invested the money he saved in a piece of farmland at Port Richmond, and endeavored, in a half-hearted way, to drive two enterprises simultaneously — with the results to be expected from one who was neither thrifty nor forehanded, however industrious he might be.

Nonetheless his move to Port Richmond was the cornerstone of whatever success he attained in after-life, for at Port Richmond he met Phebe Hand. Phebe (so the family spelled her name) was a sturdy, buxom girl, product of a strata of colonial society several pegs above the Vander Bilts. She was born at Rahway, New Jersey, daughter of prosperous farmer folk, moderately well-educated for the time. One of her uncles was Major-general Edward Hand, Adjutant-General of the Continental Army during the Revolution, who, as a Colonel, had commanded a rifle regiment with distinction at the battle of Long Island. There was good blood in Phebe; her people were used to thinking for themselves; they were willing to fight and die for something so intangible as the right not to be taxed without representation. Phebe, herself, had been left a competence by her maternal grandfather, and the proceeds of this had been invested in Continental bonds. Why? Because sentiment guided the Hands in such matters. The Vander Bilts, in the same situation, would have bought lands or houses or an interest in a vessel — and they would have had something to show for the investment. Rosy-cheeked Phebe had nothing but a wad of worthless script. But the Hands were just as willing to work as the Vander Bilts. Phebe found employment as what we would call a mother's-helper in the family of a clergyman at Port Richmond. So she met young Cornelius.

This young Cornelius — of whom we shall soon be thinking as old Cornelius — must have been a handsome devil, if he was anything like his children. Big, fair, open-faced. Strong, physically, but without much vitality. Rather credulous, almost childlike, willing to believe what anyone told him. Well-intentioned, but usually in difficulty.

Phebe was an altogether different kind of creature. The one picture I have been able to find reveals her as an old woman. It is a mighty strong face, a square, massive face, with heavy folds of flesh, a straight mouth a trifle drawn down at the corners, and eyes that seem to glint humorously from under thick brows. The forehead is high, the nose well-formed. You'll see shrewdness in that face, determination, kindliness. It's a face anyone would stop to look back at, noting it in a crowd. That old woman had *lived*. She had done a job. She had known every degree of hardship; she had suffered, yes, and triumphed, and neither been warped nor spoiled. But the funny thing about it is that nobody would remember her today if it were not for one of the nine children she bore. All the achievements of her indomitable will go for nothing; her single excuse for being is that son — as, I suspect, she, herself, would be glad to admit, proud to admit.

When young Cornelius came acourting her there was more of fun than wisdom in her features; her lips curved in laughter; her eyes shone with the exuberant joy of youth. She had never heard of such a thing as a steamboat, and she would have fled in terror, sensible as she was, if she had seen a locomotive. How she would have jeered if somebody had told her she was to sail up the Hudson in vessels that threshed their way with paddle-wheels and ride on land in stage-coaches that clanked on rails. Ah, but would she have jeered if prescience had foretold it should be her son who would help to establish these marvels as daily factors in the country's life? She came to believe that son capable of any accomplishment; he was her "Corneel." Even when she trudged about her household tasks, starry-eyed, big with the imponderable elements of life and destiny, she sensed that this was no ordinary burden. How she exulted over him, fiercely, savagely, then and in years to come, she who was to walk nine times this road of pain.

I imagine she married her Cornelius as much out of pity for his gangling awkwardness and footless ways as because he had a handsome face and honest blue eyes. Then again the Port Richmond clergyman's house was no bed of roses for a young girl who was both self-reliant and ambitious. She wanted to be her own mistress; she was that type of being. It irked her to be subject to another will. Better poverty under her own roof than a safe corner in a stranger's house. Better the labor of child-bearing and child-rearing, if the children were her own, than tending the stranger's child. Perhaps she saw a chance to mold her Cornelius anew. But I think not, for the face of the old woman who was laughing Phebe Hand shows no trace of disappointment or regret, whatever else it may contain. Perhaps, after all, she loved her Cornelius.

At any rate, they were married early in the year 1787. They could afford no honeymoon, so they must have walked direct from the home of the clergyman, Phebe's protector, to the tiny house on Cornelius's farm in Port Richmond. I wonder what they talked about. The Constitutional Convention, and whether General Washington would be King, and when would a shilling be worth face-value? No, I expect Cornelius told her how much grain the chickens needed, and to be careful the black sow didn't roll on her litter, and that Betsy cow, she milks mortal skittish. And she? Well, she clung to his arm, and gave a little skip every few steps, and then tried to be dignified, and ended by looking up at him sidewise, so that he stopped his lecture and squeezed her hand. It was a cold day, with the snow level and white, and a sparkle of ice in the ruts of the road. They were awfully happy, happier than they should ever be again, poor dears. As a couple, they were to know little save the sheer drudgery of existence.

Those were the days of imprisonment for debt, and the fear of jail, or, at best, servitude within prescribed limits for the benefit of the creditor, was a recurring nightmare to every poor man. It can seldom have relaxed its grip upon Phebe's husband, and since he was honest as well as poor it must have plagued him more than the generality. Without her he would scarcely have escaped the actual terrors of committal. For, as I have indicated, he combined an inability to concentrate upon any one object with a singular flair for unfortunate speculations. Every likely tale convinced him. If he did succeed in collecting a walletful of shin-plasters he must entrust them to the first Tom, Dick or Harry who buttonholed him on the Ferry Road. That is, if Phebe did not chance to catch him first. In time, she learned his failings, and made it a point to be handy if money was to be paid him in any considerable amount. He surrendered it to her, meekly enough, protesting, perhaps, that he might have a tenth interest in one of them ferry-lots that was to kite for Jericho come spring. Whereat Phebe would laugh shortly, and peck a kiss at his stubbly chin. What's a ferry-lot when thar's bills due? No, no, my man, this goes into the clock whar we kin find it come need.

A remarkable receptacle, that clock of Phebe's. Every shilling she earned herself or could wring from the sparse acres of the farm or save from her improvident husband's fingers she tucked away behind its swinging pendulum, then locked the door and hid the key in a corner she alone was privy to. She was the planner of the family, was Phebe. She stood between her growing brood and want, not once, but time and again. No matter how dark the prospect, she never faltered, never yielded hope. If Cornelius was out of work in winter, the bay frozen on top of a bad harvest, she patched their means together by hook or crook, did odd jobs, herself, baked, scrubbed — and when it was necessary, dug up the key to the clock and carefully counted out shin-plasters to keep the family from starvation. Once Cornelius came home in utter despair. He was dead-beat, there was a mortgage due on the farm, and he hadn't a cent to meet it — I got my comeuppance, Feeb. Git the children, and we'll share 'em 'round with the fam'ly. Phebe laughed in his face. How much you want, Corny? He sank by the hearth with a groan. Three thousand dollars! And thar ain't nobody kin help me out. She laughed again, sternly, the mirth of the warrior who has not fought in vain. I guess thar is, then, she told him. And she fished out the key to the clock, opened its gayly-painted door and rummaged beneath the pendulum. Count 'em, she bade her amazed spouse. If three thousand's what you need, thar's three thousand, Corny. And mind you don't lose a shillin' of it goin' up to Squire's.

Such was the mother of the Commodore, a woman of a great heart, high-spirited, as heroic in her sphere as any soldier who ever entered battle. A fighter who would not quail, who scorned to count odds; but who was never too proud to think ahead to avoid unnecessary perils.

III

PHEBE HAND's fourth child, and second son, was born on May 27, 1794. For some unknown reason they named him Cornelius, after his father and greatuncle. He was a lusty brat, and from infancy was notable for his stature, his wilfulness and his readiness to think for himself and go his own gait. When he was six years old he nearly foundered a farm-nag in a race with a negro boy two years older who did as well for a neighbor's horse. Needless to say, Cornelius won. At this early age he was adept at all sports and games, could swim, row or sail a boat, wrestle and use tools with proficiency. He gave every evidence of possessing a good mind, but he had no use for school. Rather than attend his lessons he would volunteer to work — although, being perfectly normal, he preferred to play.

In build, as he grew on toward adolescence, he was like his father, big-bodied, rangy, tow-headed, blue-eyed. Superficially, a Dutchman. In features, as in character, however, he showed his mother's blood. He had her nose, her humorous glint of the eyes, her sweep of brow, her square chin and jaw; and what saw him through the struggles of life was the mingling of determination and foresight she bequeathed him. They had been no more than that in her; in her son they amounted to vision. Surging yeastily in his soul, they made of him a seer. Not, in any sense, a dreamer, of course. No, that he never was. But one of those amazing folk who are gifted with an extra sense, enabling them to comprehend the demands of the future. Able, too, to plan far ahead, to advance slowly, step by step, regardless of the turmoil of the present, toward a goal unseen of ordinary eyes beyond the horizon.

I am not pretending that such metaphysical qualities were evident in the tousle-headed, bare-legged bantling who cursed and scuffed his way to leadership amongst the ragamuffins of Port Richmond, but the traces of them were there in embryo. Even then, just breeched, he was beginning to outthink opponents, and particularly, his parents. He evaded going to school more often than not, as I said, by his wily offer to work. And when he had to work he was a genius at suggesting to other boys reasons why they should help him, long, long years before Tom Sawyer was born. He could meet an emergency with an adroitness seldom found in an adult. By the time he was ten his father permitted him to make trips in the periauger, sitting very square and self-reliant in the stern, hand on tiller, eye on main-sheet. Hi, thar, Corneel, the other boatmen would hail, ye better watch out. Thar's sharks off'n Robin's Reef. Aw, go to hell, Cornelius would reply. A pithy lad in his speech. In after years, the street urchins of New York would wait hours on the curb for him to pass, just on the chance of picking up a new cuss-word.

Some years prior to his winning independence of school the family were crowded out of the Port Richmond house. There were too many boys and girls to find beds for. So they went to live in a magnificent residence of five rooms on the Stapleton shore, close by the present location of the Quarantine Station. Phebe Hand's constant vigilance had had some effect upon their fortunes, but the principal cause of increased prosperity must have been the waxing usefulness of the older children. Young Cornelius, for instance, had been supporting himself practically by odd jobs ever since he was six; and if the others were not quite as capable as he, still, they were healthy, husky young animals, and had a mother who knew how to compel the best from them.

They all worked hard. Frequently they had no leisure for play. A generation later, young Cornelius — in his turn, become old Cornelius — used to tell a story of one of his rare "holidays," promised him as a reward for diligence in hoeing potatoes. He and his chum, Owen, were to have the periauger the following Tuesday, and sail up to New York for a good time. But when Tuesday morning came, and Cornelius and his friend went down to the beach they found the elder Vander Bilt pitching hay into the periauger's open hull.

"Now, look sharp, Corneel," quoth his father, "here's the periauger for ye. I've done pitched in more'n half the hay. You'n Owen kin pitch the rest. Take her up the Bay, and unload at Whitehall same as usual. You kin play on the way — both ways, goin' and comin'! And here's sixpence for ye, Bub."

Somehow it didn't seem exactly like a treat to the two boys. The Commodore always chuckled when he recited the incident, but he was wont to add slyly:

"A boy kin git fun out of 'most anything, and Owen and me got some fun out of that — but we was jest as tired that night as if we'd been workin'."

Responsibility seemed to fall naturally to his portion. When he was eleven his elder brother died, leaving him chief lieutenant of his parents, and childhood was definitely behind him. From that day he did a man's work, did it creditably, and throve on it, physically and mentally. Naturally, school was out of the question; education, for him, concluded with very partial mastery of the simplest elements of the three R's. He could write an awkward scrawl; read a printed page, if the words were not too long; figure ordinary sums in business. But of the fundamentals of economics, history or geography he was as ignorant as a black slave in the South Carolina rice-swamps, let alone that he had no cultural foundation at all. He wasn't interested in story-books, either. Why should he have been? He was living as romantic a story as any novelist could invent, and that sufficed for him. First and last, I expect, he was naïvely wrapped up in himself, in what he was doing, hoped to do, had done. A spontaneous egotist. It was always impossible for him to explain his success. All he knew was that he succeeded because he did certain things which occurred to him. It was a question of instinct, rugged natural intelligence reacting to the promptings of the spiritual force that was born of his father's pertinacity and stubborn courage and his mother's gift of foresight and initiative. But it was mostly his mother; the electric energy of her character made the sluggish Dutch blood sparkle in his veins, prompted him to a resourceful daring his father regarded with uneasy distrust. He was Phebe Hand's boy. And he, himself, was first to admit it when he was of an age to comprehend the significance of his beginnings.

It goes without saying that he was a source of bewilderment and vexation to his father. Helpful he might be, worthy of confidence; but the dissimilarity between the two made for mutual annoyance. It was Phebe who bridged the gap, who reconciled slow-thinking father and inarticulate son. She was vaguely proud of Corneel, a little disturbed, also. What could she make of a twelve-year-old, who cursed and labored like any grown man, whose mind pounced to decisions with tigerish suddenness, who was small boy for one fleeting moment, then treated his parents with the condescension of age? Did she see in him those qualities which raised her uncle, the General, to distinction? For there was more Hand than Vanderbilt in young Cornelius. The flame that burned in him, flaring brighter in every draft of adversity, was the flame that had nerved a handful of Pennsylvania Rifles to withstand the shock of Cornwallis's grenadiers.

There was, for instance, the occasion in his thirteenth year when his father, unusually aggressive, took a contract to lighter the cargo out of a vessel stranded near Sandy Hook, and transport it to New York. The elder Cornelius was engaged on another job — the lightering enterprise had fallen to him unexpectedly — and was obliged to confide execution of the contract to Corneel as an alternative to splitting the profits with an outsider. But if he had misgivings, the boy had none. The difficulties and responsibilities were meat and drink to Corneel, and he swaggered about his task with a brawny efficiency that wrung admiration from the workmen his father hired. The leettle devil, they exclaimed to each other. Will ye hark to him cuss — and the milk ain't dry on his lips!

He bossed a small fleet of lighters and their crews, and three wagons, with teams and drivers, to haul the unladen cargo from the surf-line across the sand-spit to the lighters lying in the Lower Bay. Which meant that he had to oversee the actual landing of the cargo, its packing in the wagons and final stowage in the lighters; he had to see to the lodging of his workmen, procure shelter for his teams, and provide food for man and beast. Perhaps it was as much by luck as by good management that he accomplished this feat without mishap. The surf was low, and the cargo from the wreck came rapidly and safely ashore; the men were so delighted with him that they put their backs into the work as they never would have done for his father.

He was tired, but very happy, when he started for home, appreciative, too, of the help the teamsters had given him, and at the first wayside tavern in Jersey he stopped to buy the best dinner the house afforded for his hungry men and bait the horses. All the money remaining in his pockets went for this purpose, and it was not until he reached South Amboy that he realized he had no cash to pay the ferry tolls over the Kill. But he wasn't at a loss. Swinging down from his seat, he strode confidently up to the ferryman.

"Say, Mister," he said. "I want to git to Staten Island with my teams. How much is it?"

"'Be six dollars, Bub," answered the ferryman.

"I ain't got it with me," Corneel remarked carelessly. "Tell ye what, if ye'll put us acrosst I'll leave one of my hosses with ye, and if I don't send ye the money in two days ye kin sell him."

The ferryman agreed to the proposition, and Corneel

took his teams home, rather more self-satisfied, if the truth be known, his vanity warmed by the rough compliments of the teamsters — Never seed such a lad! Lift the hide off'n a bull without it knowed it. Hi-yi, he could talk money out of the ground.

But his father piped a different tune.

"Why, ye dratted fool, s'pose something happened to that hoss? S'pose something happened so's I couldn't find the money? S'pose — I never heard of such a fool boy. Pawnin' a hoss for grub! Here, you git six dollars from your Ma, and fetch home that hoss 'fore it's stole."

"The men had to eat," growled Corneel. "We was tuckered out, and the hosses was dead-beat, too."

"Well, ye could wait a mite longer, I guess. That was ferry-money, not eatin'-money."

"I'm goin' to git ye the damned hoss, ain't I?" snarled Corneel. "And 'tain't my fault. Ye'd oughter have give me enough for eatin' and ferry. I can't think of everything."

And so on, until Phebe intervened.

"Shoo! Now, thar ain't no use to say any more, Pa. Corneel, you hush up. Hsssh, I tell ye! Thar's no blame to the boy; the drivers 'ud never work for us ag'in if we didn't take keer of 'em. And you, Corneel, you show a little respect for your Pa. It'd make any man crazy, thinkin' of losin' a hoss in times like these. Not a word out of the pair of you! And come morning Corneel can trapse back to Amboy, but thar's no sense in his goin' tonight, and him worn to his bones. Draw up; supper's hot."

It was inevitable that father and son should not pull together; and as Corneel grew older the tension between them was aggravated. It irked the boy, with his ready wit and bold self-reliance, to be curbed by his father's plodding spirit. He was a better man than his father, and he knew it. He passed early out of adolescence, and at fifteen was a strong, wiry youth, combative, horny-handed, amazingly sure of himself, respecting no one but his mother. In the circumstances it wasn't surprising that he succumbed to the universal lure of healthy youth, and decided to run away to sea. Every day he saw the ships sailing by, cloudy specters in the twilight, brave pyramids of gleaming canvas when the sun shone and the choppy waves of the harbor rippled under sharp cutwaters or smashed asunder beneath the bluff bows of dingy coasters. The romance, the glory, the beauty of the spectacle never stirred his consciousness; but the suggestion of adventure, of perils to be countered and emergencies to be met, roused in him a fierce hunger for change. Out there, beyond the Narrows, stretched pastures greener than any he had ever known. He would lie in the grass in idle hours, and watch the procession flit past Quarantine, muttering to himself the identity of each craft:

"A Limey — bet she took hell; look at the salt on them bulwarks. Cripes, thar's a Portugee. Mebbe she's a slaver. That Yankee bark, she was bound for the Gold Coast last fall. Gawd, wouldn't I like for to be on that Injyman — looks like a man-o'-war with all them guns — bet she'd give a pirate the bellyache."

He'd curse softly, venomously; then rise up and purge his resentment in a beating administered to one of his fellows.

St. Paul's Church and Broadway in 1831, showing that traffic presented its problems even in the early 19th century

"Damn ye, didn't I tell ye not to come sneakin' 'round here ag'in? Git down thar, and unsnake that fishin'-tackle. Git! Or I'll hammer the guts out of ye."

Yes, he would run away. He knew just how he would do it. Some morning at dawn he would slip up to Quarantine, and row out to the first likely craft that appeared. A sober boy would be snatched at by any skipper starting a long cruise. He rehearsed the scene many times. What you want, boy? Whar ye bound, Mister? Naples, but what's that to you? Thought ye might have room for a hand. Shore! Ketch this rope, younker; you kin begin sluicin' that pack of drunken wharf-rats we call a crew.

Corneel must have had some imagination, hidden deep down in what nowadays we call the subconscious, for he derived a distinct thrill from recapitulation of such a scene. Afterward, he supposed, there would be fights, bloody, devastating fights, kicking and gouging, knife-work, perhaps. He'd show 'em. . . . There'd be a storm, and one of the mates would be washed overboard, and he'd take the wheel . . . Or maybe it would be a mutiny. He'd stand in front of the gray-haired captain, and batter down the miscreants with a broken oar. . . . And he'd come home a mate. He could hear the captain shouting as they tacked into the Narrows — Catch her up, Mister. That'll do. Easy, there. Slack off, Mister. Guess we better take in them stuns'ls.

Yes, he'd run away. That was all there was to it. He was sick of working for somebody else. The old man was no good, anyhow. Always grumblin', and fussin', and never sure for two months what he wanted to do.

Pack of silly gals clutterin' up the house, mewin' and squeekin'. Babbies howlin' for pap. He was sick of it, he was. He'd run away, and git to be a sailor.

Somewhere about this stage in his deliberations he thought of his mother. He saw Phebe, her last baby — and it was to be the last, too — only two months old, going cheerfully, sunnily, from one household task to another, an ear to half a dozen demands upon her time and patience, seldom out of temper, always helpful, and, rigorously impartial as she was, yet revealing continually that soft corner in her heart reserved for her oldest son. He could hear her voice, now — Corneel, take off them wet boots. Here's a mess of warm porridge. One of you gals find him dry socks. Did you git that money from Crawford, son? Your Pa was dependin' on it. I declare, now! I jest don't know what we'd do without you, Corneel.

No, he decided regretfully, he couldn't run away unbeknownst to her. He never reasoned this out in his mind. He had no clear perception why he shouldn't do it. He didn't know the meaning of the word chivalry, and it would not have entered his head to kiss the stout, ruddy-cheeked person he called Ma, unless she insisted upon it — and then he would have blushed, and sworn to himself. But all the same there was a confessed obligation to her. And to himself. It was the submission to duty which had come to him with the Hand strain, the same instinct that sent old Edward Hand into battle at the head of his Rifles, and moved Phebe's family to sink their savings in Continental bonds.

So he went, and bared his heart to her.

"I'm goin' to sea, Ma."

"You, Corneel? Why, you ain't but a child."

"I'm risin' sixteen, and I nigh got my growth," he asserted doggedly.

"Heavenly days!" She surveyed him brightly. "What'll your Pa say?"

"I don't give a da— I don't keer what he says. I've worked enough for him."

She weighed the bitterness in his glance, and sighed. Not easy for her, to have bred an eagle in this bovine family.

"But it's a terrible life at sea," she argued. "I know you don't have an easy time, son, but it might be harder. Sailors git knocked around awful. You don't git proper food to eat, and it's cold and wet —"

"I don't keer," he interrupted, more sullenly than ever. "I'm tired workin' for somebody else. Pa, he never gives me a chance. He don't know he's alive. He's that slow —"

"You can't miscall your Pa to me, Corneel." Her tone was stern, if kindly. "And you hadn't ought to be selfish. We're a big fam'ly, and you the only boy that kin help. Whar'd I be, without you? Your Pa, he does his best, but what with the babbies, and the gals' clothes, and debts, we don't never seem to keep more'n a step or two from the almshouse."

"Well, what's the use of my stayin' here?" he persisted sullenly. "Pa won't give me a free hand. All I kin do is what he'll let me. And it's like I said, he don't never know from one month to the next what he wants to do hisself."

Over in the corner of the kitchen the youngest baby,

another Phebe, whimpered hungrily; and Phebe Hand walked slowly to the cradle, stooped, crooning softly, lifted the tiny thing and offered her breast.

"Thar, now! Thar, easy, honey, easy. Ain't you the greedy poppet?" And to her son, as she settled herself in a chair:

"Corneel, I jest won't have you go, not with my leave and goodwill. I need you, son."

Her voice was placid, but it throbbed with undertones that prickled the corners of Corneel's hard, young eyes.

"That's easy for you to say," he answered, scuffling his feet. "But I tell you thar ain't no use in my stayin'. I'll never git anywhar with Pa. He never gits anywhar hisself, and he'll fix me the same way."

She said nothing for an interval, her attention apparently concentrated on the baby she nursed.

"What'd you like for to do?" she asked suddenly. "If you don't go to sea?"

He was taken aback for an instant, but his answer was prompt and assured.

"Aw, Ma, if I had a boat of my own I could make more'n Pa right now. Thar's good money in the harbor, and I kin find it."

"Honest money?" she inquired, her eyes intent on his face. "None of this smugglin' from furrin ships?"

"Sure, honest," he assented, with a trace of eagerness. "I'd make reg'lar trips daytimes, and nights, in fine weather, I'd run parties over that wanted to see the sights on the Battery. Pa, he ain't run reg'lar for years, and I jest know I could make me a heap of money, 'soon as folks knowed I was dependable. That's what counts, Ma. You got to make folks believe you'll allus run. If they kin depend on you, they'll deal with you."

"But you ain't got the money for a boat, son," she reminded him.

"N-no," he stammered. "But — but if somebody was to lend it to me, I'd pay it back, Ma. And I could give ye a sight more help 'n I do now. Honest, I could."

She patted the child in her arms, and lowered it gently into the cradle.

"How much would a boat cost?" she asked, crossing to his side.

"I know a dandy periauger over at Port Richmond you kin buy for a hundred dollars. It'd hold twenty passengers."

The eagerness was now outspoken in his face. She smiled drily, pride battling with scepticism in her mood.

"A hundred dollars is a lot of money for a boy who ain't sixteen. And I've got to speak to your Pa fust, Corneel."

She glanced at her redoubtable clock, ticking away portentously upon the mantel-shelf over the fireplace.

"But you will?" he prompted her. "You will speak to him, Ma. Ma, if you help me git that periauger, I'll make you a thousand dollars a year. Honest, I will!"

There was more scepticism than pride in her answering smile.

"Shucks, if you paid back the money that'd be a heap, son. But you run along. I'll talk to you tomorrow after I see what your Pa thinks."

She did talk to the elder Cornelius that evening, but

I suspect it was a matter of form. Wise Phebe already had made up her own mind, and that was all that was necessary. It was foolish to try to clip an eaglet's wings. If he would fly, fly he must — or perish, broken-hearted by constraint. And Phebe was convinced that her eaglet, given opportunity, would develop lusty pinions, even if she had no conception of the heights to which he should soar.

In the morning she called him to her.

"I talked to your Pa," she announced, "and we're agreed you kin have the hundred dollars, if you'll earn it."

"Sure, I will," he burst in. "I'll work —"

"Wait till I finish, son," she counseled. "Maybe you won't feel so brash."

His face fell.

"Why, I kin —"

"Kin you plough the eight-acre lot over to Port Richmond?" she interrupted. "Kin you plough it betwixt now and your birthday?"

A black shadow of gloom settled upon him. The eight-acre lot! It was so stony that it had never been planted. And today was May 1, 1810. His birthday was the twenty-seventh, a day short of four weeks distant. Twenty-seven days in which to clear and plough eight acres! But, as always when he encountered opposition, his determination was strengthened. His fists tightened belligerently.

"Sure, I'll git it cleared and ploughed," he declared. "You wait —"

"And planted," Phebe amended. "Your Pa wants it planted to corn."

He swore under his breath.

"I'll git it planted," he rasped. "I'll show you and Pa ye ain't as smart as ye think ye be."

A quizzical light twinkled in his mother's eyes.

"I don't know as I'd like that, Corneel," she returned.

That morning he tore through the neighboring district, rounding up cronies.

"Want to go sailin' whenever ye like?" he demanded of each. "All right. I kin buy a periauger for myself, if I plough and plant our eight-acre lot over to Port Richmond. Give me a hand, and I'll remember ye when I git her."

Labor was volunteered enthusiastically. None of the boys could boast his own boat, and it struck them all as highly desirable that there should be one available in the crowd. They looked forward to a long summer of moonlight sails and fishing-parties; and Corneel, listening to their excited jabbering as they rooted out stones and weeds, and harrowed and ploughed, was aware of an occasional desire for laughter. His assistants were the first flock of sheep to come under his sheers, and he enjoyed the situation. For he had no intention whatsoever of dedicating his summer to loafing. What he had promised he intended to perform; anyone who helped him could ride free in his boat. But as to abandoning it to the pursuit of pleasure — No chance! He was going to pursue dollars.

The field was planted the day before his birthday, and he limped into the kitchen at Stapleton, lame and sore and stiff in every limb; but prouder than he was ever to be again in the eighty-three years he lived.

"Well, Ma, your field's sowed," he said.

She crossed over to the clock on the mantelpiece, and unlocked the door of her safe. Perhaps there was a suspicion of moisture in her eyes as she counted out a little heap of soiled notes and silver.

"I kind of thought you'd win, Corneel," she answered. "But it don't never hurt to have to work for what you want. You ain't so likely to lose it, then."

His arms went around her swiftly.

"You ain't goin' to be sorry, Ma," he mumbled. "No, I won't wait for supper. Goin' right down to Port Richmond, and git me that periauger 'fore someone else comes along after her."

The following morning, the morning of his sixteenth birthday, he was at the ferry-landing at Stapleton, ready for passengers. It was a glorious, keen May morning, a breeze snapping over the bay and ruffling the whitecaps. His heart was glad and proud. He had his own boat; he was his own master. He grinned delightedly at the exclamations from the folk at the landing — Hi, thar's Corneel in his new boat! Say, Corneel, whar'd ye steal her? Hey, Vander Bilt, what ye got thar, a Liverpool packet? And a chorus of juvenile outcries. Hey, Corneel! Oh, Neeley, ain't we goin' fishin'?

Fishing! He sneered at the idea.

"I'm takin' passengers and freight for Whitehall Landin'," he said coldly. "Eighteen cents one way, and a shillin' if ye come back."

Sixty years afterward he told how he felt that morning.

"I didn't git nigh the satisfaction out of the two

millions I made in the Harlem corner as I got out of steppin' into my own periauger, h'istin' my own sail and puttin' my hand onto my own tiller. Yes, sirree, that was the biggest day I ever had."

For that matter, it was the biggest day in Phebe Hand's life. She felt strangely at peace, her cares and worries assuaged, as she stood in the doorway of her cottage, and watched Corneel's periauger dart out from the ferry-landing and square away for the distant huddle of roofs that was New York.

BOOK TWO

THE FERRYMAN

I

NEW YORK was a sprawling country town, with pleasant, tree-lined streets, and green grass-plots, its two- and three-story houses clustered beneath the spires of Trinity and St. Paul's, when young Cornelius Vanderbilt — Van Derbilt he wrote himself, instead of Vander Bilt, the style of his father's generation — started his ferry service between Staten Island and Whitehall Landing at the end of May, 1810. In the years since the Revolution it had overtaken and passed Philadelphia and Boston in point of population, but it was still a long way from being the country's metropolis, and should not attain that proud eminence until after the Erie Canal was opened, and the traffic of the West began to pour overland to its factories and docks.

Broadway was built up only as far as Grand Street, which was not yet in existence; most of the buildings were below Fulton Street; above the City Hall were fields and pasture-lands. The East and North Rivers were much wider than they are now; Water Street, Front Street, South Street and West Street were to be won from the turbid waters by a protracted process of filling-in. The center of business was in Hanover Square and lower Pearl Street, although the residences of the citizens were sprinkled indiscriminately in every district — for example, Philip Hone, the diarist, lived in Cortlandt Street, and De Witt Clinton in Cherry Street. Broad Street was lined with old Dutch houses, their gable-ends to the sidewalk. The Collect Pond, a ten-acre lake, covered the site of the Tombs Prison and the Criminal Courts Building and stretched downtown as far as the present approaches to the Brooklyn Bridge. What is now Canal Street was a brook rippling between huckleberry fields into the Hudson.

Life was simple and unostentatious. Of diversions outside the home there were next to none. Dinnerparties, rather than dances and card-games, were the accepted form of private entertainment. Militia reviews and musters provided the opportunities for young men which sports do today. Champagne was just commencing to be drunk by a few persons of radical tendencies, but port and Madeira were the accepted wines of a gentleman; whiskey and rum were the tipple of the poorer classes, used only for punches in good society. That common vegetable, the tomato, was entirely unknown; ice was a rare luxury; and strawberries, popularized by William Sykes of the Bank Coffeehouse in William Street, were coming to be regarded as a proper fruit for breakfast and dinner, where formerly they had been served only at tea. The fashionable hostelry was the City Hotel. There wasn't such a thing as a club or a gambling-house, and the one restaurant was a shop in William Street, kept by a negro named Billy, to which merchants resorted for coffee and cakes in the evening. The most prosperous newspaper was *The Mercantile*, with a daily circulation of 2,500.

Essentially, the city, in those days, was an English county-town, with all the social prejudices and formalities of the eighteenth century superimposed upon the economic snobbery of a community of successful merchants. I said above that life was simple and unostentatious, but don't mistake me. In a strictly social sense, it was highly complicated. There was a vast gulf between the well-to-do and the poor, a direct inheritance from the class-feeling which had persisted in the midst of all the clamor over equality before and during the Revolution. And this is the more perplexing because there were then no slums, such as unrestricted immigration was to smear from the Five Points to Harlem. The population was fairly homogeneous, almost entirely English-speaking; even the Dutch families, like the Vanderbilts, had assimilated the language and point of view of their surroundings — as was not the case amongst the Dutch in the upper part of the State for some years to come.

There was a mellow dignity, a high-flown courtesy, overspreading the city's daily life, which brought out in violent contrast the crude violence of young Vanderbilt's character. At sixteen he had elaborated the tactics he practiced to the day of his death. He was honest in his dealings with all men; he would go to any extent to make good his word; he tried to set a fair price on his services. But he was absolutely unconciliatory; he didn't care what people thought about him. He said whatever came into his mind, and if a customer didn't like cussing that customer might deal elsewhere. He wasn't interested in social graces. He saw no point in speaking softly. He didn't want anyone's favor. And if he didn't like what was said or done to him he burst out with picturesque vigor.

"What ye kickin' about?" he'd snap at the merchant who remonstrated over some incivility. "I done what ye hired me to, didn't I? Well, what the hell's it to ye how I talk? I don't give a —" variously-assorted epithets — "what ye say, yourself. A man's tongue's his'n, I figger."

Of course, he had to be fearless and skilful to succeed with such methods. He was also willing to work harder than any competitor; and he would drive himself to exhaustion to make the swiftest trip. Once, when his periauger was becalmed in Buttermilk Channel, between Governors Island and Brooklyn, a rival boatman started to pull ahead. Cornelius took his pole, and thrust the clumsy craft along through the shallow water, putting every ounce of strength he possessed into the effort. Jake Van Deuzen, the other boatman, was older and heavier than he, but Vanderbilt reached the Brooklyn shore ahead. The passengers, who laughed and applauded him as they scrambled onto the wharf, never knew that he accepted their congratulations so grimly because the butt of the huge pole had pierced his chest to the bone. The scar was on him when he died.

Savage, curt, uncouth as he was, there is something very appealing in the earnestness with which he tackled work the moment he was his own master. Every morning, when the New York-bound passengers appeared at the Stapleton landing, they found his periauger waiting, his lean, broad-shouldered bulk squatting in the stern. In a few months his boyish features became slightly worn. Little grooves ran from the corners of his mouth to his nostrils; his frosty, blue eyes, which had a disturbingly non-committal stare, were enmeshed in puckering wrinkles. He seldom had sufficient sleep, for, if the weather was fair, after he had completed his regular schedule, he would embark a boatload of young revelers who wanted to stroll arm-in-arm in the moonlight behind the row of mossy cannon on the Battery and become hilarious on glasses of flip in the parlor of Fraunces' Tavern.

"Come along, Corneel," they'd invite him, stepping ashore, Jacks and Jills, carefree and turbulent enough to draw irate letters from Pro Bono Publico and Anxious Parent in next day's *Evening Post*.

"Got to git a snooze," he'd answer shortly, and curl up on the stern thwarts.

Strictly speaking, he had no youth. He never learned how to play. And while he was in the habit of asserting that he "hadn't no time for sich fooleries," it is impossible not to feel that any youngster as sane as he was, as chock-full of animal spirits, would have enjoyed a sally or two up the primrose path had the opportunity come to him.

But he had his reward. At the end of his first year as a ferryman he tramped up from the shore to the low-roofed house on the Ferry Road, kicked the mud off his boots, and stamped into the kitchen, where his mother was cooking supper. Phebe Hand was tired; it had been a long day, with children crawling under her feet and a querulous husband to humor. But she managed a bright smile for her favorite, the only one of her brood who showed the gumption to rise above the squalid surroundings in which they were born.

"Why, Corneel, we ain't seen you for supper in a coon's age!"

"Been too busy," he returned. "How's Pa?"

"Poorly, son. He don't seem to have much luck. He says it's a lot harder since you went to ferryin'."

Cornelius grunted.

"Remember that hundred dollars you give me to buy the periauger, Ma?"

"'Tain't that, son," she denied anxiously. "We got enough with what you give us every week. Your Pa, he kind of feels you're doin' more'n you ought to."

Cornelius grunted again, and fished out his wallet.

"Well, I got that hundred dollars to pay back to you, Ma —"

"No, no! You keep that, Corneel. You done all —"

"And here's a thousand dollars I saved, besides," he pressed on, a grin softening the rigor of his young face. "Guess that'll ease things for Pa, eh?"

Phebe Hand was in tears.

"But you oughtn't, Corneel! And however did you git eleven hundred dollars? You ain't been up to any tricks?"

His lips tightened.

"Tricks ain't good business, Ma. I jest worked hard, that's all. Didn't I tell ye, if ye'd help me git that periauger, I'd do better for ye than I could workin' for Pa?"

His father came in as he spoke — a gray, battered wreck of a man, disheartened by a lifetime of failure.

"What's that, Corneel?" The elder Vanderbilt's tone was flat, hardly interested. He sank wearily on a chair. "Glad to see ye, Bub. Wish ye'd git in oftener." And mildly curious, to his wife: "What ye cryin' for, Feeb? 'Tain't never Corneel?"

She blubbered convulsively through the folds of her apron:

"He — he — he's givin' us the hundred back for the periauger — and — and a thousand besides."

Old Cornelius — who once had been young Cornelius, lively and gay — straightened in his chair.

"What's that? A thousand dollars, Corneel?"

The son nodded somewhat sullenly.

"Whar'd ye git it?"

"Ferryin'."

"Ferryin'! Gawd, Bub, that's more'n I ever made." Corneel's expression was faintly derisive.

"Sure," he assented. "Ye got to stick to ferryin' to make it pay. Like I tol' Ma last year. Ye got to make folks know ye'll run, come hell or high-water."

"I do wisht ye wouldn't cuss so, Corneel," his father protested weakly. "'Tain't seemly in a younker."

Phebe Hand rounded angrily on her husband.

"Who are you to talk of cussin', and yourself just takin' the Lord's name in vain? Can't you thank the boy for doin' right by us? Where'll you find one of his years with as old a head, and as willin' to work for others? Answer me that, now!"

The momentary stiffness evaporated from Old Cornelius's backbone. He slumped lower in his chair.

"I ain't much account," he said, and there was

NEW YORK HARBOR AS IT APPEARED FROM THE HEIGHTS OF STATEN ISLAND IN TH
THE OCEAN ST

OF STEAM. NOTE THE SQUARE–RIGGED MAN–OF–WAR IN THE NEAR DISTANCE, AN⋮
IT AT THE RIGHT

sadness underlying the flat quality of his voice. "But I done what I could, Feeb." He looked at Corneel, standing so tall and gaunt in the flickering firelight. "Bub, ye been a good son to us. I ain't findin' fault with ye. Ye allus knowed what ye wanted. I guess that's what done it. A feller ought to know what he wants." He hesitated. "I take it kindly ye fetched us that thousand dollars. 'Sure ye kin spare it?"

"I give it to Ma, didn't I?" growled Corneel.

Phebe Hand caught her arms around his neck before he could dodge her — he was never one for public emotion.

"Son, I'm proud of you," she cried. "But I ain't surprised, not a bit."

"Aw, for Christ's sake, don't take on so," he grumbled. "Thar ain't nothin' to it, 'cept work and givin' folks what they want."

"Well, and if it wasn't for you we wouldn't be givin' the gals new prints this summer," exclaimed his mother, in a state between laughter and tears.

II

CORNEEL was equally successful during his second
year as a ferryman. He gave his mother another thousand dollars, and had funds left to buy shares in several
more periaugers: his initial venture as a capitalist. But
what really started him toward prosperity was the War
of 1812, which began a few weeks after his eighteenth
birthday. The declaration of hostilities in June threw
New York into a panic. There was a flurried mustering
of militia, and contracts were let for the erection of forts
at Sandy Hook, the Narrows and the Sound entrance
to the East River. Merchant vessels were converted
into privateers; the few men-o'-war of the Navy were
outfitted and provisioned. The consequence was a
boom in harbor traffic, which lasted throughout the
period of the war. Corneel and his associates were
almost the only class of citizens who derived any genuine profit from the wretched struggle.

It is typical of him that he seems to have had no
urge to enlist, one point in which he evinces remarkable
similarity to his father and uncles. But there is this
important difference between his status and that of
Old Cornelius during the Revolution: Corneel was
relatively well-to-do for a young fellow, and could
easily have afforded to take a year off, at least, for
service in a privateer, a service which presented speculative possibilities of prize-money. His family need

not have suffered any serious inconvenience by his absence. There was so much demand for the periaugers that Old Cornelius might have been relied upon to keep things going, even though he could not have handled the full volume of traffic that Corneel did. But Corneel preferred to remain at home, and look after his own interests — as he had a perfect right to do. Many other young fellows were averse to volunteering for a war that was unpopular in the northern trading centers.

His attitude toward the war is interesting, and I emphasize it only because of the evidence it affords that the influence of his mother's blood on his character was strictly limited. From the Hand strain, as I have said, he derived that intelligent aggressiveness, which, grafted upon the dogged tenacity of his father's family, produced his remarkable joint qualities of driving power and vision. But his gift of vision was entirely selfish in its application — unconsciously so, yet, nonetheless, selfish. He envisioned a chance, an opportunity, an invention, a trend in commerce, not as it would react to the advantage of the community, but in terms of his own profit. There was in him nothing of that will to public service, which moved families like the Hands to sacrifice their energies and wealth to the attainment of an ideal.

Indeed, Corneel never knew the meaning of the word ideal. Life, to him, was simply a question of battling for what you desired, regardless of whom you trampled on. The country, the state, the city, were abstract words; they had no concrete significance — no more significance than politics, except as he happened to discover that some politician or party principle impinged upon his affairs. In all his career he only voted twice, and I don't suppose that he had genuine personal convictions upon any major social question, unless he was vitally concerned with it. Ethics? Religion? They were empty phrases, until old age put the fear of the grave upon him. But he wasn't frankly, intentionally antisocial, understand. He simply had no conception of life, save as an egocentric proposition. It was himself, Cornelius Vanderbilt. Not Cornelius Vanderbilt and John Doe and Mary Roe.

He was naïve about it, naïve as a child. He couldn't comprehend that he would be considered unselfish or noble or patriotic, if he surrendered his growing business, and went off to fight for something hazy about "seamen's rights," "no impressment" and "Injun devilries." What he could comprehend quite distinctly was that if he went away he must lose a large part of the traffic he had spent two years to develop; somebody else, who didn't go, would profit by his absence.

So he stayed home, and prospered, laying the foundation of the immense fortune he was to win unaided, as honestly, I think, as any great fortune was won in America. It seems a contradiction, doesn't it, to couple honesty with selfishness? And it is contradictory that, in the long run, all he wrought so selfishly, with absolute indifference for others, was of distinct social value. But he seems to have had a natural flair for rightness in his undertakings, a basic sincerity of purpose, bedded upon an untutored conception of economics as the art of building structures of permanent worth. That, probably, was his secret: he was a builder by instinct. In the language of Wall Street, of which institution he was the granddaddy, a bull, never a bear. But remember, too, that he was never a hypocrite. He would have mocked at anyone who claimed that he worked for the public good. Consciously, he did nothing of the sort. He worked for the hand of Cornelius Vanderbilt. Happily, what was good for Cornelius Vanderbilt was good for America.

Altogether, then, it isn't difficult to understand his attitude toward the war, but for one thing. And that is his willingness to stay out of any fighting anywhere. He was a natural-born, fist-flinging, ear-chewing scrapper. He loved to fight. His dominance over rival boatmen was secured by his physical ability more than by his industry. At eighteen, he was unbeatable at fisticuffs, wrestlin' frontier style — an atrocious species of combat — wrestlin' ketch-as-ketch-kin or just plain hammer-and-tongs brawlin'. There is a story of him in this era of belligerence, which recites that he was riding up Broadway, very gaudy in a red, white and blue sash and cockade, leading a contingent of eight hundred Staten Islanders in a civic parade, when a certain local pugilist, who rejoiced in the name of Yankee Sullivan — how familiar it sounds! — derided him from the sidewalk. What mattered the dignity of the procession to Corneel? He slid off his horse, draped the sash over his shoulder and proceeded to pummel Yankee Sullivan in the gutter, while the eight hundred Staten Islanders formed a ring to bar the interference of indignant militia officers, members of the Cincinnati and the Honorable the Justices of the Circuit Court.

How could such a fightin' fool keep away from the Niagara frontier or the sanded decks of privateers like the *General Armstrong* of glorious memory? Corneel would have enjoyed himself privateering; he ought to have reached the quarter-deck eventually. And that would have meant fat prize-money in a successful cruise — but there weren't so many successful cruises as the casual reader is disposed to think, and some thousands of privateersmen did their war-service on Dartmoor. Corneel, with his usual canniness, may have reasoned this out. He didn't, even as a youngster, approve of speckelatin', and privateering was a form of speculation, which appealed to the mania for that form of enterprise dormant in most Americans. Corneel could have bought shares in more than one well-armed private man-o'-war; but he didn't, which would seem to imply that he declined to consider warfare as a legitimate business. If he wouldn't risk his person against the Bloodybacks, you may be sure he wouldn't risk his dollars, each one dripping with muscle-grease.

On the whole, though, I reject the idea that he was restrained from enlisting by an absolute degree of financial caution. He had more than his undeniable preoccupation with his business affairs to deter him, for, astounding as it may seem, this ruthless young Hercules was in love, and he was as much concerned with accomplishment of his suit as he was with holding the harbor-traffic which came to him.

III

WORKING as steadily as he did, Corneel encountered few girls of his age, unless they happened to travel as passengers in his periauger. Any night he wasn't working he was so utterly weary that his one ambition was for uninterrupted sleep. And since his theory of conduct was to grab what he wanted as soon as he saw it, it is likely that he settled his fancy on the very first girl who attracted him. In fact, that is as certain as anything can be in the misty traditions which are all there is to go upon in describing his early career. For the object of his affections was his first cousin, Sophia Johnson, daughter of his father's sister Eleanor, and quite as much of a Vanderbilt as himself. He had known her from infancy, taken her for granted as a tow-headed lass running barefoot, like himself, around Stapleton and Port Richmond; and suddenly, meeting her in the moonshine on the Quarantine Road that eventful summer of 1812, decided there was something mysteriously attractive about her.

An aspect of his infatuation which has both pathos and humor is that Sophia, in person and character, bore a strong resemblance to his mother, who was probably the only human being he ever treated with consideration. It is as if Corneel, sensing in himself the impulse for marriage, and groping blindly, haltingly, over the unfamiliar ground of feminine intercourse, struck off at a violent tangent the moment he saw a creature who seemed to possess those qualities which endeared his mother to him. But the truth was that Phebe Hand and Sophia Johnson were only superficially alike — Sophia, brave and courageous as she was, of necessity lacked the bright valor which Phebe inherited from a family reared in the tradition of social responsibility. Then, too, they married vastly different men; there was a wide gap between Phebe's Cornelius, plodding, spiritless, inept, and Sophia's Corneel, who took as he wished, asked no man's leave for anything and battered a path upward from poverty, heedless of toes crumpled or hearts broken.

You see my point? It would be unjust to let this criticism of Sophia rest unqualified. She wasn't such a woman as was Phebe Hand; but that wasn't her fault. Such as she was, the product of innumerable biological processes, fusions of human strains that wandered confusedly across the lower reaches of life, she justified herself by deeds. She was to work as hard as her Corneel, yes, harder — and be abominably mistreated by him. She was to provide the means for lifting him finally above the crowd of strivers — and little reward she had from him for it. She was to push her children into luxury by the sweat of her body and the labor of her two hands — and at the last most of them were secretly ashamed of her. Success? Riches? Yes, she was to taste both, but I think they were sour in her mouth. There is no more pitiful figure in this story. She tried so honestly, she was so unselfish, she achieved so much, she was so deserving. And yet . . . and yet . . . I do not think Phebe Hand would have failed at the last as Sophia Johnson did. Phebe would have been able to handle the cold, blistering selfishness of such a husband as her son turned out to be. That is the difference between bright valor and stolid courage.

To the end of her life, Phebe looked upon Sophia with good-natured contempt. The poor creature, why wouldn't she talk up to the rascal? she'd mutter to herself, standing squarely, in her plain gown and cap, to see her son and daughter-in-law out after a visit. That's no way to treat Corneel. I'd learn him, if I was in her shoes. And she'd chuckle, turning to go indoors, for she understood her son. Ah, he's not one to give an inch to, not him! Little respect he ever had for them that spoke him soft, and less for them that wouldn't fight him.

Still, any man was lucky to have a wife like Sophia Johnson. And a man who had a wife like Sophia, and a mother like Phebe Hand, couldn't very well have helped succeeding.

In the beginning, of course, Corneel was as deeply in love with Sophia as his nature permitted. He was ardent, but imperious; affectionate, but quite selfish. They must do always as he wished. Even in his courtship, which rather swept the poor girl off her feet. He was so big, and masterful, and sure of himself. At eighteen he had the craggy face of a man of twenty-five, with a man's thews and sinews. It never entered his head that he couldn't do as he pleased. So soon as he perceived that Sophia possessed some quality which made her desirable he launched his attack; and despite opposition of a serious nature, pressed it relentlessly.

"Sophia," he announced in his curt way, "I'm agoin' to marry ye."

"Why — why — Oh, Corneel!" she fluttered.

"I am," he repeated.

"But thar's Pa and Ma —"

"They'll be glad ye got me." There was no more vanity than humility in his tone. "I'm a good pervider, I am."

She wondered why he didn't kiss her, and nervously contrived an opening for him; but he ignored it, frowning out upon the bay.

"Got to see my folks about this," he said abruptly. "Got to git my ferry goin' right, too. Mebbe we better not step too fast."

He started away from her.

"Why — why — Corneel," she exclaimed softly. "Ain't ye goin' to —"

"Don't be pawky, gal," he commanded.

But he thought better of it, retraced his steps, and kissed her, strangely timid.

"Ye don't kiss like ye done it very often," she whispered, rubbing her cheek on his rough coat.

"I don't hold with kissin'," he answered stiffly. "But I — like ye, and I'm agoin' to marry ye — soon as I kin git things fixed up."

It wasn't so easy getting "things fixed up." He was under age, for all his success, and his parents were strongly opposed to the match.

"My heavenly days, Corneel," exclaimed Phebe Hand. "Whatever put such an idea into your head?"

"What's the matter with it?" he demanded angrily.

"Well, you're nothin' but a boy —"

"That's what ye said when I wanted the periauger. I was old enough to pay for it, and I guess if I earn enough to support a wife I'm old enough to git married."

His mother pulled him down beside her, a suspicion of tears in her eyes.

"That ain't it, son. The Lord knows you're better able to support a faml'y than most of the lazy, wuthless —"

The elder Cornelius chimed in irascibly from his chair by the kitchen fire.

"Now, Ma, ye had it right the fust time. Leave it at that. We jest can't afford for Corneel to go and take on other responsibilities. I ain't the man I used to be, and I say it to my shame, but it's the truth, and I dunno what the gals'd do, if it wasn't for what he brings in."

Corneel snorted contemptuously.

"If that's your worry, forgit it," he admonished. "I ain't goin' to quit ye when Sophia 'n me git married."

Phebe Hand fought to control her tears. This was the first time she had felt obliged to dispute her favorite's wishes, and it hurt.

"That's jest it, Corneel," she said quaveringly. "It's you 'n Sophia. If it was any other nice, seemly gal —"

"What's the matter with Sophia?" he demanded, scowling.

"Oh, not a thing, not a thing! As neat and tidy as they come, none of your shiftless, goggle-eyed wenches, forever moonin' after new ribbons and fallalls. But —"

Phebe paused uncomfortably.

"— She's your cousin, son, and fust at that."

"What of it?" he challenged.

"'Tain't right nor healthy for folks as nigh kin as that to —"

He roared with blustery laughter.

"Might think we was brother 'n sister, to hear ye, Ma! Damn me to glory, don't ye know thar's fust cousins marryin' every week? And no harm come of it."

"But sometimes it does," she persisted. He could never roar *her* down, this swaggering lad. "You can't tell. And 'tain't healthy to mix kin-blood."

His father spoke up in acquiescence.

"Your Ma's right. You oughtn't to cross us, Corneel. We're your parents, and we know more'n you, even if you be the best ferryman on the Bay."

The son bent bushy eyebrows in an icy glance; Old Cornelius looked away — at the floor, into the fire, up at the clock ticktocking on the mantel, the clock which was Phebe Hand's reserve magazine in the family's ceaseless battle with want; most of the money stowed behind the swaying pendulum now came from Corneel.

"I guess if I know how to run my business, I know who I kin marry," growled the boy.

The Dutchman in Old Cornelius waxed stubborn.

"Runnin' a business is one thing; gittin' married is something else," he insisted. "God knows I don't hanker to go agin ye, Corneel, for ye're a ready worker, and generous, if ye do be short in respect whar it's due. But ye're a minor, and truth's truth — and ye don't git married with my say-so."

Corneel stood up, his face a thunder-cloud.

"Thar ain't nobody alive kin talk to me like that," he bellowed. "Find someone else to feed ye."

But his mother ran between him and the door.

"No, no," she cried. "You can't go thisaway, son.

It's too important to decide in a temper, gittin' married is. We wouldn't have you make a mistake."

"All Pa thinks of is the money I give him," snarled Corneel.

Old Cornelius ventured a mild protest.

"'Tain't so much for me as it is for your Ma and the gals — not that I blame ye, Bub, for holdin' it ag'in me. Only I don't have no luck, and my strength ain't what is used to be. But leavin' me out, what your Ma says is true, and 'tain't right for cousins to marry."

Corneel was unappeased.

"That's foolishness," he declared harshly. "If ye was to hire Fulton to tootle it on his steamboat whistle, it wouldn't be more foolish. Lots of cousins marry, and no harm done. And Sophia 'n me are agoin' to."

Phebe Hand caught at his coat in a rare gesture of affection.

"Oh, son, not in the face of Pa 'n me that love you, whatever you think! We're only tryin' to figger for your own good."

His scowl faded slowly.

"Well, not straight-off," he conceded. "That ain't my plan, nohow. I want my war-work to git amovin' faster. And we need a house, and all that. But when I git ready I'm agoin' to marry her — and you folks and old man Johnson better not try to stop me. 'Twon't git you no profit, I kin promise you *that*."

After he had stamped out of the kitchen, slamming the door behind him, Phebe Hand sighed.

"He ain't one to be curbed," she muttered, as much to herself as to her brooding lesser half.

Old Cornelius shifted his chair closer to the flames; life seemed to be getting colder and colder, he reflected. A few years back he would have caned Corneel for such an exhibition of disrespect, tried to, anyway. To-night — it wasn't in him. No, it just wasn't in him.

"I dunno, Feeb," he answered dully. "I been thinkin' for his best."

She glanced up quickly.

"You'd oughtn't to have said that — about needin' what he brings us," she accused. "I ain't never had to press him to his duty."

"No, you ain't had to," agreed Old Cornelius, temper flaring in a shadowy imitation of his son's; "but me, what about me, eh? Think he ever shows much respect for me, his own Pa? Not him!"

Phebe Hand was oddly disturbed. In her heart sorrow contended with pride. She realized, very poignantly, the differences of character which barred father and son from any comprehension of each other.

"It ain't that he means anything, deary," she said sadly. "It's — it's jest his way. He's goin' far — and he gits impatient 'cause we can't —"

"He'll go far, with a fust cousin for wife," fussed Old Cornelius. "Have a batch of idiot babbies, I s'pose."

Phebe Hand came, and rested her swollen, calloused palm on one of her husband's gnarled fists; she had an aching for contact, for the understanding she only occasionally realized they were denied, and if their spirits might not meet, why, then, the touch of fingers twining awkwardly must serve instead.

"It's him that's marryin'," she said. "Don't forget

that, Pa. And it's true no harm comes of cousins marryin', more often 'n not."

"It was you shouted 'bout it," he pointed out impatiently.

"Yes, and mebbe I'd oughtn't have done it," she confessed. "Sophia's a good gal. She ain't got all the spunk I'd like her to for livin' with Corneel, but then — Humph! I dunno whar you'd git a gal to match him that way. And she's well raised; her mother's no slouch."

"He's too young."

There was a high note, almost a whine in Old Cornelius's voice. Phebe's fingers encircled his, quieting the tremors that emotion sped through his workworn frame.

"He'll soon be nineteen — and they kin wait a few months, I expect. He as much as said he would, Pa."

"Oh, well, if ye got to take his side, Feeb!" said Old Cornelius weakly.

"I dunno but I *have* got to," she returned. "And you, too. What chance we got to stand off Corneel? Ever see anybody do it, Pa? You can't stop that boy. If we say he can't marry, he'll up and run away, and Sophia with him — and we'll have Eleanor and all the Johnsons down on us. No, deary, you be guided by me, and make the best of it — seein' 'twon't do us no good to make the worst."

There was a space of silence, while the flames purred and the indomitable clock ticked away the seconds. Old Cornelius slumped lower still in his chair.

"I s'pose so," he assented more wearily than ever.

It was as if a muffled voice in the dumb languor of

his brain clicked off a repetition of syllables, keeping time with the swing of the pendulum:

"Now — indeed — you — will — be — Old — Cornelius — now — indeed — you — will — be — Old — Cornelius — now — indeed — you —"

IV

CORNEEL and Sophia were married on December 19, 1813, a few months after his nineteenth birthday. There was a party, of course, a rough, rowdy merry-making, shot with the coarse humor of peasant minds. Afterward the happy couple, with some difficulty, eluded self-appointed entertainers, and fled up the muddy road to the tiny hutch which was to be their home, barred the door against pursuit, and, perhaps, guffawed secretly at the raucous witticisms which resounded through the night. In the morning Sophia commenced her household tasks, and Corneel sailed his periauger from Stapleton to Whitehall Landing. It was what they had expected to do; they knew no other way of living; and they were entirely satisfied with their lot. Sophia was ambitious only to satisfy Corneel. Corneel wanted only to drive ahead, faster and faster, to earn more money and acquire more power. And power, to him, connoted boats. Nothing more, for he had as yet no tangible end in view.

But how the lad worked! Up with the daylight, home, occasionally, for a snack at evening, then away again. Sleeping, as often as not, whenever chance offered on the bottom-boards of the periauger. No ordinary youth could have stood the pace of these years; it was Corneel's brawn that pulled him through. But probably that is a half-truth. Brawn would have wearied, without the abounding vitality which animated him. And he had keen wits, always ready to seize upon every advantage he encountered, not to speak of that battling aggressiveness which cowed antagonists and won friends and customers.

He was afraid of nobody. Place and authority left him unabashed. When Matthew L. Davis, the Commissary-General of the troops in garrison in the far-flung defenses of the port, accused him of joining in the activities of the smuggling ring that worked in coöperation with traitorous New England merchants to introduce forbidden goods procured by them under license from the British blockaders, Corneel assailed the officer with his fists, and was pried off his victim by amused bystanders. Since no punishment was visited upon him, I suppose he was innocent of the charge and regarded as righteously indignant. As a matter of fact, it is extremely unlikely that he was ever a smuggler. For one reason, he had plenty of lawful business on his hands, and for another, he nourished a consistent distaste for illegal enterprises. He was honest in a downright, practical, unhypocritical sense — a feller's a damfool to steal; 'tain't wuth it.

One effect of the incident, however, was to diminish the amount of army work which came his way, and he turned to extending his connections with private parties. When Davis presently was relieved, and the new Commissary-General advertised for bids for provisioning the harbor forts for a period of three months Corneel was the one boatman in the harbor who did not file for them. His father remonstrated with him.

"Thar's money in that contract, Bub. Ye'd oughter —"

"Thar ain't a shillin' in it," interrupted Corneel. "Seen the bids?"

"No, but —"

"Thought ye hadn't," Corneel chuckled grimly. "Feller that gits the contract is to be exempt from milishy duty. The damn cowardly pups are so feared of the Redcoats they're makin' prices that won't pay for their time, let alone give 'em a profit. Every bid's lower 'n the last one. And I don't aim to carry cargo at a loss."

Old Cornelius wasn't a fool. In this instance, anyway, he saved his more alert son from a blunder of omission.

"Ain't ye makin' a mistake, Bub?" he inquired.

"Mistake? Hell, no!"

"Well, now, I ain't so sure. Kinder figgerin' them Army fellers is purty dumb, ain't ye?"

Corneel's attention was caught.

"Huh? How ye mean?"

"If you 'n me kin see why them bids is so low, can't other folks?"

"Mebbe," Corneel assented doubtfully.

Old Cornelius became more positive.

"Sure, they kin," he persisted. "And if them Army fellers have any sense —"

"They ain't," scoffed Corneel.

"I wouldn't be too sure, Bub. This new Commissary, he looks like he means business. If he's sensible at all, he'll know ye can't git dependable service from a contractor that's takin' a loss for a purpose."

"'Might be so, if 'twasn't that every feller 'cept me has filed low," answered Corneel.

"Well, try it," urged his father.

"Nope, too late. And my bid would be so high above them skunks' the Commissary 'd drop dead of fright."

"Try it," repeated Old Cornelius. "'Twon't do no harm. Jest send in an honest bid."

"Mebbe I will," agreed Corneel.

He did, and the day after the bidding closed, being in New York, decided to stop at Army headquarters to learn what had happened. There was less formality in those days than there would be now, and he penetrated without difficulty to the office of the Commissary-General.

"What about them harbor fort bids?" he asked, sticking his head in the door.

The officer looked up from the desk at which he wrote.

"Sorry, but the bid has been let."

Corneel started to walk off, then curiosity pressed him further.

"Who got it?" he asked again.

"Man named Van Derbilt." The officer noted the surprise registered in the lean, young face. "Why?" he went on. "Know him, do you?"

Corneel gulped.

"Sure — that is, Mister — he — why, I'm —"

The Commissary-General broke into a laugh.

"Oh, so you're Van Derbilt?"

Corneel nodded.

"Say, Mister," he exploded, "how in hell did I git it, with all them damned blatherskites 'way below me?"

"Because the blatherskites were 'way below' you,"

returned the officer. "We want a contractor who is bidding to do our work, not one who is trying to escape militia duty. If I have my way, every one of those rascals will go in the next draft."

Corneel stumbled to the street in a daze.

"By God, the old man was right," he muttered to himself. "Don't that beat —"

This army contract doubled the work he had to do. During the daytime he operated his ferry service. At night he transported a load of provisions to one of the forts. As there were six of them, and their stores required replenishing weekly, that meant six working nights a week. He never saw his family, except on Sundays; and then he usually slept all day as well as all night. But he completed his contract without a hitch, and this led to other engagements. The Army officers said that if you wanted a job done right Cornelius Van Derbilt was the man for you. They talked to merchants they met in the taverns and coffee-houses; Navy officers and owners of privateers would send for him when they had cargo or stores to be transferred. Very soon he was obliged to hire or subsidize others to carry out certain contracts, but all really important work he attended to himself.

His wartime reputation is illustrated by an incident which occurred on a raw, blustery fall day when Admiral Cockburn's blockading squadron, for target practice and to divert stale crews, bore down on the fort at Sandy Hook. The northeast gale carried the rumbling of the cannon miles across the waters of the Lower Bay; people scrambled up the hills on the Staten Island and Brooklyn shores, peering out to sea. Were the British really coming in, at last? Cockburn had threatened to "lay the town in ashes." The British had tremendous naval strength off the coast, a score of ponderous seventy-fours, dozens of racing frigates. In a duel with the hastily improvised forts and militia artillerymen no one knew what might happen. It was imperative to discover the situation at Sandy Hook.

An epauletted staff-officer appeared at the Stapleton wharf, panting with excitement.

"Who's the best boatman here?" he appealed to an anxious group.

"Van Derbilt," answered one. And others chimed in: "Sure!" "Young Van Derbilt." "Corneel, he's your man."

The officer sought out Corneel.

"Can you sail me to Sandy Hook?" he asked.

"If ye don't mind bein' under water part way," replied Corneel.

"I don't mind anything, so long as I get there," rejoined the officer.

Driving his periauger, close-reefed, Corneel reached Sandy Hook early in the afternoon. The British had sheered off, rather because of the storm than for any puny damage the fort batteries had done. But the garrison, in the first hectic glow of victory, were disposed to think that they had really defeated a serious attack, which was likely to be renewed when the wind shifted. Ammunition was low, and reinforcements would be necessary to hold the post and resist a possible attempt at a landing. It was necessary to carry word to headquarters in New York.

Corneel was appealed to again.

"Can you make it, my lad?"

"Sure, if ye don't mind sailin' under water," he reaffirmed.

So he cast loose a second time, and the periauger scudded away before the wind, a shivering group of officers clutching the weather gunwale for dear life. They were all soaked to the skin when Corneel ran alongside Whitehall Landing, a crowd of curious boatmen and citizens braving the wet to hear the news from the front.

"Who fetched ye?" clamored the boatmen as the officers climbed the landing-stairs.

"Young fellow named Van Derbilt."

"Who? Corneel?" And then wonderingly amongst themselves: "What ye think of that, eh?" "Christ, I wouldn't go out in this for any price." "I guess thar ain't no one but him could have made it."

His pertinacity secured prompt results. Even his cold, off-hand manner, his hard tongue, his attitude of constantly carrying a chip on his shoulder, won him business. He was a personality. People couldn't forget him. In an age when there was still a good deal of class feeling his independence commended itself to all save the conservatives at the top; and these conservatives, who, in New York, were usually merchant gentry, didn't permit class feeling to interfere with trade. They admired a young man who was faithful to his word, ready to labor unstintedly and careful of his money. For Corneel was no spender. A shilling was a shilling to him. He actually had a respect for the twenty-five and fifty cent shin-plasters, issued by Jacob Barker's Bank, which were the recognized currency in New York.

All his earnings were promptly stowed away, not behind the pendulum of a clock, which had been his mother's thrifty, if unproductive, habit, but in some safely profitable venture, which might be relied upon to produce returns.

He and Sophia lived as simply as ever. She did her housework, and bore children at a fairly consistent rate — the first one came in the fall of 1814; and he, to do him justice, was every bit as relentless toward himself, at a moderate estimate, performing the tasks of two strong men. But it goes without saying that young people could not do what they did, and not pay a price. Poor Sophia was laying the seeds of an illness which would make for tragedy, and Corneel, eating irregularly and toiling prodigiously, was acquiring chronic dyspepsia, slowly weakening his heart and undermining other organs. An ordinary man, yes, an ordinary man of unusual strength, who attempted what he did, would have died at forty. Much of Corneel's success is explained by the fact that, despite his self-abuse, he lived to be an octogenarian. His vitality was unquenchable.

But in these days of his youth he laughed at warnings. Sophia, conscious of his indefatigable efforts, proud of his success, had no thought of saving herself. No, she must keep pace with him; it was a point of honor with her. If he made money, hand over fist, she must save at home, cut down unnecessary waste, do without coddling. A new baby? Well, there would have to be a midwife, to be sure, and one of her sisters in for a week afterward; but more assistance would have shamed her. And whatever else happened, there must always be warm food on the stove, in case he came in unexpectedly. If he was angry and sullen, as he was sometimes, plagued by vague longings and ambitions hardly coherent, or vexed over deals that had fallen through, she must keep the baby quiet, and leave him alone, without seeming to avoid him. He wasn't an easy man to live with, as she learned to her cost. And there was always hanging over her the shadow of her mother-in-law. She never won to the place she might have had if Corneel's mother had not been Phebe Hand. For it was to Phebe that Corneel went in his rare moments of confidence, when vanity or a plethora of emotions sundered his usual shell of aloof indifference, and he had to talk, to parade his ambitions and devices and preen himself in the sunshine of feminine admiration. Nobody like Ma to understand a feller. Sophia agreed with him docilely. She liked and respected her mother-in-law. It was her ambition to approach measurably Phebe's competence.

V

As Corneel's means increased so did the scope of his ambitions. He had launched his fortunes in a periauger, and he was anxious to make all he could out of small boat traffic; but he determined to transfer his interests gradually to the coasting trade. With his first war-earnings he built the schooner *Dread*, a handsome, swift little craft, in 1814. The following year, in partnership with a brother-in-law, Captain De Forest, he built a larger schooner, the *Charlotte*. The *Dread* was intended for service to Long Island Sound and other nearby ports; the *Charlotte*, however, was up to lengthy voyages north and south.

In common with most other boatmen Corneel looked with utter contempt upon the clumsy, noisy steamboats, which Messrs. Fulton and Livingston were operating on the Hudson and adjacent waters. All very well for passengers mebbe, if ye want to git a cinder-bath afloat, but thar ain't no room into the contraptions for cargo. No, sirree, I guess bulk goods'll allus go by sail. That was young Corneel's dogmatic stand. He couldn't see, in 1815, that steamboats might ever be different from what they were then. Indeed, he, like all his class, was instinctively prejudiced against the new invention. Its sponsors were tryin' to take the bread out of his mouth.

He was impervious to argument. Until the advent

of the *Clermont* and her successors, the trade between New York and Albany, at the head of navigation on the Hudson, was carried on in so-called Albany packets, heavy, bluff-bowed sloops of unmistakable Dutch ancestry. These vessels were a tradition of the river; there hadn't been any change in their design in two centuries. They weren't large enough to be comfortable, and with a fair wind they required thirty-six hours for the journey. The first rattly steamboats of Fulton's design cut the time in half; but Corneel refused to be impressed. Who wants to hurry cargo? he demanded. What's the use? Besides, like as not, ye'll have your goods burned up by the damned sparks. Foolishness! Ship by sail, and git thar safe and sound; calicos ain't hurt for a few extry hours afloat.

So he shut his eyes to progress, and addressed himself to building up a prosperous little sailing fleet — which was just as well, in the circumstances. Steamboats were a monopoly, and a crude, young boatman would have had no share in the profits the owners of the patents were bent upon keeping to themselves.

Summertimes, after the war, he devoted to harbor traffic, supervising the operation of his Staten Island ferry and a number of other periaugers. In the Fall he went to sea in the *Dread* or the *Charlotte*, sailing up the coast to New England or south as far as Charleston. Sometimes he would carry regular cargoes for merchants. But if trade was slack and a cargo wanting he would undertake a flyer as a floating peddler. He might run down to Delaware, and pick up a shipload of melons to be retailed to the Hudson River towns. Or he would buy a load of shad in the river, and sell it in Philadelphia. He liked this kind of business; he was his own capitalist; all the profits, wholesale, middleman's, transportation and retail, were his. So, whenever the chance occurred, he played his own hand.

Bold, vigilant, resourceful, he possessed the qualities of a commercial magnet. Generally, business came to him; but he was never quiescent, awaiting it. He liked to have a long list of jobs staring him in the face. He liked to be able to say to a merchant:

"Sorry, Mister. Ought to have spoke to me yesterday. I got a cargo for Stonington next week."

He bought out his brother-in-law's share in the *Charlotte*, and built a third schooner in 1816. Although people continued to speak of him as "that young Van Derbilt who runs the Staten Island ferry," he was much more than a ferryman now. In a small way, he was become a factor in shipping. His future seemed assured. If he continued at his present rate he might shortly expect to add ocean packets to his coasters. But that trick of vision, which Phebe Hand had bequeathed him, gave warning that he was sailing a false course. He couldn't help noticing, on his voyages up the Hudson and through the Sound, how the steamboats hissed past him as he tacked back and forth against adverse winds. For several years, as I have said, he joined in the staple derision of the other boatmen. Why, they have to carry so much fire-wood thar ain't deck-room for a mortal to pass! Ye can hear the racket them injines make from the Battery to Communipaw. And they keep a feller hoppin' 'round all the time with a bucket of lead to solder b'iler leaks.

But his uneasiness increased. More and larger steamboats were built, and whenever they were not discriminated against by legislation they were able to hold their own and finally draw traffic from the river-sloops and coasters. Finally, Corneel obtained a passage in the *Fulton* to Albany and back, and devoted himself during the trip to studying the engine and methods of operation. His doubts were strengthened. Improve the hulls and deck-space, according to simple methods which were suggested at once to him, and the superficial disadvantages of the novel craft would be minimized.

He mulled over the problem for months, listening to every argument he could obtain from either side to the controversy, for one of his salient characteristics was his readiness, despite his constitutional pugnacity, to revise or recall any opinion in the light of facts grasped by his common sense; and on December 31, 1817, when he was twenty-three years old, he reached a decision. Balancing his ledger that day, he ascertained that he owned three vessels and $9,000 in cash, all acquired in the seven years since he bought his periauger. This was his capital, the surplus produced by his business, which was swelling from year to year. He had reason to be proud, ample excuse to stick to his course; prosperity was a certainty. But he courageously resolved to scrap outright the instrument of his gains.

"B'ilers," he muttered, closing his ledger. "Thar's whar the money's goin'. Steam's bound to beat sail, if ye give folks comfort and stowage."

BOOK THREE

B'ILERS

I

CORNEEL was none of your hesitant deciders. As soon as he had taken his stance he leaped.

"Goin' to sell the ferry," he announced to Sophia that evening.

Her broad, placid features revealed only slight surprise.

"So ye kin git full time for coastin'?" she inquired.

"Goin' to sell the schooners, too," he answered.

She eyed him now with open amazement.

"Why — why — What ye fixin' to do, Corneel?"

"Dunno," he growled.

"Nothin'?" she pressed. "Ain't ye — ain't ye got a job to hand?"

"No." And after a pause: "Figgerin' on steamboatin'."

Amazement was displaced by perturbation in her expression.

"But ye ain't never done no steamboatin'!"

"Sure," he agreed. "Time I learned."

She bent over a pot slung above the fire for what seemed to her a long time — stirring — stirring.

"Well, we got aplenty money put by," she hazarded at last.

A hint of quizzical humor warmed his blue eyes.

"Sure, we got enough," he assented. He heaved himself up from his chair. "Goin' to see Ma," he said.

Phebe Hand received his news with quite as much surprise as Sophia, but it did not show in her face.

"Steamboatin', eh?" she commented. "That takes a pile of money, Corneel."

"It takes a pile of knowin'," he returned.

"I s'pose you know your own mind," she went on dubiously; "but it sounds more like your Pa than anything you ever did, hoppin' out of a good business into something else."

"I ain't failed yet, have I?" he demanded touchily.

"Land's sake, no! But —"

He wagged an impressive forefinger at her.

"I done a heap of thinkin', this last year. Mebbe if I went on like I have I'd do better 'n I hope to; but I don't guess so. B'ilers have it over sails, Ma. 'Tain't no use talkin'. You fire up a steamer, and she goes, head-wind or no wind. The main thing is to work out a way to make steamboats profitable. They ain't built right, and that's what I aim to do — build 'em right."

She was still doubtful.

"That's a mighty big order, Corneel. Mr. Fulton invented steamboats, and he had the Chancellor and all the rich folks to help him; but he couldn't make 'em no better 'n they are."

"What did he know 'bout ships?" jeered Corneel. "Not a damn thing! I bet you before I git through I'll have steamboats bigger 'n a seventy-four, goin' ten miles an hour."

"How you talk!" sighed Phebe Hand. "Fust off, son, you ought to find a job."

"I will," he said confidently. "Only — only" — a rare fit of shyness overcame him — "I want for you to believe in me, Ma. I don't keer what the rest of 'em say, but you —"

She sighed again.

"I guess I kin believe in you," she answered. "But for the Lord's sake, Corneel, don't you start changin' 'round for a habit. If you're goin' in for steamboatin', stick to it, till you're the biggest steamboat man thar be."

"You jest watch me," he advised grimly.

But finding a job, a job at all commensurate with his past achievements, wasn't so easy, he discovered. A condition almost of anarchy prevailed in the steamboat business. It seemed as though the people, with the odd perversity often displayed by democracies, were bent upon thwarting the establishment of this new method of transportation. There was, as yet, no doctrine of Federal jurisdiction over navigable waterways, and the State of New York, in granting a monopoly of steamboat traffic to Robert Fulton and Chancellor Livingston, had entered into controversies with all the neighboring states, and at the same time practically inhibited progress or improvement, which could come only from competition. New York also assessed a tax upon steamboat passengers, which, in the years 1817 and 1818, when Corneel was first beginning to be interested in b'ilers, produced a revenue of $41,440. Trips of less than thirty miles were untaxed, from thirty to one hundred miles cost fifty cents, and one hundred

One of Daniel Drew's steamboats navigating the Hudson

miles or more one dollar. Naturally, travelers considered this tax when they went ajourneying, and if they were not in a particular hurry elected the sailing packets, which were more comfortable, if less speedy, than the primitive steam craft. The trip from New York to Albany by steamboat cost $7, a largish sum in those days.

As always in American history, an attempt to create a monopoly excited widespread hostility. Men were alive then who remembered having seen John Fitch steer his screw-propelled steam yawl around the Collect Pond in 1796, the same John Fitch who had operated on the Delaware in 1786 the first steamboat to traverse American waters, who in 1788 had operated another steamboat on a twenty-mile voyage from Philadelphia to Burlington and in 1790 had run this last vessel as a regular passenger packet on trips totaling a thousand miles. Poor Fitch! A Yankee ginseng peddler in the Ohio country, once a captive of the Indians, he had come East with his great invention, hoping for modest wealth, inoculated with the fine, unselfish patrotism which flowered in the Revolution. He offered his idea unconditionally to Congress, but Congress was too preoccupied with the problems of erecting a commonwealth to have time to appreciate it. So he did what he could with the scant private capital he secured, and when that was exhausted, and shipping merchants continued to flout the practicability of steamboats, he returned West to Kentucky, a broken, disheartened man, and drank himself to death in a log cabin in the wilderness.

But Fitch was merely the most important of eight different men, who built sixteen steamboats — of which fifteen were actually operated — in America before Fulton's *Clermont* was launched. John Stevens, of Hoboken, progenitor of a famous engineering family, later to be one of Corneel's competitors, built a screw-propelled vessel in 1803, which he operated as a ferry between New York and Hoboken. There are other instances. And if we go abroad, Denis Papen, a French engineer resident in Hesse, in 1707 had built and run a steamboat on the Rhine. In 1781 a second Frenchman, M. de Jouffroy, built a paddle-wheel steamer one hundred and forty feet long, which was operated successfully in 1783 in the presence of a committee of the French Academy of Sciences.

There is, in fact, not the slightest shred of evidence that Fulton invented either the steamboat or any important detail of its machinery. The hull of the *Clermont* was built for him — under his nominal supervision, it is true — by Charles Brown, a New York shipwright, who had done work previously for Nicholas Roosevelt, one of Fulton's associates in the enterprise, and himself a dabbler in plans for steam-driven craft. The engine and boiler were constructed by Boulton and Watt in England. Fulton's contribution to the development of the steamboat was his assembling of the products of other men's experiments, and his procurement of the interest of Robert R. Livingston, Chancellor of New York, who had built — or caused to be built — in 1798 a boat, which was driven alternatively by stern-wheels or by endless chains of paddles. Through Livingston Fulton secured financial assistance, while the Chancellor's political influence obtained the partners in 1811 the grant from the State Legislature of a monopoly of steam navigation in New York waters for a term of twenty years. Opposition boats must either pay a royalty to the monopoly or be forfeited to it.

Monopoly, of course, produced stagnation. Notwithstanding the boom in shipping which followed the War of 1812, there were but eight steamboats on the Hudson by 1816, the year after Fulton's death, and probably not more than this number in all the rest of the country together. But the monopoly was gradually breaking down under its burden of animosity. The Fulton-Livingston organization made a half-hearted attempt to exert their authority on Western waters, and presently abandoned it. In the East they did somewhat better, but their success was limited. Neighboring states rebelled against what they considered New York's outrageous demand to control interstate steam traffic. Connecticut refused to permit the vessels of the monopoly to ply to her ports. New Jersey, after a period of fast and loose, finally decided to fight for the rights of her citizens, and this was where Corneel found his chance to become a steamboat skipper.

It is a sidelight on his character that he entered the battle on the side of the independents. Corneel was always against any monopoly — that he didn't exercise, himself. He was against the steamboat monopoly, too, because his business judgment warned him it was bound to lose. And another reason, his principal one, indeed, was that an ambitious young man, who intended to be a steamboat operator some day, could not expect any assistance in that direction from the monopoly. But his family and friends thought he was crazy — that is, everyone except his mother. Heard what that fool Corneel is up to? My grief, fust he sells his schooners and the ferry, then he hires out to this feller Gibbons. Goin' to git hisself busted flat as a pie-plate — his old man to a T. Yes, boys, I guess blood will tell. Always shiftless, them Van Derbilts.

Even Sophia gulped down her tears when he told her.

"I'm goin' with Mr. Gibbons," he said curtly. "Cap'n of his ferry from New York to New Brunswick."

"Will — will he pay ye well, Corneel?" she asked timidly.

"Thousand dollars a year."

The tears squeezed between her eyelids.

"Why, Corneel! Ye saved three thousand a year these last three years."

He glowered at her.

"Give me a chance, and I'll save ten thousand a year. Stop that cryin'. I ain't agoin' to starve ye."

He hesitated.

"Got a job for ye, too," he added, softening his tone. "Thar's a tavern at New Brunswick, Halfway House they call it. Passengers lie thar over night goin' to Trenton to take the Philadelphy boat. 'Tain't never been run right. Gibbons says if ye'll run it we kin have what we make."

"Oh, I'll do anything I kin to help ye, Corneel," she quavered, mopping at her eyes with a corner of her apron. "But it seems kind of fearsome to go away so far, and the children so young, and — and — ye'll be from home more often, I s'pose."

"Cryin' won't mend it," he answered gruffly. "Do ye good to git rooted up."

Phebe Hand knew better how to handle him.

"Is it what you want, Corneel?" she asked.

"It ain't much, Ma," he admitted frankly; "but I didn't expect much. I got to figger on goin' slow the next ten years, mebbe."

"That's a long time," she remarked. "Kin you stand it?"

"Me? Sure. I wouldn't wonder but Sophy'll make more out of the tavern than I fetch in."

"I won't see much of you?" she hazarded.

He grinned light-heartedly.

"Much as I kin manage," he assured her. "Sophy'll allus have a bed for ye in the tavern."

"I guess Sophy'll have her hands plumb full," Phebe Hand observed drily.

II

THOMAS GIBBONS was a Georgian by birth, a man of independent means, who had settled in Elizabeth — then called Elizabethtown — New Jersey. As an investment he had sunk some of his money in a ferry, which linked certain Jersey towns with a more comprehensive system of steamboat and stagecoach lines joining New York and Philadelphia, the property of Aaron Ogden, a former Governor of New Jersey. Both Gibbons and Ogden possessed coasting licenses issued by the Federal government. Ogden, in addition to his coasting license, had purchased from the successors of Fulton and Livingston the right to operate steamboats in New York waters. Gibbons had not entered into this latter arrangement with the monopoly because his vessel did not enter New York's jurisdiction; but the monopoly contended that, inasmuch as his vessel was really a part of the system of interstate traffic operated by Ogden, he should also pay a royalty to it, as Ogden did.

In support of this contention, the monopoly brought suit against Ogden and Gibbons in the New York courts, and the learned Chancellor Kent, in an opinion bristling with precedents, decided that Ogden could not be held liable for damages or violation of the privileges of the monoply, but that Gibbons must comply with the monopoly's terms, notwithstanding the fact that his vessel was simply a feeder for Ogden's lines and did not operate outside New Jersey's territorial waters. This was bad enough for Gibbons, but his indignation was measurably increased when Ogden brought pressure to bear on him to yield to the monopoly, threatening otherwise to boycott his steamer. The immediate consequence was the separation of the partners, and the determination of Gibbons to launch an opposition ferry between New York and New Brunswick, as part of a new steamboat and stagecoach line, by way of Trenton and the Delaware River, to Philadelphia. Ogden promptly brought suit against him individually in the New York courts, backed by the full weight of the monopoly's political and financial influence. Indeed, the suit of Ogden *vs.* Gibbons should really have been inscribed on the court dockets Monopoly *vs.* Gibbons, for it was the monopoly, screened behind the imposing figure of the former Governor of New Jersey, that moved with implacable determination to crush this audacious pretense at independence.

In the opening of the contest Gibbons had distinctly the worst of it. He was obliged to construct an organization out of nothing at all, seizing upon whatever elements were handy to him; and the weakest link in his chain was the very one upon which the monopoly's suit was predicated: the New York–New Brunswick ferry. To maintain this he had only the one steamer which formerly had served as feeder to Ogden's service, the *Mouse of the Mountain*, a cranky, unhandy, disreputable, little craft, cursed with the reputation of never being on time and often failing to complete her trips. Furthermore, the crew of the *Mouse* were exposed to a ceaseless campaign of sabotage and persecution, while her master was harassed by a stream of court orders, injunctions and complaints of violations of municipal ordinances. Her runs became more and more irregular, and were about to cease, when Corneel heard of Gibbons's difficulties, and applied for the job of bluffing the monopoly.

He was just the man for the place, and the place offered the kind of work he preferred. He was building something; he was learning how to make steamships pay; and he had a gorgeous fight on his hands, with heavy odds against him. Those years with Gibbons were probably the happiest of Corneel's life. They aroused every combative instinct in his character. Opposing him were efficient antagonists, better equipped, more liberally financed — for Gibbons dared not risk much capital in the struggle; and bolstered by the might of the law. To help him he had very little aside from his own grit and initiative, although he derived some back-handed assistance from the growing resentment of public opinion in New Jersey, which stirred the Legislature to enact a law of retaliation upon the monopoly, providing for the seizure of vessels of any corporation navigating the state's waters, which was party to the confiscation of any vessel belonging to a Jerseyman. This law had the important effect of deterring Ogden and the monopoly from libeling the *Mouse*, but similarly it concentrated their energies upon the hazing of the little steamer's master.

Corneel wasn't loath to snatch up the gage of battle. Damn sharks! Think ye kin skeer me? I'll take all ye kin give, and holler for more. He hurled himself upon the sluggish ogre, bred of Fulton's and Living-

Courtesy of New York Central R. R.

THE FIRST STEAM RAILROAD TRAIN OPERATED IN THE STATE OF NEW YORK. TRIAL TRIP OF THE DE WITT CLINTON, LEAVING SCHENECTADY, SEPTEMBER 24, 1831, ON WHAT IS NOW THE NEW YORK CENTRAL AND HUDSON RIVER R. R.

ston's greed, with the pugnacity of a prize-fighter and the enthusiasm of a crusader. The ferry service and its dependent lines had been running at a loss. He studied the situation for a week, then went straight to Gibbons.

"Out to make a profit?" he demanded of his employer.

"Certainly, Captain Van Derbilt."

"Got any idees for it?"

"Why, what do you mean? I am willing to do anything in reason."

"Give me a free hand, hey?"

"If it won't cost too much, Captain —"

Corneel snorted contemptuously.

"Got to spend *some* money, if ye want to make anything. Can't run a ferry that won't run."

"What do you suggest?" Gibbons asked uncertainly.

"Let me fix the *Mouse* so she'll git whar she starts for. And I fire and hire my crew, no questions asked."

"If it won't cost too much money —"

"It won't."

And it didn't. With his practical knowledge, gained in planning his schooners, Corneel supervised the remodeling of the *Mouse*, so as to make her less uncomfortable, if not more comfortable. He hunted up a machinist who put her engines in order, and hired an engineer who could be relied upon to keep them going. He weeded over Gibbons's employees, discharged the inefficients and sweated the ones he retained — for one of his peculiarities was an ambition to get out of others as much work as he did, himself. He seldom succeeded in this, but he never was discouraged, not even when he was branded as a hard-hearted oppressor of labor. Hard-hearted he was, and no question; but few men worked for him one-half as hard as he worked for himself.

The running expenses of the ferry dropped, under his management, and the number of passengers increased. In six months he had the line paying a profit, and at the end of the year he persuaded Gibbons to allow him to have a larger steamer, the *Bellona*, built to his specifications. In the meantime, too, Sophia was performing the great exploit of her drab life. She went to New Brunswick, with her children tagging her heels, three of them, probably — she and Corneel were too busy to write down birth-dates in the family Bible, and there has been some doubt as to precisely when most of their offspring entered the world — and found the Halfway House a mess of filth and vermin. She was all by herself, without Corneel's rough tongue and masterful ways to spur her on, without Phebe Hand's mocking humor to stiffen her courage. But she turned up her sleeves and kilted her skirts, anchored the children in a corner of the stable-yard and addressed herself to the emergency with an efficient vigor her mother-in-law couldn't have excelled. That was a brave lass!

Toiling long days, and sleeping short nights, she cleaned and fumigated the tavern from cellar to attic, oversaw its redecorating and refurnishing, reëstablished the service departments. In a few days she transformed it from the blackest plague-spot of the road to the most attractive stopping-place between New York and Philadelphia; and quite as many travelers elected to patronize Gibbons's Union Line because of Mrs. Van Derbilt's Bellona Hall, as it was rechristened, as because of Corneel's smooth-running ferry, which could now be relied upon to complete the trip from the Battery pier to the head of navigation on the Raritan River on schedule time and in any and all weathers. The Union Line was really the Van Derbilts, Corneel and Sophia. They saw to it that passengers from New York, who disapproved the monopoly, were afforded the opportunity to travel as comfortably out of the monopoly's sphere of influence as could be done via Ogden's licensed steamers.

But this was success, and the success of the Union Line prompted the monopoly to more strenuous endeavors to break Gibbons and his resourceful lieutenant. The *Bellona* they were afraid to touch lest they precipitate the seizure of one of Ogden's steamers by the New Jersey authorities; and Gibbons, himself, was careful to keep out of reach of the New York courts, so that he could not be served in a personal action. But Corneel was subject to prosecution for contravening the rights of the monopoly, in personally operating an unlicensed steamer in New York waters, and the day came that a writ of arrest was issued for him. Gibbons wanted to take him off the run, and substitute another skipper.

"I'll give you the Delaware steamer, Van Derbilt. Her master can handle the *Bellona*."

"Like hell," Corneel retorted gustily. "Let the" — assorted epithets — "ketch me fust."

For sixty consecutive days the *Bellona* was boarded by officers with writs for her master. In the early phase of the contest, Corneel's tactics were to hide near the gangplank as the steamer reached her dock, wait until the officers had passed it and then skip ashore. There he would remain under cover — he had plenty of partisans on the waterfront — up to the moment of sailing, when he'd jump aboard at some point aft of the gangplank, and shout the order to cast off before the sheriff's deputies could pursue him. After this ruse was discovered, he constructed a secret closet in the hold, and at the first appearance of the deputies would stow himself here during the *Bellona's* stay at her pier.

Several weeks of the game of hide-and-seek drove his baffled antagonists to adopt the scheme of intercepting the *Bellona* in the harbor; but Corneel spotted their picket-boat in time, and was safe behind the sliding-panel of his closet when they boarded. After cogitating another week or two, the attorneys for the monopoly concluded to sue out writs against all the *Bellona's* crew for contempt of court. Warning was dispatched to Corneel, however, and on his next trip from New Brunswick he left the crew ashore, taking with him only a young woman to steer, while he attended to the engines. Who was the young woman? I wish I knew. The scanty records are silent, probably discreetly so. Of course, she may have been one of his younger sisters, all of whom were accustomed to the water and the handling of boats; but I sadly fear the incident was an early demonstration of Corneel's later inclination toward a diversity of playmates. Sophia was tied fast to her child-bearing and the management of Bellona Hall. He must frequently have been lonely. And he was not the man to deny himself diversion, if he had a hankering for it.

At any rate, the young woman was with him on this

trip, a very capable young woman, apparently. When the sheriffs boarded the *Bellona*, triumphantly confident, there she was, perched atop of the cabin, clutching the clumsy, old-fashioned tiller with both hands, petticoats billowing in the breeze, a polite smile welcoming the officers of the law. You Mis' Vanderbilt? they wanted to know. She accorded them a shake of the head. Where's the Cap'n? A shrug and a merry twinkle. Where's the crew? A faint giggle. All by yourself, eh? A tinkle of laughter, in which the amused passengers joined.

The sheriffs cursed privately, and set themselves to search the vessel; but not a sign of the crew could they find. Fires were burning under the boiler; a fair head of steam was on; cargo and baggage were properly stacked; the cabin and decks were swept and clean. And the girl at the tiller the one representative of owner and master! They searched a second time. They interrogated the passengers, who thought it all a great joke. They threatened the girl on the cabin roof — but their writs didn't apply to her, and she laughed at them until they tumbled into their own boat, very free now as to oaths and vehemently threatening the future comfort of all concerned in the hoax, their wrath in no degree assuaged when they beheld the *Bellona* mysteriously gain headway, in response to a heel-tap on the cabin-roof.

Another jape of Corneel's was to allow himself to be captured in broad daylight, on the Battery wharf. His enemies were delighted. At last this obnoxious fellow was to be punished for his innumerable insults and impertinences; and they promptly shipped him off to Albany to answer before Chancellor Kent for contempt of court. A rigorously legalistic gentleman, the Chancellor, conservative in his views and impressed with the necessity of maintaining the dignity of courts. He could be depended upon to put this insolent young ruffian in his place. But Corneel was strangely unperturbed; and when he was arraigned for trial he completely flabbergasted the court by producing papers to prove that for the day of his arrest, and for that day only, a Sunday, on which the Gibbons line did not run, he had hired himself out to D. D. Tompkins, who held a license from the monopoly.

Perforce, he was released, with a deal more bad language, and scorching comments from the Chancellor upon the unwary attorneys who had suffered themselves to wander into his trap. The waterfront roared its approval — B'God, ye can't beat a Dutchman! Say, did ye hear what Van Derbilt done to Ogden's crowd? If them fellers don't watch out, Corneel 'll have 'em indicted for runnin' their own boats.

Thanks largely to the single-handed fight which Corneel was waging, Gibbons about this time induced the New Jersey Legislature to enact a second retaliatory law, threatening with imprisonment any officer of New York, who arrested a citizen of New Jersey for the offense of operating a steamboat in defiance of the monopoly. Consequently, Corneel's next quip was to kidnap a deputy sheriff, who boarded the *Bellona* in search of him as she was on the point of leaving the Battery. A signal from their captain advised the deckhands to draw in the gangplank, and the deputy was compelled to choose between jumping overboard and a journey into the jurisdiction of the hostile state. He took his chance with Corneel, and I cannot find that any harm came to him thereby; but the persecution of the *Bellona's* skipper seems to have eased up after this incident.

Perhaps, though, this was due as much to Gibbons's willingness to contend for his legal rights as to Corneel's more elementary strategy. The Georgian brought suit on his own account against Ogden in the New York courts, and appealed from the decision of the Court of Errors — then the appellate court — to the Supreme Court at Washington, laying a path, had he but known, for one of those granite decisions, by means of which John Marshall was to seal the unity of the states. But the members of the Supreme Court, a century ago, were also required to sit on the Federal Circuits, so that four years passed before the case of Gibbons *vs.* Ogden appeared on its docket for argument, and in the meantime the irregular warfare over the *Bellona* lapsed into what might be called armed neutrality.

Instead of fighting, the monopoly tried bribery. Ogden sent an emissary to Corneel, who offered him $5,000 a year and command of Ogden's largest steamer. It was five times what he was earning; but he refused it.

"I'm agoin' to stick to Gibbons," he said doggedly. "He's treated me square; been as good as his word. Besides, I don't keer so much 'bout makin' money as I do 'bout makin' my p'int and comin' out ahead."

The logic of his career is comprised in that last sentence. He liked to make money, yes, but he was never willing to sacrifice his ulterior purpose to making a little more money in the present than he might make if he followed another course, which seemed to him to lead in the direction he had planned for his efforts. He always wanted to "make his p'int," and his p'int, in this case, was eventually to establish himself as an independent steamship operator, which was next to impossible so long as the monopoly — blind, selfishly pig-headed, intent on meager immediate profits — was shackling the development of river traffic in every state. To win to the future Corneel desired, he *must* see the monopoly's grip shattered; his fortunes were inextricably tangled with those of Gibbons; and with his usual grim tenacity of purpose he never allowed himself to forget this principle.

His mental attitude during the twelve years he devoted to mastering a new field of enterprise is a striking indication of the essential greatness of his character. I can see him, once his mind was made up, crossing to Staten Island to talk with his mother. Phebe Hand was living alone, but for several of her younger daughters; Old Cornelius had died — died so unobtrusively that the date is never mentioned. And how glad she must have been, when Corneel poked his head in the kitchen door, for she seldom saw him these days. Where d'ye keep yourself, Ma? said he. And why don't ye move over to New Brunswick? Ah, she answered, I'm no hand to roost in other folks' houses. And anyway, thar's the gals — I've got to see them married fust, son.

Then he told her of this offer from Ogden, finding sly pleasure in the way her eyes expanded at the news. Five thousand dollars a year! Heavenly days, son! And jest for runnin' a steamboat — paid out by the week, eh? Jest like that, Ma. What d'ye think? Her keen, old eyes scrutinized his forbidding, craggy face, so bold, so indomitable. Think? says she. I guess I think same as you. He grinned, with an openness he showed none but her. What *do* I think, Ma? Huh, says she, you think you kin do better if you wait. His grin widened. That's God's truth, Ma — and didn't you tell me not to keep achangin' my mind?

Her chuckle must have been good to hear.

I was worried a mite 'bout you, Corneel, when you jumped into this steamboatin' so sudden; but you stuck to it, and done what you said you would. Keep astickin', and thar ain't nobody kin keep you from buyin' your own steamboat yet. I don't aim to stop with one boat, he snapped. Phebe Hand leaned over, and yerked him in the ribs, good-temperedly, as a mother bear bats a forward cub. Now, don't you talk too brash, son, she chided. One steamboat is more'n you ever had before — and mebbe as much as you're likely to git.

III

FINALLY, in February, 1824, the Supreme Court reached the long-pending case of Gibbons *vs.* Ogden, which, in so far as the court's jurisdiction was concerned, turned upon the construction of the provision of the Constitution granting Congress the "power to regulate commerce among the several states." And during the subsequent weeks we may be sure that Corneel studied every newspaper that came to hand and eagerly interrogated the travelers on his ferry who hailed from Washington, for, aside from his personal interest, few legal causes in our history have aroused as general contemporary appreciation of their significance as this did, with its direct application to business and its more subtle implications as to the division of authority between the states and the Federal government.

Both parties to the action had made elaborate preparations for the battle. Originally, the monopoly had retained the services of the great Maryland advocate, William Pinkney, in his prime reckoned the strongest orator at the bar; but Pinkney died in 1822, and his place was filled by Thomas J. Oakley, Attorney-General of New York, who was noted for deep learning and a cold, logical intellect. Assisting Oakley was Thomas Addis Emmet, whose style was as warm as the Attorney-General's was impersonal. Gibbons had briefed Daniel Webster, only recently come into his own, flushed with his victory over Pinkney in the Dartmouth College case. Webster's assistant was William Wirt, but it is no criticism of Wirt to say that in this case Webster was everything. The New Englander's argument set the capstone on the edifice of his fame which was to be unchallenged for a generation.

Opening on a moderate and conciliatory note, recounting the plausible claims of his opponents and paying graceful tribute to their integrity, he passed swiftly to the offensive, stressed the intention of the Constitution to confer upon Congress authority to regulate interstate commerce, and asserted that if the court upheld the monopoly there was no reason why Virginia should not claim the right to control the navigation of the Chesapeake, or Delaware deny the waters of her bay to any commerce she pleased. Within a month Marshall announced his decision, in accordance with Webster's views. The Chief Justice ruled that the possession of a Federal coasting license was all a shipowner required; no state had the power to demand or extort additional qualifications; Gibbons might send his vessels anywhere in New York waters, without paying tribute to the monopoly.

In point of fact, there was no monopoly. It ceased, automatically, to exist.

Of Marshall's major decisions, this is commonly reputed to have done most to cement the union of the states and to bolster the influence of the Federal government. But really it is a moot question whether its economic consequences, immediate and in the future, were not of more importance in the nation's life. Gibbons and Corneel and others who thought as they did must have maintained this opinion, for, as they saw things, the first result of Marshall's decision was to release business from the nagging control of a horde of petty bureaucracies. Its effect upon steamboat operation and domestic commerce was electric. In the ensuing five years the country shot ahead farther than it had gone in the intervening period since the *Clermont* puffed up the Hudson. Where steamboats had been rarities, they soon became common; their exhaust-pipes racketed in the forests along the Ohio and the Mississippi, and in the older-settled sections of the East they rapidly replaced the handsome sailing packets, which had been able to withstand the half-hearted competition prevailing while the monopoly maintained its deadening pressure upon transportation.

But the spiciest, the most amusing, aspect of this early struggle against what today we would call "a conspiracy in restraint of trade" is Corneel's share in it. There is something comical about the way in which he always bobs up on the side of progress and constructive business. He, who was to be shouted at, denounced in the press, for manipulating his interests to wring the last dollar from a reluctant public, whose name was to become synonymous with immense wealth arbitrarily employed! He, whose whole career was guided by selfishness, and yet contrived invariably to work for the general good! It's amazing, contradictory, inexplicable — and the truth.

To him, in common fairness, should go a slice of the credit for the monopoly's defeat. It was he who made money for Gibbons to pay Webster, whose lucid arguments convinced Marshall, whose dicta reduced the pretensions of the monopoly. And what was more important, perhaps, it was he who dramatized the issue, simplified its abstruse legal technicalities to a point where the most ignorant citizen could understand how they reacted upon himself. Waall, I declar'! Them rich fellers won't let Cap'n Van Derbilt earn his livin'. Wonder what the country's comin' to? Don't skeercely seem right a man kin say everyone builds a steamboat has got to pay him somethin' of what she makes — not when Fitch and Stevens was workin' 'round these parts years afore Fulton come home from France.

It was a fine stroke for freedom, that decision. It paved the way for the Federal government, years hence, to undertake systematic supervision of the railroads, although few people — and certainly, neither the monopoly nor Gibbons nor even so wise and far-seeing a young man as Corneel — at that time entertained any serious conception of such a ridiculous means of locomotion as would require vehicles to be confined to a pair of parallel rails. And no less, and without delay, did it pave the way to increased success for Corneel and riches for Gibbons. Once they were safe from the monopoly's oppressions, Corneel boosted the prosperity of the Union Line until it was paying Gibbons a profit of $40,000 a year, and in an unrestrained excess of emotion Gibbons raised his salary to $2,000. What interested Corneel more, however, was that he was afforded wider opportunities for trying out his theories of operation. He embarked upon a policy of expansion, which is sketched in the appended advertisement, itself a complete picture of the transportation methods preceding the railroad era:

UNION LINE
For Philadelphia and Baltimore
through
To Philadelphia in One Day!
Twenty-five miles

of land carriage, by New Brunswick, Princeton and Trenton! The splendid new steamer, *Emerald*, Captain C. Van Derbilt, leaves the wharf, north side of the Battery, at 12 o'clock noon, every day, Sundays excepted. Travelers will lodge at Trenton, and arrive at Philadelphia by steamboat at 10 o'clock next morning!

Fare Only Three Dollars!

For seats, apply to York House, No. 5 Courtlandt Street. New York, September 15, 1826.

The *Bellona*, under another master, left New York at a later hour, having come from New Brunswick that morning; her passengers, as of old, reached Bellona Hall in the evening, slept there in charge of Sophia, and continued by stagecoach in the early morning to Trenton, whence they were relayed by steamer to Philadelphia, arriving in the evening, about twenty-four hours after leaving New York. It was far and away the best service between any two important cities in the country, and was regarded as comfortable and speedy. But Corneel was not satisfied; all his life he was never to be satisfied, which isn't so odd when he was working for himself, but deserves comment in the period that saw the fruits of his ingenuity swelling another man's purse.

He was constantly altering the Union Line's vessels, and building new ones as often as Gibbons would let him. Besides the *Emerald*, he had built the little *Caro-line* in 1820, the following year the *Fanny*, in 1822 the *Thistle*, in 1824 the *Swan*, in 1826 the *Citizen*, and two years after that the *Cinderella* — all for Gibbons, some augmenting the New York–New Brunswick ferry, others sent around to ply the Delaware. Each vessel was an improvement over its predecessor, his unflagging effort being in the direction of combining speed with comfort and adequate baggage-room, the last the most difficult problem of all, since wood was the fuel employed and ate up much of the hold-space for bunkerage. Many people thought his ideas fantastical. Three-hundred-foot steamers to Albany! Haw-haw-haw! But they were careful to be polite to his face. He was as fond of a fight as in his youth, when he had to rely on his fists to help him hold the traffic he obtained for his periauger. In 1827 he was fined two penalties of $50 for refusing to move the *Thistle* from a wharf, in order to furnish a berth for the *Legislator*, a competing steamer. You see him doing it, don't you! Haul out my steamer for any lousy, back-scratchin' this-and-that! Come and make me, damn your eyes! I've tanned the hide off better men 'n you, ye —

Naturally, he was no easier to live with as he grew older, and harder, and more sure of his destiny. Bellona Hall didn't see him for weeks at a time. Aw, I can't help it, Sophy. Christ, gal, I got work to do. What? Another kid? How d'ye do it? No, send for Ma. I ain't a midwife. Waall, all right. I'll be down next week, then.

Sophia didn't weep, at least not when he was by to flail her with his harsh tongue; but, however much of a cow she was, she had feelings. There were nerves buried beneath the rounded contour of her ample figure. There were tear-ducts in her eyes. Her heart was impulsively loving, affectionate. She knew, too, that she was playing her part in the family's progress toward that mysterious goal which Corneel spoke of in occasional moments of intoxication with his own personal magnificence — I tell ye, gal, I'll show 'em all. Thar ain't a one but kin l'arn from me. Wait a couple of years more, and I'll have folks talkin' 'bout me from Paulus Hook to Niagara.

The steamboat operators of the Hudson, the Sound and the harbor were talking about him already. The room at 457 Washington Street, which sufficed him for office and lodgings, was becoming a meeting-place for restless young merchants, traders and mariners, who enjoyed his salty speech or desired his advice in matters of shipbuilding or management — and there were many such kindred souls, more from year to year. He had a reputation for common sense, a quick shrewdness at solving knotty problems. When strangers asked why they should be concerned with the opinions of a foul-mouthed harbor-rat like young Van Derbilt, his friends would point to one of the occasions on which he had displayed his singular ingenuity. A favorite instance was his exploit of freeing the ship *Elizabeth* from the ice which had frozen her into her pier-slip at the foot of Rector Street.

The *Elizabeth* was the first vessel dispatched to Liberia with redeemed slaves by the African Colonization Society. She was to have sailed in January, but the combined efforts of her crew and the company of

A VIEW OF UNION SQUARE IN 1858

From a rare engraving

her convoy, the *Siam* frigate, could not work her free; as fast as a passage was cut it froze over again, and the miserable darkies crowded in her 'tween-decks were perishing with the cold. Corneel happened by one afternoon while the cutting parties were on the ice, and remarked casually in his rough way:

"The dam' fools! They're agoin' at it wrong. Why, I could git her free in a day."

A bystander reported this to the agent of the Colonization Society, who knew Corneel by repute, and ran to call him back.

"Cap'n," panted the agent, "did you honestly mean that you could work the *Elizabeth* into the stream in a day?"

"'Sure did," vouchsafed Corneel, biting a chaw of tobacco.

"How?"

"What'll ye pay?"

"What do you want?"

"Humph," rumbled Corneel, "I'll do it for a hundred dollars."

"It's a bargain," exclaimed the agent. "When will you do it?"

"Have a steamer ready to tow her out at noon tomorrow."

"At noon?" doubted the agent. "But —"

"I'll have her clear," rasped Corneel.

At six o'clock that evening he reappeared with five men, three pine planks and a small anchor. What had prevented the ship working clear was a belt of thin ice, two hundred yards wide, which intervened between the slip and the hard-frozen channel. No man could stand on this ice, but Corneel, lying flat on one of his planks, with the anchor in front of him and trailing a length of rope, crawled forward to the end of the plank, then had two more planks pushed up to him, and shoved these in front. When the ice commenced to sway under him he simply pushed the anchor forward to the full length of his three planks, and presently it sank through and took bottom. He then made his way back to shore by the same methods which had carried him so far, and had a small boat hauled out by the anchor-rope to the edge of the thin ice, where his men could go to work hacking a channel in the heavy floes. The *Elizabeth* was clear at eleven the next morning, an hour before the time he had set.

In a closely centered community like New York, in the third decade of the last century, such a performance was talked of at every dinner-table the day it happened. News was scarce, events were humdrum. There were only one hundred and twenty thousand people in the little city; and across the East River Brooklyn was a village of seven thousand. The fashionable district lingered around the Battery, stretching up Broadway and Greenwich Street as far as Courtlandt Street. Grand Street, which, a few years back — do you remember? — had been surveyed, but not built, was now a staid residence thoroughfare, and the lower farms out Greenwich Village way were slowly yielding to the demands for suburban lots and red-brick blocks. There was actually a post-office in the parlor of a private house at the corner of William Street and Exchange Place; but postage was so expensive that letters were sent by private hands whenever practicable — every traveler kept a corner of his carpet-bag for his friends' correspondence. Poor persons only wrote in times of birth and death, if at all. Wood remained the sole fuel, and there wasn't such a contrivance as a stove or a furnace even in the houses of the rich merchants, who pridefully drew the attention of out-of-town visitors to the fact that no less than twenty-five of the leading families boasted two-horse carriages.

Yes, New York and Corneel were growing up together.

IV

B'ILERS were bustin' sails on every river in the East. On the Hudson and Long Island Sound the handsome sailing packets, with their brasswork and mahogany fittings, cosy cabins and wine-lists and obsequious negro stewards, were fluttering, broken-winged, into the limbo of dead ships. And Corneel, totting up his resources and casting a perceptive eye about him, decided the time had come for his next leap into the dark. He went to Gibbons in the summer of 1829, and announced his purpose.

"Sorry, but I'm agoin' to quit ye, Mr. Gibbons."

"Why? What's wrong, Captain?" Gibbons was all solicitude. "If it's a question of money —"

"No. Goin' to run my own boats."

Gibbons's solicitude became anxiety.

"See here, Van Derbilt, I can't get along without you."

"Waall, I don't guess that 'd be my fault," Corneel opined mildly. "Allus done what I could for ye."

"Oh, you've done splendidly. But that's the trouble. We've simply got to have you."

"Sorry," repeated Corneel. "I done made my plans."

"I'll double your salary," offered Gibbons.

"I don't figger on takin' salary from anybody. Goin' to be my own boss."

Gibbons clutched eagerly at this last declaration.

"I'll sell you a half-interest in the line. Name your own price. Pay for it when you please — pay out of profits."

Corneel pondered gravely.

"No," he concluded. "The business ain't big enough."

"Not big enough?" Gibbons protested incredulously. "I'm taking $40,000 a year out of it."

"Yes, and it ain't likely to grow much more," Corneel explained. "I'm goin' into the River and Sound business. That's whar the big money'll be. Plenty of competition."

"Yes, competition," replied his employer. "And competition cuts rates."

There was indulgence in Corneel's voice.

"Sure, and if ye don't have competition, ye don't have competitors to skin. Thank'y, Mr. Gibbons, but I'll quit the end of the season."

Gibbons wrung his hands.

"It will ruin the line," he cried. "I'm not a steamboat man. It will ruin the line."

It did. Thomas Gibbons, prosperous, intelligent, courageous gentleman that he was, was no more than a husk, animated by Corneel's pugnacious executive ability. He could sign checks, and he knew theoretically the operations of the Union Line; but it wasn't in him to go out and fight for traffic or take a cranky engine apart or inspire in lazy underlings a mad willingness to break their backs for him. As I had occasion to say once before, the Union Line really was Corneel — or, rather, Corneel and Sophia. Without them, it simply petered out.

Poor Sophia, though, was as set against her Corneel's new venture as was Gibbons. She had been torn up by the roots when they left Staten Island for New Brunswick, and she dreaded repetition of the experience. Bellona Hall, all things considered, was the happiest home she had ever known; her boys and girls had comfortable, healthy surroundings; she, herself, had won many friends. And in a corner of the tavern, too, had died her baby, Francis, the only one of her brood not to reach maturity.

"I jest love this place, Corneel," she pleaded chokingly. "The childern was born here. I got friends, awful nice friends, ladies that wear silk dresses on Sunday."

Corneel snorted.

"Plenty of women wear silk dresses in New York. Wouldn't wonder but some of 'em wear silk weekdays, Sophy."

She fought back her tears.

"Ye allus twist 'round what I say," she cried. "'Tain't that, and ye know it! It's — it's — oh, I'm happy here. And the city's big, and nobody'll keer for us, and the childern 'll have to play in the streets."

"'Twon't do the younkers no harm," growled Corneel. "Do 'em good, mebbe. Sharpen their wits. Cain't afford to raise a passel of farmers."

"But why we got to go? Ye said Mr. Gibbons offered us half the business."

"'Tain't enough. Wouldn't do it for the hull business."

Sophia wrung her hands.

"It's allus money ye want — more 'n more 'n more. Never content! Why, we got $30,000 put by, now."

He nodded.

"That's why I kin afford to set up for myself."

"But — but I saved most of that, Corneel. And ain't I got a right to say what we'll do?"

"Don't be a fool, gal," he bellowed, suddenly angered. "What I make ye all share in, and if ye'll only stop atryin' to haul me back I'll lift ye whar ye never hoped to git. Silk dresses on Sunday! Hell's delight, I'll have ye drivin' in your coach, with a nigger on the box."

"I'd liefer stay here," she sobbed.

And he stamped from the room, cursing.

The day afterward he paid one of his rare visits to Staten Island.

"Goin' to quit Gibbons 'n take the fam'ly to New York," he told Phebe Hand. "Buy me a steamer 'n start up a line on the Hudson."

Her bright, squinty eyes, deep-set in her plump face, scrutinized him with merry indulgence.

"Another jump, hey?" she commented. "What's Sophy say?"

"I left her bawlin'."

"Purty nigh her time," Phebe Hand observed indulgently. "You *do* try a woman, Corneel. But she'll come 'round." A chuckle, a smothered jelly-quake of a chuckle. "Yes, I guess she'll come 'round — 'fore you git through with her. You 'n your steamboats! I never seed such a man."

BOOK FOUR

RICHES

I

WHAT a racket and clamor there was that day on the New Brunswick wharf when the Van Derbilt clan swarmed the guards of the *Emerald*, New York-bound. There must have been at least nine children, all girls but one: a stolid, uninteresting boy, with narrow, squinty eyes that somehow minimized the effect of a nose that was a replica of his father's masterful beak, and a good, square chin. This was William Henry — named for William Henry Harrison, hero of Tippecanoe and destined to be ninth President of the United States, a hard-fighting, hard-swearing, hard-drinking, frontier soldier-politician after Corneel's own heart. Young William Henry Van Derbilt, known to the family as Billy, was nine years old, and regarded with testy contempt by his redoubtable father. He didn't seem able to live up to his name — a pindlin', stoopid younker. And anyhow, it must have been pretty difficult to be one boy against eight girls. These girls, by the way, were typical of the Vanderbilt women, strapping, capable, rather handsome, young creatures. Handsome, that is, in a healthy, animal sense, well-built, well-thewed, with aggressive, husky intellects.

There was Sophia, too. Ah, poor Sophia! She was big with child again, the third of her sons, and the second to live. Proudly, fondly, she and Corneel would give him his father's name; and all his life he would be a cross to them, weak, drunken, epileptic, a forger, a gambler, a thief, his natural failings accentuated by the harsh treatment of a parent who had neither understanding nor sympathy for weaklings. But this, mercifully, was veiled from Sophia, this and much, much more of travail and suffering. I think she would have sought the black waters of the Raritan had she sensed a tithe of the misfortunes awaiting her. It was enough, surely, to stand on the *Emerald's* deck, and watch the dwindling group of friends on the wharf, the tiny smoke-puff above the chimney of Bellona Hall, with its memories of achievement that had justified her to herself in moments of mental anguish, when the remorseless hammer of Corneel's will beat, beat, beat, upon a soul that was never intended for conflict.

She could not see for tears. Her heart was so full of woe. She remembered her coming to Bellona Hall, the first overwhelming hopelessness with which she had surveyed its delapidation, the rush of courage that had stimulated her, the determination to prove to Corneel that she could carry her share of the family's burden. She remembered the lonely days and nights when he was away from her, weeks and months at a time in winter, longer and longer intervals as his ambition pushed him farther afield. Her hand went instinctively to her waist as the child in her womb stirred in response to the tumult that racked her, and she seemed to feel again the sudden pulsation of birth-pangs, and the floor cold under her feet, as she stumbled out of bed and cried down the stairwell for aid. A stranger among strangers, none of her own at hand to comfort her in her agony! The mere recollection of it, after years, made her shudder. The flickering candle-light, the muttering voices of negro servants and neighbor women, a whimper of frightened children, the shadows that converged upon her in toppling waves of darkness. It wasn't the pain she minded most, for that she was used to. No, it was the loneliness. But people had been kind. Fresh memories recurred to her: the friends who had thronged the wharf, little incidents from day to day, the night baby Francis died —

Corneel's hand was clamped roughly upon her shoulder.

"What ye cryin' for, Sophy?"

"Oh, jest — jest — well, it's kind of hard — leavin' what a body's used to — and good friends — and all."

"Huh! Never seed sech a waterin'-cart. Forgit it, gal. Folks'll think I'm abusin' ye."

"Oh, no, Corneel! But — but it ain't as easy for me as 'tis for ye to move 'round. And I was mighty happy in the tavern. I feel like I — well, like I'd done all I could. I don't hanker none for the city."

He snorted derisively.

"Allus ag'in change, that's your trouble. Fust, ye didn't want to leave Staten Island 'n go to New Brunswick — and now, I'll be damned for a sucker if ye ain't abawlin' 'cause ye're leavin' New Brunswick. Next thing ye know, we'll be movin' out o' the city to go back to Staten Island, and live like gentry. And ye'll holler and cry wuss 'n ever, and tell me ye jest can't abear the country no more!"

Sophia resolutely strangled her sobs, and dabbed at her eyes with a damp kerchief. She was conscious of a suggestion of injustice in Corneel's indictment, but there was no indignation in her voice.

"Oh, no, deary. I ain't agoin' to stand in your way. Thar ain't nothin' I wouldn't do for ye. And if ye don't like for me to cry, I — I" — gulp — "I won't. Honest, I won't! But — but" — gulp, gulp — "I'll never have friends ag'in like them we're leavin'. A body's only young once, Corneel."

"So I figger," he answered, with a trace of grimness. "And if a man don't make his pile while he's got his stren'th he's a gonner. Here I be, thirty-six, and a passel of kids on my hands, and Gawd only knows how much longer I got my health. If I don't clean up quick, Sophy, I don't clean up atall."

"Oh, but ye will clean up," she protested, with ready loyalty. "Ye allus done what ye set out to do. Thar ain't a man like ye — no, nor one kin beat ye. Only — only —"

"What?" he inquired good-temperedly, as she hesitated.

"I wisht ye'd stay home more."

He shifted his feet uncomfortably under her wistful gaze.

"Hell, gal, a feller as busy as I be is lucky if he kin stop long enough to cram his belly," he growled. And as her face fell, added hastily: "But I reckon I kin git home oftener now ye'll be in the city. I don't aim to run a boat, myself. I'm agoin' to hire cap'ns, and use my time to work up business for 'em."

Her hands sought the lapels of his weather-stained peajacket.

"I'll be awful glad, Corneel," she said softly.

But he drew away from her, always averse to sentiment, and especially in public.

"Aw, ye talk like I never come home," he snapped. "Tryin' to give t'other passengers a treat? This ain't a yacht." His eyes blazed with an egotism that was sublime in its intensity. "But wait a few years. I'll have a yacht. Ye'll be proud to be called Mis' Van Derbilt, then. Yes, sirree, I'll have more'n all these high-toned swells, like the Clintons, and old Hone, and Sim Draper, and Minturn, and Hoffman, and the rest of 'em. I'll have more'n Astor, by Christ!"

"Sure, ye will, Corneel," she applauded indulgently, in no wise believing, but complaisant as a good wife should be.

There was a hint of dissatisfaction in his answering glance.

"Think so, do ye?" he returned vaguely. "Huh! Better go git a cup of tea in the cabin — wash your face. Hey, you younkers! Want to see the in-jine?"

A chorus of delighted cries hailed this unusual demonstration of parental indulgence.

"Oh, Pa!" "Kin we, honest, Pa?" "Pa, kin we steer?" "Say, Pa, Billy says he kin run a in-jine."

"Does, does he?" Corneel commented upon this last remark. "Bill, I guess ye're one of them fellers thinks he kin do 'most anything, hey?"

And Billy retired, quenched and sullen, to attend his mother's tea-drinking in the cabin, while Corneel, proud of his flock of gals, strutted like a rooster, childishly vain of his parenthood, of his personal accomplishment in begetting such purty critters, of his unchallenged masculinity. Preening his authority for their admiring gaze, he shouted orders at the crew, importantly hail d acquaintances at the landings, pointed out places of interest, his older daughters fluttering and squawking and exclaiming "Oh, Pa!" "Reeley, Pa?" and hauling their infant sisters wherever he led them, until tired wails impelled him to send the hull push to the cabin. "Damn the brats! Tell your Ma to hush 'em up. I cain't be bothered."

They reached New York late in the afternoon, and straggled ashore at dusk, shrinking from the terrible crowds, awestruck by the innumerable vessels at the piers and lying at anchor in the harbor, goggling at the endless perspective of houseroofs and chimneys, dazed by the clattering hoofs and wheels on the cobbles. "I'll bet thar's ten thousand people in this place!" "Oh, Ethelinda, do for mercy's sake, ketch aholt of that bag!" "Here, you Billy! Come out from under them carts or I'll chuck ye into the river." "Phebe Jane, cain't ye put one foot in front of t'other?" "Hey, Pete, I want ye to git Andy 'n take them boxes and stuff over to Stone Street. Here's a shillin' apiece for ye, and I'll grind your heads together if ye keep me waitin'." "Corneel! Corneel! I'm plumb sorry, but ye got to give me a hand with the babbies. I *cain't* carry M'ree 'n drag Sophy." "All right, all right. Gimme Sophy. Now! Are ye all ashore? Well, come along, come along! What ye waitin' for?"

They started to cross the Battery park, and Sophia, the baby a dead-weight in her arms, would have collided with a slim, little, old gentleman in the black coat and smallclothes of an elder day, who was staring over the water at the distant gap of the Narrows, if he had not stepped aside.

"Beg pardon, ma'am," he apologized, bowing like a Frenchman from the hips. And then his beady, black eyes lit on Corneel, following in Sophia's wake, the younger Sophy clutching one hand, the other upholding a battered carpet-bag. "Ah, Cap'n Van Derbilt, how d'ye do? Moving, eh?"

"Howdy, Cunnel Burr," acknowledged Corneel. "Yes, movin' the hull kit 'n caboodle."

The little, old gentleman in black cast a curious glance at the group of children, sturdy, ruddy-cheeked, yellow-haired, each one laden according to his or her degree, and a melancholy smile lit his sallow features.

"You are blessed, sir, you are blessed," he said, and turned away to continue his scrutiny of the harbor.

Sophia craned back over her shoulder as Corneel prodded her on.

"Who's that?" she demanded.

"Aaron Burr. Who'd ye think?"

"What? Him that was in the duel — and was President —"

"Vice-President, gal."

"But what's he lookin' at Staten Island for?"

"He ain't lookin' at Staten Island. Folks do say he comes down to the Battery to look for his darter. She was sailin' home years ago — and never come. But the damned old fool keeps alookin' and ahopin'. Every fine evenin' ye'll see him here."

"Ain't ye 'shamed to talk like that of him?" reproved Sophia. "And him so polite and kindly."

Corneel chuckled unctuously.

"Ye ain't the fust woman to speak for him, Sophy. And they was allus sorry afterward."

"Mebbe they wasn't so sorry," Sophia retorted cryptically. "Did ye see him look at the childern?"

"He didn't offer to give us a lift with 'em," panted Corneel.

"And him so old!" She peered behind her again at the little, black figure etched clearly against the immensity of the sky between two clumsy cannon. "He looks dreadful lonesome, Corneel."

"If he's lonesome it's his own fault. A feller gits his chance. He cain't ask no more."

Sophia ignored him.

"Alookin' and ahopin'," she murmured. "I guess that's all 'most anybody kin do."

But Corneel had hustled in front of her, out of hearing.

"Git up, younkers," he was calling. "Don't be 'feared of the hosses. This is Stone Street — and that's our house down thar aways."

But the children were unimpressed.

"That leettle place, Pa?" "Aw, Pa, thar ain't no grass." "Pa, whar do we play?" "Pa, kin we *all* git into it?"

Corneel dropped the carpet-bag, and wiped his streaming face with a bandanna. He was, for him, somewhat crestfallen.

"Hark to that," he appealed to Sophia, as she reached his side. "Never kin tell what'll please younkers. Complainin' already, they be. Jest 'cause they ain't agoin' to live in a tavern — in the country!"

"They'll git used to it," Sophia answered sadly. "S'pose we go on in. I'm a mite tired."

II

Sophia and the children were as unhappy as they were uncomfortable in their Stone Street tenement, but Corneel was deaf to every plea. Waste any of his capital on unnecessary rent? Huh, not me! Ye'll be askin' a kitchen-wench next. Thought ye didn't like movin', hey? Fine, solid, two-story-and-attic, brick houses, in the newly opened blocks uptown — in the vicinity of Bleecker Street, say — were for rent at $300 a year; but Corneel considered $300 a year extravagant for a man who must buy and operate steamboats in competition with opponents who could afford to drop the equivalent of his $30,000 capital on one unsuccessful deal. Ye got to pinch, Sophy, pinch it tight. And Sophy meekly obeyed. To give him justice, though, he didn't fare better than his family. Up early, working late, snatching a meal when the opportunity offered, sleeping scarcely at all, he was straining himself as he had not since those war-years when he laid the foundation of his meager fortune.

It was his biggest fight, when all is said and done, a fight against odds that would have defeated most men a dozen times. He had nobody but himself, just the money he and Sophia had scraped to save, the technical skill he had so painfully acquired, and the commercial instinct — that mysterious flair for the right course to follow — which had been born in him. He *had* to win.

He didn't dare to lose a single trick. He must outguess his opponents, bluff them, skeer 'em off. And all this with whatever vessels he could pick up cheap, buying usually on credit, relying on the profits a boat would earn to complete her purchase price. He couldn't, in this preliminary stage of his venture, undertake to build steamboats according to his own designs, as he wished to do, starkly confident that with his knowledge of the peculiar problems of operation he could make substantial improvements, both in reduction of running expenses and in increased comfort for passengers — exactly as he had done with Gibbons's boats.

But despite his handicap, he did not play safe. He was never one for defensive tactics. On the contrary, as he had boasted to Gibbons that he would, he addressed himself to attacking existing lines, to providing competition. He had two alternative objectives in adopting this policy. His opponent must either buy him out or sell out to him. The idea never entered his head that he could be driven to the wall, and so far as can be learned, he never was forced to cover. At the very beginning of his operations, he tackled the strongly established firm of Robert L. Stevens & Son, that firm, you will recall, which actually antedated Fulton in steamboat operating in New York waters. There were no more enterprising men in the new field of transportation than the Stevenses. They had vision, engineering ability, ample capital. But Corneel went at them, tooth and nail, slashing rates to what seemed a suicidal extent — and probably would have been suicidal, too, if one of his bluffs hadn't worked.

Taking an occasion when friends of the Stevenses

were present, he announced casually that he "guessed
the Hoboken crowd had got their bigness to fight," and
when doubt of this was expressed he added, still casually, "oh, I kin stand any trouble they kin make for
me."

"You haven't enough money to fight the Stevenses,
Cap'n Van Derbilt," protested one of his hearers.

"Ain't, hey?" answered Corneel. "What I ain't
got, Gibbons has."

"Do you mean to say that Mr. Gibbons is backing
you?" demanded another friend of the Stevenses.

"If I ain't got 'nuff money, I guess Gibbons has,"
returned Corneel, with a blunt evasiveness that carried
conviction.

The conversation, of course, was reported to the
Stevenses, and had all the more effect upon them because Corneel promptly cut his rates again. The Stevenses knew that their competitor had bought vessels
from Gibbons, and considering the relations which had
existed between the Georgian and Corneel, were not
disposed to question the ambiguous language of the
threat. So they surrendered.

"There's no sense in fighting a madman," they said.
"We'll quit rather than lose a fortune in this absurd
rate-cutting."

But Corneel wasn't left to enjoy the fruits of his
victory unchallenged. There was a lean, whining-
voiced, shifty-eyed individual named Daniel Drew,
who kept the Bulls Head Tavern at Twenty-sixth
Street and the Boston Post Road (Third Avenue), the
resort of the cattle-drovers, who brought their steers
to the city from upstate. He had been a drover, him-

self, had made money selling "watered-stock" to old Heinrich Astor, John Jacob's brother, and the other local butchers, and thanks to parsimoniousness and a knack at questionable trades was become a moderate capitalist like Corneel, who experienced a stroke of bad luck at this time, which Drew seized upon. The rickety little steamboat *General Jackson*, which Corneel's brother Jake ran between New York and Peekskill, happened to blow up, as those primitive steamboats very often did; and Drew and some of his friends bought a new boat, the *Water Witch*, to put on the run, reckoning that the Van Derbilts would be unable to acquire a substitute for the *Jackson*, which, in accordance with Corneel's invariable custom, was uninsured. But anyone who reckoned that Corneel would take adversity lying down was hunting himself trouble. Where he found the money I don't know, most probably he used only credit. At any rate, Corneel obtained the *Cinderella*, a better boat than the *Jackson*, from Gibbons, and started in to cut rates as he had done against the Stevenses, with the result that Drew and his associates lost $10,000 the first year. But Drew, also, was a fighter after his fashion; he induced the Peekskill people to supply him with more capital, and proceeded to cut rates faster than Corneel. When the fare was down to a shilling — twelve and a half cents — Corneel bought him out, and looked around for someone from whom to retrieve this irksome expenditure.

Being Corneel, he decided to devote himself to the treasury of the Hudson River Association, which operated a prosperous line to Albany. The most prominent figure in the Association was Dean Richmond, a member of the Albany Regency, the term applied to the group of politicians representing Martin Van Buren in control of the Democratic party in the State. Richmond was very powerful, politically and financially, one of those men who make themselves felt in the under-currents of business, the last man, one would suppose, for an upstart such as Corneel to challenge. But Corneel's answer to that would be that it don't never pay to fight with pikers. At any rate, he employed against the Association the same tactics Drew had used in the struggle for control of the Peekskill route. He put two steamboats on the Albany run, cutting rates as rapidly as the Association would meet them — and presently concluded an agreement to withdraw from competition for ten years, in consideration of substantial payments made.

These incidents occupied several years, and by no means represented the sum of his activities. But he confined himself to steamboat operating, refusing all propositions to embark a dollar of his capital in the new-fangled railroads, which were spreading a network of debts and speculation over the country along with their ill-laid rails and road-beds. "No, sirree," he answered a man, who wanted him to buy stock in the recently incorporated Harlem Railroad, "I ain't got nothin' ag'in you railroad fellers, but I'd be a damned fool to sink my money into a business that sets out to compete with steamboats. You kin have my good wishes, but that's all."

He had personal reasons for distrusting railroads, for he was a victim of what is said to have been the first serious railroad accident in the country, in October,

1833, when a number of cars were pitched off a thirty-foot embankment of the Amboy Railroad, in New Jersey. Several of his ribs were broken, and one of his lungs was punctured, while his body was bruised so severely as to be monstrously swollen; he staggered home to New York, and sank, fainting, in a chair beside Sophia. "Git the doctor," he bade her hoarsely, the air whistling in his punctured lung. "Purty bad — but I kin — fool 'em yet." Sophia responded to the emergency, as she always did. One of the girls was dispatched with Billy, and she contrived to put Corneel to bed. Luckily for her — luckier still for Corneel — the young practitioner the children fetched home was Jared Linsley, destined to become one of the most eminent physicians of the next forty years. Dr. Linsley spent three weeks by Corneel's bedside, one night bled him three times, and with Sophia's patient nursing, saved him from almost certain death.

He was up again as soon as his wounds were healed, scorning the indulgence of convalescence. "Ain't got time to be sick," he snapped at all objections, and not Phebe Hand, herself, fetched especially from Staten Island, could budge his stubbornness. "You heed me, and leave him be," his mother advised anxious Sophia. "That boy never would do what anybody else wanted. His own way is his way, and you might jest as well be agreeable as fretty, seein' you can't hinder him, once his mind's sot." And to Corneel, indulgently reproving, she added: "Son, you want to remember you ain't got but the one life, and if you up and bust yourself, thar's a sight of things you might git to do that you won't." "Huh," growled Corneel, "if I don't git outside damned quick ye'll all be in the poorhouse — and me in jail. Gimme my razor, Sophy — and them clothes ye hid on me." And as she wrung her hands, silently weeping, he exclaimed brusquely: "I tell ye, I cain't *afford* to be sick no longer."

There was something of exaggeration in his fears of insolvence. The bare fact is that in the first five years of his independence he made $30,000 a year; but it is equally true that his commitments were extensive, his capital investments very heavy and that he was seldom in a position to command sufficient liquid assets. He was compelled to try for a quick turnover, and, egged on by the restless ambition of the man who knows he is capable of greater enterprises, was never satisfied with what he attained. He was looking forward, year by year, to enlargement of his scope of operations, selling off, whenever he could, the crude, cheaply constructed vessels of his initial fleet, and cautiously building boats modeled after his own plans. But fortunately for him, his limited resources continued to prevent him from embarking upon much new construction, for an invention was at hand, which should revolutionize steamboat design almost overnight and render obsolete every vessel in existence, in the East, at least.

On June 13, 1836, the *Novelty* steamed from New York up the Hudson to Albany, against the tide, in twelve hours, burning anthracite coal under watertube boilers by means of a forced-draft system, the invention of Dr. Elijah Nott, President of Union College. She required twenty tons of coal, costing $100, for the voyage, as contrasted with forty cords of wood, costing $240, previously consumed. It was estimated that the expense of operating the *Novelty* would be reduced $19,000 in a single season, and the steamboat men of the city turned eagerly to Nott's invention. The consequence was a forward spurt in transportation comparable only to the change occasioned by the original adoption of steam as motive power. Coal-burning steamers were infinitely cleaner than wood-burners; there wasn't so much fire-risk; they required less fuel-space; and they developed increased speed. The era of the floating river-palaces was at hand, those stately vessels, which, for close upon a century now, have been one of the characteristic elements of a distinctively American civilization.

Think what it meant to the nation, this discovery that "black rocks" would produce a steadier and more intense combustion than wood. In 1820 the whole quantity of coal sent to market from the Lehigh mines was three hundred and sixty-five tons. In 1830 only 7,000 tons reached New York by the Delaware and Hudson Canal, and this was for household consumption. But in 1839, just three years after the *Novelty's* trip, the Pennsylvania mines produced more than 1,000,000 tons, and of this amount New York took 122,000 tons, by far the greater proportion for motive fuel, since furnaces were unknown, stoves were rare, and houses usually were heated by open fireplaces burning wood rather than coal.

Yet it wasn't simply that the inventions of Nott and other men, working contemporaneously along similar lines, made coal-mining profitable, stimulated a new industry and involved the scrapping of practically all the vessels then employed in river, lake and harbor transportation. It wasn't simply that the idea of a forced-draft furnace brought about tremendous improvements in methods of communication, foreign no less than domestic. These immediate results were largely mechanical. The really important repercussions of the shift from wood to coal, on land as well as afloat, were social in their application. The fabric of the nation was tightened; intercourse was freer; traffic became more fluid; and — most significant of all — there was an unprecedented development of wealth, notwithstanding the existence of what often amounted to political and financial chaos.

New York, like all the rest of the country, was growing so fast that it hurt. "Brickbats, rafters and slates are showering down in every direction," recorded a contemporary. The staid Federalist era was a thing of old men's memories. Gone was the aristocratical atmosphere of the earlier years of the century, when property — which meant gentility — had ruled, when the Mayor was a creature of the State Council of Appointments, sitting at Albany, when it still meant something politically to be a Patroon or allied to a Patroon's family, when the suffrage was narrowly restricted. The last slave had been manumitted a good ten years past now. The population, people said with awe, would soon be 150,000, while across the East River Brooklyn claimed 10,000 inhabitants and the ability to subsist itself independent of the Pierreponts' gin distillery — oh, shades of Prohibition!

Physically, the city was in process of rebirth, thanks to the terrible fire of 1835, which, starting at nine o'clock in the evening of December 16, in the store of Comstock

DANIEL DREW

From an old engraving

& Adams, in Merchant Street, a narrow, crooked alley rimmed by high-built warehouses stored with drygoods and hardware, had burned all night with increasing fervor until far-away crowds in Philadelphia and New Haven, aroused by the mobilization of their own fire companies in response to Gotham's appeal, had been able to see the crimson glare of the flames reflected upon the sky. A clean sweep the fire made to Coenties Slip, north to Wall Street and west to Broad Street, destroying the most valuable area of the city, a quarter of a mile square, at a cost of more than $20,000,000, a frightful loss for the period.

But the city was undismayed. Events moved so rapidly that no one stopped to count the cost. Democracy was in the saddle, a raw, rowdy, cocksure Democracy, all for casting adrift from the conservative methods of business inherited from the eighteenth century and the connection with the mother country. Build, speculate, never heed the cost, pyramid upwards. Banks? Hell, any feller can start a bank — all you got to do is print money. In Washington the Frontier was paramount, illiterate, ignorant, hard-boiled, old Andrew Jackson, the Playboy of the West, handling the economics of national business with the same ruthless, partisan asperity which he had employed upon his Kentucky and Tennessee militia in 1812. There had been a panic in 1833, there would be another in 1837. Firms crashed, banks closed, real estate values collapsed. Technically, the country should have dissolved, but it bobbed up serenely after each calamity — just like New York. South Carolina threatened to secede; the tariff, the whole question of national revenue, became the sport of sectional politics — and within two years the national debt was extinguished! The nation possessed a vitality which could overcome enough politico-economic bunkum to explode the Old World.

The stars in their courses, forces beyond human control, fought for America. Nothing could stop its progress, no man, no heresy. And in the midst of all the turmoil and chatter, the brawling and sedition, the hysteria, the scrambling after false gods, the surrendering of old values for a mingling of claptrap and shoddy idealism, a new era was being ushered in, and no man was quicker than Corneel to realize its implications or had more influence than he upon its trend.

III

In this Year One of the Age of Coal, 1836, Corneel doubled his income to $60,000, and in the ensuing three or four years reaped such a harvest as to merit his inclusion in a list of the city's rich men, a list which embraced sixteen millionaires, of whom an early biographer of Corneel remarked in 1886 "most of them are now forgotten." Not that Corneel was a millionaire as yet, you understand. Indeed, he ranked quite low on the roster of success. "Cornelius Van Derbilt, $750,000," recited the compiler, "of an old Dutch root; has evinced more go-aheaditiveness than any other single Dutchman ever possessed. It takes our American hot suns to clear off the fogs and vapors of the Zuyder Zee and wake up the phlegm of old Holland."

That note of patronizing approval furnishes a key to his standing in the community at forty-odd. He was respected by the more conservative merchants and shipping-men as a rough, uncultured fellow who possessed a knack at operating steamboats; but none regarded him as a serious leader in the city's commercial life. As for the Society of the day, it politely passed him by. He was never invited to those formal dinners, for instance, which Moses H. Grinnell — of Grinnell, Minturn & Company — gave to the great merchants, the luminaries of the bar, the handful of prominent professional men. Rare feasts, those dinners, where

Washington Irving, Chancellor Kent, Richard M. Blatchford, Simeon Draper, Robert B. Minturn, J. Prescott Hall, Charles H. Russell, the Curtises, William H. Aspinwall, Ogden Hoffman, Charles A. Stetson, Russell Colt, James Watson Webb, John Ward, Charles King, Samuel B. Ruggles, James Brown and many others thrust their knees under the mahogany, cracked walnuts and drank prime Madeira, sang songs and framed jests, with an easy gentility the world was soon to lose.

And Corneel was never asked to the cosy dinners given by Philip Hone, in Great Jones Street — that house to which the former Mayor had moved from 235 Broadway, in response to the remorseless pressure of trade, even as, long years past, when Corneel was a gangling urchin, he had been obliged to quit his first home in Courtlandt Street — to meet Captain Marryatt, or Miss Fanny Kemble, or the elder Wallack, or Mr. Cooper — in the days when Mr. Cooper was recognized as a hundred per cent American, or, later, Mr. Dickens. You would never have encountered Corneel, either, at the Italian Opera in Mrs. Hamblin's Theatre or at a first-night at the Park or the National. He and Sophia, I regret to say, didn't receive invitations to the famous fancy-dress ball, which the Brevoorts gave in their new house on the Fifth Avenue — at Ninth Street, you know.

The sad truth is that the Van Derbilts were not received. They were quite hopelessly *nouveau riche*, *déclassé*, outsiders, those awfully common Dutch farmers from Staten Island, an *army* of children, and he swears frightfully. She? Oh, an impossible frump.

One of the finest aspects of Sophia's character is that she didn't, as Corneel would say, care a tinker's damn for all the finicky, highfalutin' fashionables between the Battery and the Harlem River, which could scarcely be claimed for Corneel, notwithstanding his constitutional self-sufficiency. It wasn't that he cared for this or that fashionable or for the blind thing called Society; but meeting practically everyone who counted in the city, as he did, he couldn't help noticing that he was treated always as a business acquaintance, never as a social equal, and it stung his egotism. Pathologically, I suspect, this was a sign of spiritual growth, an indication that his horizon was widening, for ten years before he wouldn't have bothered how men regarded him. Even now, he refused to make advances or alter his mental attitude. He was aggressively, belligerently coarse in speech and manner, all the more so because of the hidden wounds to his vanity.

Sophia, on the other hand, was genuinely careless of what strangers thought of her. She wasn't, bless her heart, the kind of woman to alter the habits of a lifetime. A workingman's working wife she had been born and raised, and all she required of life was the opportunity of service. Servants rather appalled her. She tried friendship, and they became suspicious or impertinent; and if she was consciously the lady with them she had a disturbing sensation of being laughed at behind her back. Fancy clothes she was distrustful of, knowing her own limitations. The theater she conceived of as being wicked, and anyhow, incomprehensible. Parties, in other folks' houses, frightened her.

To her, in fact, Corneel's snowball of wealth represented only a means to secure for their children the education and social advantages she had been denied. Herself, she craved nothing — unless it was an occasional morsel of attention from that irascible, cantankerous, gingy-mouthed husband of hers, who was prancin' all over the map every mortal moment, weekdays *and* Sabbaths.

"I vow and declar' it's all a body kin do to find out if he's into the State," she'd complain to Phebe Hand. And Phebe, plump, positive, sure-footed, scarcely older in appearance than her daughter-in-law, would flash bright eyes a little scornfully at Sophia, and observe: "Corneel ain't one of your home-stayin' lazybones, gal. Thank your stars you got a man 'll hustle for his fam'ly, and ain't content to tie down to one job. Look at Jake!"

"Yes, Ma, look at Jake," retorted Sophia, assertive for once. "He runs a steamboat, and his wife knows where he is and when he'll be home."

"And he's Corneel's hired man," jeered Phebe. "A good lad, and I'm his mother to say so; but Corneel's wuth ten of him. It takes brains, Sophy, to make money out of other folks' sweat."

Sophy shook her head.

"I'd jest as lief not have all this money, Ma," she said sorrowfully. "We was happier on Staten Island, even when Corneel went to sea. Now — I dunno — it's like as if we had to work for the money 'soon as we git it."

"We!" scoffed Phebe. "And I see you givin' up what you have! Think of the childern, and don't talk foolish."

"I do think of the childern," answered Sophia. "I figger they was jest as happy in New Brunswick. They had enough to eat, and a roof to their heads, and friends and all."

"Not the kind of friends they got now," asserted Phebe. "A passel of daughters need husbands. Your gals 'll marry gentlemen in New York, real gentlemen in high hats and broadcloth, like Mr. Allen that comes acourtin' Ethelinda. In Brunswick they'd be lucky to git honest farmer lads."

There was a drawn look in Sophia's gentle face.

"Yes," she assented, "I s'pose they'll marry gentlemen. And then they'll be ashamed of their ma that's old and plain and ain't never learned to talk right."

"Fiddlesticks!" exploded Phebe Hand. "What a pore-spirited critter you be! Nobody ain't ever ashamed of *me*, my gal, and what's more, ain't agoin' to be."

Sophia didn't have the wit to say so, but after all, Phebe was Corneel's mother — and Phebe Hand. Which was very different from being Sophia Van Derbilt, of undiluted peasant stock, and merely Corneel's wife.

Not that Sophia was terribly, devastatingly unhappy. She was too placid, too self-effacing, to feel more than occasional spasms of loneliness. I do not think that she was even very jealous of Corneel's absences and inattentions. His will had bent her to humility, and all the strength of her being was poured into the one channel of childbearing and the nurturing of her children. Three were born to her after they came to New York: Cornelius Jeremiah, the family's blacksheep, another girl, and a third boy, George, the sole

one of the children to excite any marked affection in
Corneel. Her children, the twelve that lived, gradually
became her one valid interest in life. Her thoughts and
actions centered around them. They, and only they,
could rouse her to defy Corneel.

It was for the children's sake that she compelled him
to move the family from Stone Street to 134 Madison
Street; and when his Hudson River Lines were successful she struck out again, in her quiet, stolid, Dutch
way, and in that Year One of the Age of Coal, 1836,
which saw his longest stride toward affluence, she
engineered a move to a really commodious house at
173 East Broadway. But she was unable to adjust
herself to city life, and the younger children were constantly discontented, so, in 1840, she persuaded Corneel
to return to the starting-point of all their migrations,
Staten Island.

She managed this with extraordinary deftness, for
her. Corneel was commencing to let himself out, in-
dulging his personal tastes, which ran chiefly to three
things: good whiskey, good cigars and trotting-horses.
And the horses rekindled in him the memory of his boyhood on his father's farm, grassy paddocks, shady, dirt
roads, the spaciousness of outdoors. Sophia perceived
the drift of his mind, and urged it carefully along.

"It's jest a shame, Corneel, what it costs to live here
into the city," she'd say. "And all we git is the house
and 'bout as much ground as ye could cover with a
saddle-blanket."

"Ye would move uptown," Corneel pointed out,
gruffly illogical.

"And no place to stable so much as one hoss," she

continued, without noticing him, "let be the childern have to play in the street."

"Thar ain't no other way to live," grunted Corneel, "less'n ye want to move into the country, up to Harlem, mebbe."

"I been wonderin' how ye'd like to build on Staten Island," she said tentatively. "Thar's enough room on the farm. Your Ma, she'd give ye the land."

"Buildin' costs money," scowled Corneel.

"So does payin' rent," she returned, "and nothin' to show for it. Ye got a position to hold up, Corneel. Thar's the childern. And 'twouldn't do ye no harm to live in the country, yourself. Ye could keep all the hosses ye wanted, and a man to take keer of 'em, and what with the change and the fresh air, I wouldn't be s'prised if it did your dyspepsy a sight of good."

"It might, at that," Corneel agreed reluctantly.

He was seeing himself, under the spell of the picture Sophia had presented, somewhat in the light of — well, not a country gentleman, but a sporting farmer. The unquenchable nostalgia of the country-born man welled up in his heart, flavored by that lurking resentment against the great ones of the city, who refused to notice him outside of business hours.

"Damn 'em," he reflected. "I'm good enough to carry thar goods, 'n help swing thar deals. But not a one of 'em ever says: 'Stop in on your way uptown, Van Derbilt, and have a snort of licker.' Dudes, lilly-livered dudes! I'm as good as they be, 'n in the coun-try —"

He jerked out of his study.

"Tell ye what, Sophy," he decided, "I'm 'bout finished with the city — for a place to live. Let's go over, camp with Ma. I'll git contracts let, and we'll build 'soon as we kin. Huh?"

Sophia inhaled a long sigh of relief.

"Oh, Corneel! The childern 'll be so glad. And I — it'll seem like goin' home."

"That's 'bout what it will be," agreed Corneel, very good-natured. "We'll show the Island folks a thing or two, hey? Show 'em what the Van Derbilts kin do."

He posted off in the morning to carry the news of his intention to his mother.

"Goin' to build, Ma," he announced almost breathlessly. "Want that lot ye allus called mine, over thar in the northeast corner on the rise toward Tompkinsville."

Phebe Hand chuckled.

"Well, now, Corneel! Chickens come home to roost, and so do Van Derbilts. I expect you'll be for makin' a mansion house — give the neighbors something 'sides snuff to chew on?"

"They'll be able to see it," he grinned. "Tall, white pillars — 'n an iron fence. And say, Ma! Kin Sophy 'n the childern come over 'n pack in with ye while I'm buildin'?"

"Course!" Her restless, bright eyes probed at his face. "Kind of feel you ain't took the city by storm, son? Got to come back, and settle down with your old Ma, eh?"

"Not — not exactly." He was shamefaced, as he would be only with her, of all living people. "We — we ain't — Ye see, Sophy 'n I — we — Well, the city folks they talk so, 'n they eat so, 'n they do everything jest so. We — I ain't had time to l'arn. I guess I never will."

"I guess you won't, Corneel," she responded. "But don't you let up on yourself. You'd ought to have a house in the country for the childern summers, anyway; but some day you'll be goin' back to the city to live. I *want* you to, son. It ain't in you to lie down on a fight, is it?"

"No, Ma," he denied, swallowing hard. "But this is a diff'rent kind of fight. These fellers, they do business with me, 'n then they forget me. I don't hanker to sit in their dining-rooms, but I jest git mad 'cause they figger I'm not enough account to ask. I'm agoin' to show 'em, Ma. You wait, 'n see."

"I'll wait," she affirmed grimly, "if it don't take too long."

IV

WHEN Corneel forced the Hudson River Association to buy him off, and withdrew his Albany steamers, he was, technically, accepting a bribe to abstain from competition; and the logical criticism has been made that the influence of such conduct must have been destructive and inimical to the public interest. There isn't, of course, the slightest doubt that in adopting this policy he was thinking solely of himself; it was a device to wring money out of his rivals; he was too ignorant of book-economics, and too selfish, even had he been less ignorant, to dream that what he did might react to the general advantage of the community. Probably, he would have laughed had the idea been suggested to him, for he was, above all things, no hypocrite. All a feller kin do is mind his own fences. But nevertheless, that uncanny faculty of his for the constructive course dictated this, as it did every important step he took. The success of his tactics stirred other men to emulation, and created competition on a scale hitherto unknown.

His place on the Hudson was filled by a number of ambitious operators. That shrewd and oily scoundrel, Daniel Drew, once bitten by any money-making scheme, could never keep away from it. Ranked with Drew — sometimes associated with him, sometimes opposed to him — were such men as Isaac Newton, Robert W. Kelly, J. W. Hancox, J. C. Corwin, and George Law.

Of this group Law was the most picturesque, after Drew — although, like all the steamboat men of his generation, with the two exceptions of Corneel and Drew, his name is practically unknown today. But in his time "Liveoak George," as he was called in tribute to his rugged pugnacity, was a familiar character to Americans. It was he, who, after the Spanish authorities proclaimed that they would not permit one of his Panama Mail steamers to touch at Havana because of articles written by her purser on the Cuban situation, appealed to Washington for support, and when the Administration refused to help him, and went so far as to withdraw the mails from his vessel and warn passengers that they traveled on her at their peril, sent her off in ballast, with the offending purser aboard.

"I'll show these god-damned dagos they can't bluff George Law," he said. "Let the Administration trim. I'll take care of myself."

The Captain-General of Cuba had threatened to sink the steamer so soon as she came under the Morro's guns; but she entered and departed from Havana harbor, unharmed. And the whole country, regardless of creed, applauded Law's gesture. Evidently, he was a man after Corneel's pattern, and it isn't strange that, although they were business enemies for years, they entertained mutual feelings of almost knightly respect and amity. Their occasional meetings were like the contacts of two rusty-armored, hoarse-voiced *condottieri*, who, in the intervals of partisan warfare, sit by the roadside to drink from the same jug and compare casualties.

All the Hudson River operators were substantially

influenced by Corneel's activities, even during the period of his absence from their field when he was establishing a web of lines covering Long Island Sound and the rich New England ports, maintaining regular schedules to Bridgeport, Norwalk, Derby, New Haven, Hartford, New London, Providence, Newport and Boston. He had the means finally to test his theories of construction, and under the spell of his restless energy river and Sound steamers became larger and faster, year after year, with pleasant staterooms, sumptuous cabins and luxurious dining accommodations. By 1840 the cost of a journey from New York to Albany, 150 miles, was $2, and this included dinner and breakfast. Hone, whose diary is as reliable a clue to the intimate life of the era as Pepys's is to Restoration London, comments on a journey he made in this year: "Travel on the North River is cheaper than anything I know of, except American shirtings at five cents a yd. I wonder people do not live on board instead of going to the Astor House."

The steamers plying out of New York, which had lagged behind the Mississippi packets, were now superior in size and accommodations. Within fifteen years of Marshall's decision, squashing the pretensions of the Fulton-Livingston Monopoly, within ten years of Corneel's entering the business as an independent operator, these vessels were substantially as comfortable as those we know. Nothing like as rapid improvement marked the railroads of the era, and while there were various technical and mechanical reasons for this, it still affords a commentary on the initiative of Corneel and his contemporaries — who acquired initiative because if they didn't they went to the wall. Only men of daring ingenuity could withstand the press of competition. Every operator was afraid to let his service down. That feller Van Derbilt hops any line that ain't got a thunderin' good balance-sheet. Christ, he'll run yer ragged with rate-cuttin', and then buy yer out at sheriff's sale. Cain't take no chance with him.

It wouldn't be honest, however, to contend that such exaggerated competition was an unmixed blessing. In the beginning, the chief emphasis of all the operators was on speed: that pet mania of our people, which, in the days of horse-drawn vehicles, required a four-horse coach to be dubbed a "Flying-Machine"; and not a month went by without its toll of explosions. On the Hudson, too, there was another menace to passengers in the practice of "flying landings." In order not to lose time, the steamers, instead of stopping and mooring to the wharves, would transfer the passengers for a certain place to a small boat towed astern. Approaching the landing, the steamer would sheer in toward it, slackening speed, and the miserable passengers would have to scramble ashore as best they could in the brief interval during which the smallboat was bumping by the piles of the wharf. Naturally, there were many accidents, and one at Poughkeepsie, in which several passengers were drowned, induced the Legislature to forbid the practice.

Having exhausted the novelty of speed, the operators turned to development of size and comfort. Corneel, as I have said, was a leader in this move from its inception. He discovered a naïve, a childish, satisfaction in building and improving things. It was always his great hobby. And nothing pleased him more — tickled his vanity, you might say — than to produce a new steamboat, which would compel rival operators to sit up nights, groping for changes to stimulate traffic for their vessels. But like all pioneers, he had the humiliation of seeing one of his imitators inaugurate the most drastic evolution of the new era. For, although he might justly claim that he was the progenitor of the up-to-date river steamer, it was none other than Daniel Drew, the drover, who built the first of the floating palaces, the *Isaac Newton*, of the People's Line, 300 feet long and with berths for 500 passengers.

After that, as you might imagine, nothing could keep Corneel off the Hudson. His deal with the Hudson River Association was terminated; his Sound lines were fairly dripping dollars into his bank accounts. So he built the most magnificent steamer that had yet been seen, proudly named her the *Cornelius Van Derbilt*, and embarked upon another of his riotous campaigns ag'in fellers fat enough for profit. Stout rivals they were, for besides Drew's People's Line, George Law was active on the Albany route, and put into commission a monster of his own, the *Oregon*, which was proclaimed the fastest vessel on the river.

This was an implied challenge, which Corneel wasn't the man to swallow. A race was arranged, with all the formality of a civic event. The vessels were stripped for action; their machinery was tuned up; select companies of friends of the two magnates embarked on each. What happened is told, in part, in Hone's entry of June 1, 1847: "A great steamboat race came off between the *Cornelius Van Derbilt*, which bears the name of her

WALL STREET FROM THE CORNER OF BROAD, SHOWING THE FAMOUS STREET IN IT
NAT

ATE BEFORE IT HAD BEEN CHANGED ENTIRELY FROM A RESIDENTIAL SECTION INTO THE
TRADE

enterprising proprietor, and the *Oregon*, Captain Law. They went to Croton Point, and returned, 75 miles, in three hours and fifteen minutes, — a rate of speed which would carry a vessel to Liverpool in five or six days. The *Oregon* gained the race, and Captain Van Derbilt was beaten for once." This entry is interesting for two reasons: it is the first mention Hone makes of Corneel, and the concluding phrase indicates that already he had acquired a reputation. But it doesn't tell the whole story. Corneel lost the race because, in the heat of approaching the halfway point, he grabbed the steering-wheel from his pilot, forgot to slacken speed for the turn and was carried on up-river, while the *Oregon* thrashed around nimbly and gained a lead the *Van Derbilt* was unable to overcome. Ah, but the air in that pilot-house was blue and sulphury with more than tobacco-smoke!

"And Captain Van Derbilt was beaten for once." But the victory didn't win much for "Liveoak George." Ground between the competition of Drew's powerful line and Corneel, who was bolstered by the immense traffic of his Sound lines, Law stood no chance at all, and ultimately sold out to Drew. Drew, as strange a figure as there is in the sweep of our history, was an adept at playing fast and loose, and contrived to enmesh his affairs with Corneel, so that the two ran along fairly amicably, even when their interests clashed, as on the Hudson. Like Corneel, the former drover had a line of steamers to Stonington, Connecticut, and for a time he employed Jake, Corneel's brother, as one of his captains. For several years, also, Corneel's oldest son, Billy, was a clerk in Drew's banking firm, Drew,

Robinson & Company. Corneel, on his part, always had a soft spot in his heart for Drew, no matter how crooked and sinuous were the policies "Uncle Dan'l" fathered.

It wasn't only that Drew, like Corneel, had climbed from a farmyard, spoke the same crude dialect and was distinguished by the same rude manners. More than this, Corneel was influenced by the tolerant contempt of a big, lusty, free-spoken, courageous man for a shambling, mealy-mouthed coward, who was saved from utter mediocrity by the almost insane cunning of a weasel-mind. Two men more unlike couldn't be imagined. Corneel, in his absolutely selfish, cold-blooded way, was honest. There wasn't an honest corpuscle in Drew's furtive body. Again and again he double-crossed Corneel, betrayed trust, cheated, lied — and Corneel seemed never to abandon confidence that he would live up to each fresh set of apologies and promises for the future. I sometimes wonder whether the relationship of the two didn't come to assume the status of a game with Corneel; he was fascinated by Drew's ability at devising varied forms of hypocrisy, and plumed himself on his skill in dodging the rascal's consummate trickery.

At any rate, about this time the two of them bought control of the Boston & Stonington Railroad, so that, with their steamers, they had direct connections with the New England metropolis — there wasn't, as yet, a railroad the entire distance between New York and Boston. It was the first venture of each in railroads, a foreshadowing of the days to come when one should wreck Erie and the other consolidate a string of weak, ill-managed roads into the New York Central system.

Corneel had learned something, you see, since he refused to subscribe for Harlem Railroad stock because
railroads would be competitors of his steamships. An
odd fallacy for a man who built his career on competition, and it proves his essential greatness that he was
willing to scrap an erroneous principle the instant he
detected its error. But so far as that goes, the biggest
single factor in Corneel's success was his willingness to
learn. Away back in the days when he worked for Gibbons he used to deliver speeches to waterfront audiences
on the iniquity of great wealth, the pernicious influence
of Astor, especially.

"I tell ye, fellers, thar ought to be a law ag'in any
man ownin' more'n $20,000. Look at Astor! Is he any
better'n you 'n me? Not by a damn sight! We work, 'n
them fellers gits — that's all."

When Astor died in 1848, the richest man in America, leaving an estate estimated at from $15,090,000 to
$20,000,000, Corneel was properly impressed. And he
looked with pained surprise at the radicals who in-
veighed against concentrations of wealth as hostile to
the people's interests. To hear to 'em ye might think a
feller didn't have a right to what was his'n.

V

Long before the founder of the Astor dynasty died Corneel reckoned his own millions several times over. Fail he did, of course, and not infrequently; but his successes were so numerous, so prolific of dividends, that nobody outside his circle of intimates would believe he ever lost a dollar. It could be said of him, as of the Hessian peddler, who created the first Trust to dominate the fur trade, that "all he touched turned to gold, and it seemed as if fortune delighted in erecting him a monument of her unerring potency."

A very different Corneel, this well-groomed figure, in top-hat and broadcloth, gray hair and sideburns neatly combed and brushed, from the flurried, untidy fellow, who had landed at the Battery under Aaron Burr's nose, with a sick wife and nine children. Aaron Burr was dead. A good many things were dead or changed. The America Burr had represented, the America into which Corneel had been born, was dying, never to be reborn, hordes of foreigners pouring in on every transatlantic packet, myriads of emigrants of the native stock pushing westward with the covered wagons to escape worn-out soils and a ferocious mortgage system, product of financial chaos. Corneel, himself, was changed, immeasurably changed — changed for better, changed for worse. Oh, he was just as violent in his speech, his nose beetled quite as belligerently, his blue eyes retained their frosty glint, he stamped around with the same impatient haste. But this Corneel, past fifty, possessed a subtle authority of manner that was quite independent of curses or a loud voice. The consciousness of power. And in the tilt of his fierce head, in the tight lines of his jaw, nature had left a hint of the volcanic ruthlessness which growing power strengthened in him.

Not, in any sense, lovable, this Corneel. Except Phebe Hand, no one loved him understandingly for his blasphemous, cyclonic self. His children feared or hated him, and he despised or tolerated all of them, but George, the youngest, a baby at this time. He was fond of George, and his fondness increased, mainly, perhaps, because George was a physical replica of himself. Billy, his eldest son, he had no use for. A sucker, a blatherskite, a lazy, wuthless dirt-digger. Billy had made the mistake of imitating his father to the extent of marrying at nineteen. Corneel regarded this precocity with suspicion. He, Corneel, was the Old Man of the Tribe, and he was determined to maintain supremacy. No young scut was agoin' to fool 'round, waitin' to tell *him* what to do.

Billy made a second mistake in picking his bride, Maria Louisa Kissam, daughter of a Brooklyn clergyman, a young person of breeding and gentility. The type was strange to Corneel, and what was strange to him he mistrusted. He resolved to hold the couple on a tight check-rein. Notice was served on Billy that he'd have to make both ends meet on his salary of $1,000 from Drew, Robinson & Company. And then Billy made a third mistake: his health broke down. He must live in the country, Dr. Linsley said. Corneel was both disgusted and relieved. The younker'll never be no good. Might as well git him off my hands now as later. So he bought his son a seventy-acre farm near New Dorp, and turned him loose to sink or swim as a farmer.

The second son, Cornelius, everyone disliked. But Corneel's hatred of the unfortunate lad was terrible. "I'd give one hundred dollars if he'd never been named Cornelius. Here I go, and make a name stand for something, and *he* comes after me!" Young Cornelius — do you remember the other young Corneliuses? — was in hot water from boyhood. He seemed to combine in his diseased body all his father's vicious tendencies, with none of the virility which was shared in some degree by his eleven brothers and sisters. He'd gamble away his last cent, fall in a fit by the gaming-table and when he recovered borrow money to continue playing. In the Gold Rush of '49 he ran away from home, shipped as a sailor before the mast, reached California more depraved than when he started, forged his father's name to a check and on his return, pitifully debilitated, was arrested and incarcerated for a while in Bloomingdale Asylum for the Insane.

As for the gals and their husbands, all Corneel asked of most of them was that they should come near him no oftener than was necessary. He was, to an extent, generous. He wanted his womenfolks to be lodged and dressed decently; but he didn't care for their company, unless he was in the mood. Two of his sons-in-law, however, were skippers in his fleet, and may be considered to have shared his good graces. Two others, Daniel B. Allen and Horace F. Clark, were able business men, and closer to him for years than any of his own children. Allen, especially, he took into his office, and employed as agent, in doing so, there is reason to suppose, preparing the ground for a feud which culminated in one of the most sensational family lawsuits in New York's annals.

It was an unnatural situation: the son-in-law preferred to the eldest son, the presumptive heir-at-law. Unfair to both of them, and a sure source of trouble. But the earliest clue to the true character of William H. Vanderbilt is that not once, either at this time or later, did he show resentment of his father's policy. He was so acquiescent, so subservient, as to reap Corneel's contempt. Yet, without personally lifting a finger, without intriguing against Allen or anyone else, he was to reinstate himself completely — twenty years hence. A man who could wait twenty years, and not miss his opportunity, deserves respect.

So much for the children. Sophia — It isn't easy to talk of Sophia in this period of Corneel's fortunes. She had everything to make her physically comfortable in the white-porticoed house on Staten Island, everything that money could buy, I mean — everything but Corneel's affection. There were servants, even a governess for the younger children. But the governess doesn't seem to have been an asset for Sophia. There were tales told by some of the daughters and sons-in-law. Long years afterward, you understand, when Corneel and Sophia were sleeping side by side in the Moravian Cemetery. There was talk about a housekeeper, as well. Not pleasant, these details. But part of the story, part of the warp and woof of life that went to make Corneel.

The break between them came after the move to Staten Island, which Sophia had planned and striven for. It was often impossible for Corneel to go home nights, particularly in winter. And Sophia's health was failing. She was become a drab, nerve-tortured hulk of a woman, exhausted, temporarily, by protracted child-bearing and the toil of the servantless days when the refrain had dinned in her ears: Pinch it, tight. Tighter, gal! But she was pitifully glad to live — exist, rather — amongst the haunts of her childhood, and took an innocent pleasure in the homage paid her as the wife of the Island's richest citizen. She was prostrated when Corneel calmly announced to her in 1845 that he intended to shift back to New York. He'd build a house in Washington Place, near the Square, which had been laid out for the swells who found the downtown districts overcrowded.

"But I don't want to live in the city," she wailed. "Ye *said* we'd stay here. I'm skeered of the city, Corneel, and of the noise, and all the people, the feet on the pavements and the eyes alookin' and awatchin' when ye go out."

"Don't talk crazy," snapped Corneel.

Her eyes opened blankly.

"I — I feel like I was crazy," she sobbed.

"Damn nonsense! Ye're jest puttin' on a tantrum 'cause ye want me to keep alivin' like a farmer for ye."

Later, he ordered out his gig, and trotted down to his mother's.

"Ma," he said abruptly, "remember ye said ye'd wait for me to show them fellers in New York? Well, I'm agoin' to do it. Lettin' contracts for a house in

Washington Place, no great shakes of a house, but purty fair. I'm too big a feller to live in Staten Island. My name means something in Wall Street."

"It means something in Staten Island, too," Phebe remarked drily. "Them fellers takin' ye in now? Figger they'll have their wives askin' Sophy for tea?"

Corneel's expression was sardonic.

"Nope! Nary a chance. And I don't keer 'bout it no more. I was foolish to let it rile me. And I got to thinkin' 'bout it. If they don't ask me to their houses, they'll have to come to mine. Same thing, ain't it?"

"Humph," said Phebe. "Mebbe. What 'bout Sophy?"

"That's one of the things I wanted to ask ye," he returned. "When I told her, she up and raised hell — talked crazy."

"She would," said Phebe largely. "You got to gentle her, but same time, don't take her too serious. She's jest startin' her change of life; all women act peculiar thataway. Tell you what. Ethelinda and Dan'l Allen are goin' on a trip to Canada. Why don't you have 'em cart Sophy along? It'll kind of take her mind off herself, and when she comes back more sensible, the house'll be there, and she'll make the best of it."

"That's a bangup idee," exclaimed Corneel. "Ought to do her a sight of good. Dunno what I'll do, if it don't, though. She's gittin' plumb selfish."

His mother emitted her brusque chuckle.

"I wouldn't say that. Trouble with Sophy is she ain't selfish. And a body needs to be a mite selfish in this world — or she gits run over by men like you."

Corneel grinned vaguely.

"Got to look out for yourself, Ma. Nobody else ain't agoin' to do it." He rose, hesitating awkwardly. "Say, I hope ye don't think I waited too long — or — or — ye ain't disap'inted?"

Phebe Hand's eyes gleamed with a reflection of the icy light in his.

"I ain't never disap'inted in what I know is bound to happen, Corneel. But you let them city people see you for jest what you are. Let 'em feel the weight of your hand. What if they don't want to eat with you? They'll be afeard of you!"

"By Christ, that's what I was thinkin'!"

He stooped and kissed her, very awkward again.

"You hadn't ought to cuss so," she rebuked him sharply. "Now, git home to Sophy — and don't be rougher 'n you kin help."

Sophia received him with fresh tears, and a babble of confused, aimless pleadings. She didn't want to go anywhere. She wanted only to remain here, with him. Wouldn't he please stay with her? He fumbled clumsily her ardent bid for a sentiment that was alien to him, and sent for several of the daughters, who gently persuaded her to accept her mother-in-law's plan. She was too tired to support the argument alone, and I suspect, subconsciously, she realized that Corneel was no longer her Corneel. All right, nobody keers what becomes of me. I'll go. I guess I'm better dead or away.

Corneel bade her good-by as patiently as his disposition would permit, and returned to his work and his diversions — these latter not always harmless — with a very frank and gusty expletive of relief. There wasn't any pretense about him, no fineness of fiber to dispute his cravings and appetites. He indulged himself, if he felt like it. And he'd damn the eyes and bust the guts of anyone that tried to stop him.

That was a busy summer, what with the building going on in Washington Place, and the Mexican War, and a new trotter or two, not to speak of several — well, diversions. He was fifty-two, but men of forty envied his physique, his tall stature, straight as an Indian's, his abdominal muscles developed like a wrestler's, his limbs gnarled and thick. There was a haughty lift to his chin that attracted people's attention, and discouraged amusement at his shocking grammar and mispronunciations. He wasn't, as he had confessed to Phebe Hand, any closer to inclusion in that company which gathered at Moses Grinnell's, notwithstanding others had been admitted in the current decade. An imposing list: William M. Evarts, Isaac Bell, Marshall O. Roberts, Benjamin F. Silliman, Nathan T. Griswold, Moses Taylor, Peletiah Perit for a few. But why should he care for arbitrary social differences? He was rolling up close to a million a year. He had power, power over some of these very men, whose table-linen was too choice for him to spill wine upon.

In the Fall Sophia returned, unimproved, her condition aggravated, if anything. She wasn't violent, but her tears and lamentations, her protests against living in the boiling hive of the city, her occasional threats to do away with herself, her continual reproaches for Corneel's inattention, aroused his implacable animosity.

"I ain't agoin' to stand her ravin's," he shouted, at last. "She's crazy, and the crazy-house is the place for her."

She was committed that fall to Dr. McDonald's Asylum in Flushing, New York, against the protests of most of her children; and Corneel moved the family to Washington Place, with a housekeeper to look after them.

This is a black chapter, and it is only fair to explain that the one version of it which ever came to light was part of the testimony given by his son-in-law, Allen, in the contest to break his will, the culmination of the feud referred to previously. Allen was a prejudiced witness, and due allowance must be made for that; but still, there is no possible excuse for Corneel's action. It was the act of a man who had temporarily lost any sense he had possessed of decency, honor and obligation. Whether he was actuated by infatuation for another woman, as Allen very patently hinted, or merely by temper over Sophia's condition, his conduct was unforgivable — as, apparently, he, himself came to understand.

The feeling against him must have been widespread. Allen testified that the governess of the younger children refused to become housekeeper, and that then Billy undertook to find one. Billy, whom Allen accuses of having refused to join with the rest of the family in repudiating Sophia's confinement, declared bluntly: "The old man is bound to have his way. It's useless to oppose him. And he's bound to fall under the influence of some woman. I'm going to appoint that woman. There's no use talking. He'll fall under the influence of some woman, and I'll have that influence."

It is true that Billy did secure a housekeeper for No. 10 Washington Place, but this housekeeper left in the Spring of 1847, when Sophia was released from the asylum, on the representations of her physicians. It is true, too, that there is no direct evidence that Corneel ever betrayed his wife in her own house; but there were plenty of nasty rumors, which some of his daughters credited. Corneel was anything but a saint. If his conscience pricked him, it wasn't because his children berated him — little he cared for the whelps! It wasn't because those nasty rumors were beginning to percolate outside the family, and might, any day, reach the ears of "an ill-looking, squinting man called Bennett, who is now editor of the *Herald*, in which scandal is retailed to all who delight in it." No, it was because Phebe Hand laid down the law to him. Most men are ornery, Corneel, but I ain't seen the beat of you. To talk about makin' your name mean something! It'll mean a monstrous fine smell, if you keep on like you're adoin'. You yank that gal out of the asylum, and fetch her home and treat her proper. Don't argue with me! She's your wife. And if she ain't able to manage you, I kin.

Poor Sophia!

VI

ALTHOUGH the tragic episode of Sophia's insanity had no direct influence on Corneel, it does seem to have marked a crisis in his career. I might sentimentalize on this theme, but that would be as ridiculous as dishonest. In private, he was no more considerate of his wife than he had been. It wasn't possible for him to be considerate of anyone, if he didn't happen to feel considerately inclined. And according to his view, he was doing all he was obliged to for Sophia, anyway. She was surrounded by luxury; she had her own coach, as he had promised her she should, in New Brunswick; she could go and come, as she pleased; there were dozens of children and grandchildren to amuse her. Why couldn't she leave a feller be, then? Hell, a man that worked as hard as he did needed a bit of fun, and thar wasn't no fun in a fat, old woman's drool.

What had happened has happened, and happens today, to thousands of couples. Corneel had grown beyond Sophia's scope of comprehension. She was the same Sophia, who had walked the Shore Road with him that moonlight night in 1811; the same Sophia, who had gone, protestingly, to New Brunswick; the same Sophia, who had accumulated the nest-egg of their fortune; the same Sophia, who had borne his children. Enshrined in her plain body, no longer pretty or shapely, were all the virtues that had made her lovable, loyal

and content to sacrifice health and comfort for his purpose. But that was exactly the difficulty. She hadn't
grown or "evoluted" — as Corneel had. Yes, as Phebe
Hand must have grown, under similar circumstances.

Corneel, despite his selfishness, was a tremendously
bigger person at fifty-odd than he was at thirty-six.
And there was almost no resemblance to the raw youth
Sophia had married. His intellect, his ego, his vices,
such virtues as he could boast, were all expanded. He
was by way of becoming a great man, while Sophia remained a simple country woman. In a phrase, she no
longer satisfied him, and this was as true mentally as
physically. After thirty-five years, they were strangers.

A sorry situation, and the bitterest factor in it was
that, speaking impartially, neither of them was to
blame, for each was the product of certain blood-
streams, certain inherent traits. One was born capable of triumphing over environment; the other wasn't.
It was written on the slate of destiny that they should
travel separate paths — nonetheless separate because
for so many years their direction was parallel. And
once their paths diverged, their spiritual divergence
was emphasized. Sophia, with regained sanity and
health, might resume her place as mistress of Corneel's
home; but the tie that had bound them was broken. All
she could do for him, now, was to keep his house in
order, and maintain the pretense that she was happy,
lest the breath of scandal besmirch the prestige of his
millions.

I said that this episode seemed to mark a crisis in
his career. It is difficult to be explicit, but I gather that
Phebe Hand's criticism, following the outspoken com-

ments of several of his children, convinced him his business reputation could not afford a possible exposure of his treatment of Sophia. For another thing, Corneel wasn't a brutal man. Ruthless, yes. Bad-tempered, even cruel. But never brutal. He derived no pleasure from torturing his wife. He simply didn't understand what had driven them apart. He was so absolutely inarticulate, as inarticulate as Sophia. And he was used to a well-run house, used to Sophia, too. She was as essential to the kind of home he wanted as a dining-room table. Essential impersonally, as a habit, you know. So, when he was made to understand the gravity of the attitude he had adopted, he abandoned it with the agility he displayed in slipping out of all his difficulties. Publicly, from then on, he showed entire consideration for his wife. I daresay he rather prided himself on his private consideration for her, also. He wasn't sensitive, himself.

The most important consequence of the episode, however, was that it awakened him to comprehension of the responsibilities of his position. Men were beginning to drop the title of Captain, and call him Commodore. He had interests, not only in Hudson and Sound Lines, but in iron works, in shipyards and in the Boston & Stonington Railroad. Downtown he was a familiar figure to passers-by, pointed out to country cousins, saluted familiarly by merchants whose names were nationally famous.

Insensibly, he became more conservative in attitude; and beneath the surface, more unsettled and discontented. He had gone far. Wasn't he going farther? Dan'l Drew, George Law and a pack of other fellers were purty nigh as far along as him. Fellers like Marsh Roberts or Ben Silliman were better known, and jest as prosp'rous. He felt that he had practically worked out the fields to which he had devoted his attention. He could continue making money in them, of course, a good deal more money, in all likelihood. But there wasn't promise of what he called "big money" in the future; and if there had been, he wasn't content to remain merely a prominent New Yorker. He had a queer, medieval pride of name, and there was dawning in his brain a hot desire to make his name a household word over the breadth of the continent.

The question was: how? And while he was searching an answer, word came from California of the shiny, yellow particles found in the tailrace of John Sutter's new sawmill on the South Fork of the American. The Gold Rush of '49 was on, and Corneel had his opportunity. In three years his name was as often spoken, from the Narrows to the Golden Gate, as the President's.

BOOK FIVE

NICARAGUEY

I

A GREAT year, '49. One of the four Shining Years in American history, ranking in significance with '76, '65 and '18. It flung hundreds of thousands of discontented or adventurous Americans across the continent. It sent hundreds of thousands of restless aliens after them. It insured the settlement of the West. It revived the slavery controversy, and in doing so, created political currents which should carry the country into the turmoil of the Civil War. But most important of all, it brought gold into American politics and business. Gold! Gold, which did not have to be purchased at a premium from the bankers of London, but could be torn from the ground, our own ground, at the mere cost of men's labor — and occasionally, men's lives. Gold, which stimulated a boom, an expansion of trade, comparable only to that the World War gave us.

In ten years, thanks to California's gold, we developed from a backward, economically dependent nation into a world power of the first rank. Our deepsea shipping increased from 1,439,694 tons in 1850 to 2,379,396 in 1860. Our foreign trade in the decade jumped from $317,885,252 to $687,192,176. Domestic expansion was at a similar rate. Railroads radiated across the Middle West and South as steamship and clipper lines fanned out of our seaports across the waters of the globe. Everywhere was the stir of travel, the hum of progress. All built upon gold, upon some $550,000,000 worth of bullion shipped from San Francisco, and employed by Corneel and his compeers as the core of the gigantic structure of credit they reared for their far-reaching enterprises in that mysterious district of New York, which was already described as Wall Street.

But the spiritual implications of California's gold, the psychological reaction it precipitated amongst our people, was more momentous than its tangible influence on the nation's life. For to it, I think, may be traced the innate conservatism of American social thought, which has been a dominant factor in shaping the national character up to the present time. During the twenty years preceding 1849, that is, from the rise of the frontier Democracy, under Jackson's leadership, the country was radical to an extent scarcely appreciated. When Corneel, as a young man, denounced New York's wealthy citizens to the idlers who hung about the Union Line's wharf, and asserted that none should possess more than $20,000, he was expressing opinions possibly shared by a majority of Americans, a very large minority, at the least. Most people were terribly poor, life was hard, the lack of proper banking facilities dislocated business and made credit dear, often usurious.

Partly as a result of this condition, partly because the spirit of the frontier was still almost universally prevalent, there was a very general spread of lawlessness. Or not, perhaps, actual lawlessness so much as disrespect of the law. It was confined to no state or section. It was political as well as financial, — in the case of the Mormon movement, discontent sought expression in a new religion, which, incidentally, was combined with economic measures designed to relieve the poor farmer and petty tradesman from the injustices to which they were exposed by what I have previously called an iniquitous mortgage system. Occasionally, even frequently, this radicalism was really revolutionary in character; and surveying it in perspective, you sense that there was ever present during those two decades a distinct menace to the republic, either from minds unbalanced or minds prejudiced. A thread of social antagonism or revolt, which we of the twentieth century might term Red, although there is danger of misinterpretation in any attempt to characterize it specifically, so wide was the range of dissatisfaction.

Certainly, there was no common ground of complaint for the Nat Turner negro insurrection in southeastern Virginia, in August, 1831, with its long list of killed and executed, and the armed rebellion, a year later, of South Carolina on the issue of nullification. Yet both were symptoms of a social *malaise* by no means confined to the South — a national wilfulness, disregard of authority, unsettlement, which tempted the ignorant to resort to force for the redress of every real or fancied wrong. The persecution of the Mormons at Nauvoo, Illinois, and in Missouri is one of the most shameful chapters in American history, and it is not an isolated instance of the fierce prejudice of the times. In 1834 an anti-Catholic mob burned St. Ursula's Convent at Mt. Benedict, Massachusetts, while religious feeling was a submerged factor in the ridiculous Forest-MacReady riots in New York in 1849, quelled by volleys which killed twenty people.

In Baltimore, during the hard times of 1835, a mob of the poor attacked banks and homes of the wealthy, and were not put down until many had been killed and injured. The year 1837 witnessed the "Patriot War" along the New York frontier, with its harum-scarum invasion of Canada; and in the following year the Empire State was convulsed again by the Van Rensselaer Rebellion, a morally justified, if legally indefensible, rising of the tenants on the last of the great Patroon estates against a medieval system of rentals. There was much of *opéra bouffe* in several of these affairs, and in none more than this bloodless dispersal of the *posse comitatus* and the consequent filling of the New York newspapers with columns of brigade, division and headquarters Orders, General Orders, Field Orders and Proclamations to the faithful militia; chartering of boats — including one of Corneel's — to move the warriors upriver against the stubborn Dutchmen; and hurricane of threats and counter-threats sizzling into compromise — quite in accordance with the Dutch tradition.

The year of New York's rebellion also saw the seizure of the Pennsylvania Capitol at Harrisburg by a political mob, which was expelled at the cost of bloodshed. The "Aroostook War" between Maine and New Brunswick occurred in 1839, and if bloodless, and withal, somewhat comical, nonetheless was the product of violent speaking and thinking. In 1842, Rhode Island staged the Dorr Rebellion, which was a genuine political revolt to overthrow the State government, with the intention of securing a more liberal Constitution, and was suppressed by force of arms. In 1844, conservative Philadelphia was convulsed by three days of rioting.

I might go on with this list at considerable length, but the incidents cited serve to illustrate the point involved. A country so frequently agitated, and by disorders so varied in their immediate causes, obviously was in an unhealthy social condition; and after making due allowance for the root-evil of slavery — which, of itself, was an economic as much as a social problem — this social condition was a direct consequence of economic conditions, due to three principal causes: too rapid expansion, deficient capital, and lack of a coördinated banking system. Indeed, so far as the last of these causes is concerned, it wouldn't be an exaggeration to say that there was no banking system worthy of the name, as we understand banking today. The poorer people deeply distrusted the bankers and money-leaders, often with sufficient excuse. They were kept from actual revolution, probably by their ability to emigrate. There was plenty of free land, and the native American was pathetically optimistic over the future in any state except the one he was born in. But an odd corollary to this was that the alien immigrants, who largely supplanted the native stock in the East, were quite as radical as the frontier folk. Speaking generally, all poor Americans, native-born and foreign-born, were radicals. That is, ag'in the Government and the vested interests.

California's gold, without their realizing it, changed the point of view of most of them. The lure of it stimulated travel, which was good for business. The capital of the country was enormously increased by the unprecedented shipments of bullion, and that boomed manufacturing and railroad-building, and made credit easier for farmers. Many, many more men became capitalists in a small way, acquired a stake in the country, and as capitalists, followed Corneel's example and turned conservatives, wholly out of patience with loose, socialistic talk. Insensibly, year by year, as the gold continued to flow East, the mental attitude of the country stiffened. Property came to mean more in men's minds. The germs of what we call Big Business were planted in Wall Street and elsewhere. Corneel, and men like him, who had been bull-headed, blustery freebooters, cheerily ready to cut the financial throat of any rival, discovered themselves possessed of vastly greater power and commenced to chafe under the naggings of responsibility.

Don't misunderstand me. There was no miraculous, overnight development of conscious thought. Corneel, for one, I am sure, had no adequate perception of what was happening, and it is doubtful whether any American fully comprehended the phenomena of this decade. How could he — or they? Things were coming too fast. All that was evident was that the nation was growing at a rate which appalled staid, old Europe, growing gigantic, leaping whole degrees of latitude and longitude at a stride — and gold was the motive power, gold which multiplied credit over and over again. They knew this. They knew gold was the life-blood of commerce, which, flowing freely, must animate the country's dormant energy. But of its more subtle operations, of the changes it wrought in men's minds and hearts and habits, they had no knowledge at all.

Corneel, even, did not know that California's gold should have a lasting influence upon his own ambitions, lifting him first from the rut into which he had been settling, then urging him forth again upon the most splendid achievement of his career, and always, at every turn, binding its spell upon his roughly aggressive disposition. He was one of gold's earliest victims, as I read him, transformed gradually from a lone wolf of Wall Street into a reluctant pillar of financial stability. He furnishes, in a way, an epitome of what gold did to the United States. A servant of the public, despite himself!

II

THE Staten Island hills wavered in the heat haze as Corneel stepped ashore from the steam-ferry at Stapleton, and took the reins of his trotters from the groom with a curt admonition: "Goin' to Ma's. Git along home, Eph — tell Mis' Van Derbilt, will ye?" Several passers-by hailed the tall figure, perched high up on the gig — "H'are yer, Corneel?" "Afternoon, Commodore. Hot, eh?" — but Corneel returned only a brief nod of recognition, gathering the reins in his big hands that had never lost the callouses worn by sheet and oar. His thoughts were far away, so far that the familiar scenes around him provoked no responsive echo of memory. But then he was singularly unimaginative, and rarely contrasted the Stapleton of 1849 with the Van Derbilt's Landing of his boyhood — or the broad-beamed steam-ferry with the clumsy periauger in which he had started his voyage to fortune. Always his thoughts were of the present or the future; the past he discounted as useless to him.

So, driving now with unwonted moderation of pace along the shady stretch of the Ferry Road, he was pre-occupied with a new enterprise, projected on a scale so grand that it should lift him amongst the world's great captains of industry. His vanity expanded pleasantly as the picture was reshaped in his mind's eye. He'd show 'em, b'God. He'd l'arn the country a thing or two.

Cornelius Van Derbilt's name 'd figger some, he guessed, after this. Nobody 'd be able to say he was jest an ignorant steamboat cap'n that made money by fool luck. Steamboats, hell! He was 'bout through with steamboats. *Steamships* for him, and the ocean 'stead of the river and Sound. Steamships — and mebbe more'n steamships. Mebbe he'd change the hull world. And he cracked his whip exultantly, turning into his mother's grounds. He was coming, as he had come so often before, to lay his hopes at her feet, boyishly eager for her approval, although he would have showered curses on whoever suggested that anyone's opinion could influence him personally.

He hitched his team, and stamped inside, bellowing: "Ma! Hey, Ma, what ye doin'?" Phebe Hand met him at the kitchen door, wiping her hands on the apron fastened about her tubby, little body, her eyes gleaming shrewdly from the creased, pink folds of flesh which tried to mask them.

"Land's sake, Corneel, let a body think," she commanded sharply. "I'm preservin'. But that's no reason to holler me deef *and* dumb."

He grinned sheepishly, stooping to peck the cheek she offered — they kissed oftener, these two, as years increased with both of them.

"Wanted to see ye," he explained. "Come straight from the ferry."

She sat herself firmly in a chair by the table.

"You ought not to work so hard," she reproved him. "At your age."

He had the grace to laugh.

"I guess I'm sort of like ye, Ma."

"More Hand than Van Derbilt," she agreed. "But I was thinkin' of the cholera. How's it goin'?"

"Bad," he answered briefly. "Twenty-six dead yest'day, eighty-eight new cases this mornin'."

"Huh! Seems like the Californy fever was enough of a plague, without *that*. Was it as hot in the city as here?"

"Hotter. But that wasn't what I —"

Her eyes twinkled understandingly. She was one person who could read him.

"Humph," she grunted. "Up to more mischief, I calc'late. Sophy says you're allus studyin' at a map."

He grinned sheepishly again, and hauled a folded sheet of paper out of an inner pocket.

"Here 'tis," he answered, spreading it in front of her. "It's Nicaraguey."

"What's that?" she demanded, peering at the blue and green blocks of land and water exposed on the table.

"It's in Central America — this side of Panama. You know 'bout Panama? George Law and Bill Aspinwall and some other fellers are runnin' steamers down thar for the Gold Rushers. Ye take a steamer from New York to Aspinwall — that's on this side of the Isthmus; they named it after Bill — and cross over by a mule-trail to Panama City, on the Pacific side, and ketch another steamer up to Frisco. Law's crowd are gittin' $600 for a fust-class passage, New York to Frisco."

"You figger you kin make 'em take you in, Corneel?" inquired Phebe.

He shook his head.

"They'd be damn fools. No, sirree, Ma, I'm goin' to open another way to Californy. You take a look at this Nicaraguey. See, thar's a river, the San Jew-on that comes into the Caribbeen Sea — that's on our side. Well, now, this river, she comes down from that big lake, plumb in the middle of the country — Lake Nicaraguey, it's called. And from the west side of the lake to the Pacific it's only a few miles of land. What I'm goin' to do is build a canal clear acrost Nicaraguey. See?"

Phebe Hand bent closer, a frown of concentration on her plump face.

"That's a powerful grand idee, son," she returned dubiously. "But it sounds 'most too grand. I should think it would take as much money as to run the Government."

"It would," Corneel assented. "Got to git the English banks to help us. But fellers been down thar tell me all ye need to do is blast the river-bed up to the lake, and then cut a channel from the lake to the Pacific — and that ain't twenty miles. It might be as leettle as twelve some places."

"Sounds too easy," reaffirmed his mother. "Thar never was such a thing as a canal between two oceans, so it must be hard to make. I kin see mountains all through this country, and they look to be high ones. A canal, if I rec'lect, has to have locks to git over mountains — and whoever heard tell of locks for big ships?"

"Nobody ever did," admitted Corneel. "But they kin be built, the engineer fellers say. No more difficult to build a canal than a railroad, Ma. And I ain't figgerin' on locks. I believe that canal kin run straight as the Hudson from one ocean to t'other."

"S'pose it cain't," she insisted. "S'pose you go in thar, and spend a heap of money — and most of it other folks' money — and don't git anywhar. What you goin' to do, then? Oh, I know you ain't failed, Corneel, and the Lord knows I ain't wantin' you to fail. That's why I'm talkin' to you. If you go, and lose the Englishmen's money, and your own, I guess you'd be back whar you started from in this room. Eh?"

He nodded unwillingly, and his gaze strayed around the low-roofed kitchen. It was the same room in which Phebe Hand had given him the hundred dollars to buy his periauger. The clock, in which she had stowed the family savings, still ticked away on the mantel over the fireplace. He was unimaginative, but no man who has known poverty ever forgets it.

"Tell ye what," he said. "I've thought purty much like ye have. And I ain't denyin' what ye say. *If* them engineers are right, we kin build the canal. If they ain't — well, I wouldn't wonder but it could swallow all the gold in Californy. Sometime it'll be done. Don't ye make no mistake 'bout that. But I ain't aimin' to bust myself jest to give jobs to a few thousand Greasers in Nicaraguey. So I'm startin' slow. We're havin' surveys made. After that I'll go to England, and talk to the banker fellers. If they're ag'in it" — he jabbed his finger at the map — "I'm goin' to organize a way to git acrosst Nicaraguey easier than 'Liveoak George's' mule-trail acrosst Panama. Steamboats up the San Jew-on and the lake, and coaches from the lake to the Pacific. And my own lines of steamers from Nicaraguey to New York and Frisco. It'll be five hundred miles shorter'n Panama — and if Law and Aspinwall kin git

$600 for passage-money, I'll charge $300, and clean up a fortune. How's that, hey?"

Phebe pored over the map several moments longer without replying. Her forefinger, its tip dotted with needle-pricks, a scald-scar on the second knuckle, traced laboriously the ocean trade-routes from New York through the Atlantic and the Caribbean to a tiny speck labeled Greytown, and from the blank western coast of Nicaragua northward to San Francisco. When she looked up at Corneel she was trying almost visibly to withstrain a smile of admiration.

"*That's* a real idee, son," she answered. "*That* even a stupid, old woman like me kin see. But your canal — I ain't so sure."

"Nor me," he owned candidly. "But she's wuth a try at."

He flushed, his lean, predatory features quivering proudly.

"I wanted ye to know — 'bout this here, Ma." He drew the map to him, and began refolding it. "I — I'm agoin' to make folks sit up, and take notice. 'Fore I git through my name's goin' to stand for something. I — Humph! — I thought ye'd like to know."

Phebe Hand blinked at a tear which persisted in oozing onto her cheek.

"I vum I ought to wear glasses," she said briskly. "That map pestered my eyes unmercifully. Why, of course, I wanted to know, Corneel. It 'pears like I'm the only person kin keep you from makin' a fool out of yourself once in a while. And if you ask my advice, don't you talk too brash 'bout that Canal. Some folks might git to think you didn't have your two feet fair on the ground."

"I ain't talkin' much to anyone," Corneel returned defensively — he was actually embarrassed. "This is jest between you 'n me."

"Sophy?"

"God, no! Why, Ma, she'd blab it right out. I ain't sayin' anything ag'in her, but she cain't keep a secret whar I'm consarned. Time enough to tell her when I go to London."

Phebe struggled with the satisfaction that would rear its head, however she strived.

"Ain't many women kin keep a secret," she observed. "You watch out for that cholera, Corneel. Be sure your green food's b'iled proper."

As he started for the door, she walked after him, light on her feet, despite her age and bulk.

"You needn't worry 'bout Sophy, if you go away. I'll keep an eye on her. . . . New trotters? You don't grudge yourself money on hoss-flesh, do you?"

He chuckled acknowledgment of the gibe, and whirled down the road in a cloud of sunshot dust. Phebe Hand permitted herself a grim smile, and glanced over her shoulder at the omnivorous clock that ticked on the mantel. So much to have come from so little. Folks called him Commodore. There were pieces about him in the paper. Sometimes she wondered whether he wasn't gittin' to be nigh as big as he thought he was!

III

Secretive as he was, Corneel couldn't keep the news of his Nicaraguan project under cover. It seemed as though all men's minds were turned toward Central America. The Mexican War had started it, of course. The doctrine of Manifest Destiny was abroad in the land, and people of very diverse political views argued determinedly that the United States must push its rule North and South until the entire Continent was brought beneath the Stars and Stripes. Not so much was said of Canada, but all adherents to the doctrine contended for establishment of our authority in the Latin countries. Southerners saw new slave states to offset the free states which should be carved out of the Transmississippi West. Northerners of jingo or Know-nothing persuasion were strong for expansion which would increase the national prestige and draw the incoming hordes of Germans and Irish from the Eastern cities. And aside from the imperialists, whose land-hunger was unsatisfied, there were the hard-fisted business men, like Corneel and his friends, "Liveoak George," Bill Aspinwall and Marsh Roberts, who perceived the value of Central America in furnishing facilities for rapid communication with California and Oregon.

Clipper ships, designed to round the Horn under royals, were slipping down the ways by scores; but fast freight and passengers in a hurry preferred to pay high for steamship transportation via Central America — it was a voyage of three to four months as against three weeks. "Liveoak George" already was reaping a fat harvest from this demand for haste. He and his associates had incorporated the United States Mail Steamship Company, which operated a line from New York to Aspinwall — now Colon; the Panama Railroad Company, which had begun work on a road across the Isthmus; and the Pacific Mail Steamship Company, which operated a line from Panama to San Francisco. The two steamship companies received mail subsidies from the Federal Government aggregating $480,000 at this time; and they did a capacity passenger business, besides deriving a lucrative revenue from bullion and light freight. In the first ten years of their existence they transported 175,000 passengers and $200,000,000 in gold. It was the spectacle of their early prosperity which made Corneel's mouth water, and directed his attention to Nicaragua. Opposition, competition, those were his watchwords.

Meeting him in Broadway, "Liveoak George" waved a stick in mock hostility and vented blasphemous accusations.

"Damn you, Van Derbilt! Why 'n hell can't you leave my syrup-kettle be? I never see such a feller for crowdin' in whenever the vittles were spread."

"*I* never see the dog fed easy vittles didn't growl at any pup tried to horn in," grinned Corneel. "Fight me off, George, or by Christ, I'll git your grub down to the lickin's."

Law chuckled derisively.

"Not you! You'll lose your shirt on this canal. All I'm hopin' is you stick to it."

"Keep ahopin', God damn ye," Corneel advised pleasantly.

Continuing on his way, he was aware of certain vague, unformed misgivings. So many people jeered at the idea of a canal. But that wouldn't have bothered him, if it hadn't been for his mother's concurrence in their attitude and his own dawning suspicion of the grandiose character of the plan. If the job could be done for $25,000,000, say, even $100,000,000, mebbe, it wouldn't be so bad. Somethin' to figger over, of course. Somethin' to be purty damn sartain 'bout. But then there was a feller name of Squier — knew the country well — claimed she'd eat up $250,000,000, and not fill her belly. Jiminy Jesus, no feller livin' could swing that deal. Well, only thing to do was go to London.

He went — early in 1850. His first trip abroad, and I fancy, not a very satisfactory one. There isn't much said of it; but I can imagine the impression produced on the Whiggery of Threadneedle Street by this lank, tobacco-chewing, foul-speaking, mannerless American. By Gad, sir, Mr. Dickens hasn't told the half. Knows his business? So does my chimney sweep. An impossible person! Wouldn't have him in my office, if I could help it, let alone my house. Corneel, however, wasn't daunted. He was as good as any Lord, and as for these banker fellers that talked funny and give ye a squint out of an eye if ye cussed, why, he thought 'bout as much of them as he did of Dan'l Drew.

The bankers he visited may not have been personally cordial, but they were interested in his proposition, notwithstanding they rejected the preliminary surveys for the canal as too inconclusive. Let him forward the more exhaustive reports then being compiled by his agents in Nicaragua. If these were satisfactory, he need have no misgivings as to obtaining the requisite capital. In fact, there was actually an element of eagerness in the words of the Londoners. England, Great Britain, was much concerned by the expansion of the United States. In 1848, a foothold had been established in Nicaragua by Queen Victoria's government, with the purpose of insuring British participation in just such a scheme as Corneel was forwarding. The comical Kingdom of the Mosquito Shore, a labyrinth of lagoons and swamps peopled by runaway slaves from Jamaica and the offspring of the degenerate Indian tribes of the hinterland, had been erected into a protectorate, under the general administration of the Superintendant of British Honduras; and by the terms of the Clayton-Bulwer Treaty, under negotiation during Corneel's visit to London, Great Britain was assured of joint ownership of any canal built across Nicaragua.

So all Corneel had to do was to prove the practicability of the scheme. British capital would be offered in self-defense, as a means of curbing the outrageous Yankees, who were threatening to chase the Union Jack off the seas, whose clippers were stealing cargoes from British bottoms in every port where the two flags had equal standing, and whose ocean steamships should soon obtain supremacy in every theater of competition they entered. But Corneel couldn't prove that a canal was practical. Definitive surveys showed Lake Nicaragua was elevated so high above both the Atlantic and

Pacific that, without locks, it could not be used — and there wasn't sufficient available capital in the world in 1850 to finance a canal 160 or 170 miles long, with double tiers of locks large enough to accommodate ocean-going vessels and rising more than 120 feet. Corneel's trip was for nothing, except that its failure urged him to greater efforts to succeed with the alternative plan of a transportation route by river and lake steamers and coaches.

He was bound he'd show them London fellers. And "Liveoak George," and Bill Aspinwall, and Marsh Roberts and the rest of 'em in New York. It took more'n one bunt in the jaw to slow up Cornelius Van Derbilt. His vanity was stung, you see. He hated to admit, even to Phebe Hand, that he had failed to put over the most impossible project.

IV

Sophia returned to Washington Place one evening from a call at Ethelinda's to find Corneel sprawled half across the dining-room table as he laboriously traced pencil marks on a large-scale map, which was pinned flat with entire disregard for the walnut.

"For goodness' sake," she expostulated mildly. "That ain't goin' to do the table no good. And the lamp's smokin' dreadful. I wisht ye wouldn't be so heedless, Corneel."

"Go down to the office, if ye say so," he growled.

She fluttered beside him nervously, lowering the lampwick, stealing a glance at the map.

"Don't talk like that, deary," she exclaimed. "This is your home, ain't it? Only it does seem a shame to sp'ile a fine, handsome table —"

"Buy ye a new one, if ye give me a chance to work," he snapped.

"No, no," she protested more nervously — Sophia was quite healthy, nowadays, self-assured, too; but she was less at her ease with this older Corneel, who bore his half-century as buoyantly as a boy, than she had been with the husband of middle age. "I don't keer what ye do to it, Corneel, but — but — couldn't ye fix things so's not to have to work so hard? Ye're allus astudyin' that map, and I thought — Ethelinda says — I mean, ye ain't agoin' to build the canal in Nicaraguey — are ye?"

A non-committal grunt was her answer. Her eyes of faded blue widened anxiously, her bosom rose and fell, as she searched for the word which would draw his attention. She wanted it so badly — she wanted to make him understand how interested she was in his undertakings. If she only hadn't been so foolish about the table! As if the table really mattered! It was just that years of practicing economy had ground into her consciousness precepts not readily discarded. A walnut table would always represent to her something to be hoarded and treasured. To Corneel, on the contrary, it was simply a necessary piece of furniture. He valued none of his possessions, except his horses and his boats. Her eyes lighted at this thought. Yes, his boats!

"I drove down to the Battery this afternoon, honey," she cried. "All the folks were ap'intin' at that new steamboat of your'n, the *Prometheus*. She was lyin' at the dock, purty as could be, with the smoke comin' out of her smokestack — and 'most the biggest steamboat thar is, folks says."

Corneel flung up that lion head of his, a mingling of amusement and resentment mirrored in his frosty eyes.

"Steamship, gal," he corrected. "Steamboats don't go to sea. The *Prometheus* is the sightliest craft in these waters. I didn't see her beat in England, either. And I'll tell ye somethin' else. She's the fust ocean steamer ever built with one man's money." A flame of high egotism ennobled his conqueror's face. "She's Cornelius Van Derbilt's, as she puts to sea. No other man owns ary dollar of her. She's mine, b'God, mine!"

Sophia was properly impressed.

"But whar ye goin' to run her, Corneel?" she ventured. "What's she got steam up for?"

"Thar's plenty fellers 'd like to know."

"But that ain't a reason ye can't tell me," she pleaded, childlike.

He began to fold up his map slowly, head cocked on one side, deliberating.

"Humph! I ain't so sure. Ye wouldn't tell apurpose, Sophy, but —"

"Of course, I wouldn't tell," she declared feelingly. "No more'n your Ma would — and ye'll tell her."

Corneel's face clouded, and he twitched in his chair.

"No, I ain't agoin' to tell Ma," he asserted haltingly. "Not — not even her. Thar's fellers like George Law would pay money to know jest what I'm up to, but I aim to beat 'em out — and the best way to beat 'em out is to say nothin' and jump quick."

Sophia was puzzled.

"Jump quick?" she queried. "What ye mean? Are ye —"

He got up abruptly, stuffing the map into his pocket as if it was something to be guarded and concealed.

"Sophy, I cain't tell ye what I'm up to. But so's ye wont worry none, I'll tell ye what I told Ma. One of these days, mighty soon, I'll disappear. But don't fidgit yourself. I'll be all right. And when I come back" — that blaze of egotism kindled in his face again — "folks won't be sayin' I bit off more'n I could chew with that canal business. Huh! The damn fools! As if I'd go into anythin' without a second load to my gun!"

"Of course, ye wouldn't, deary," assented Sophia, both placated and perturbed. "But if ye're goin' to sea ag'in I do hope thar's someone to look after ye right. What with the dyspepsy and that heart trouble ye had two years back —"

"I ain't got time for dyspepsy," Corneel interrupted grimly. "Nor heart trouble. Nor fam'ly. I got a hell of a job to chew off."

Sophia, greatly daring, reached up and kissed his ruddy, clean-shaven cheek. She forgot, in that moment, the insane asylum and all the other woes of recent years. Once more, if only for a breath, he was her Corneel, and she shared with him his dreams of conquest.

"So long as ye chew 'nuff, dyspepsy won't bother ye none," she said. And as he moved toward the door: "Ain't ye comin' to bed?"

"Not yet awhile," he answered evasively. "Got to go 'cross the Square."

But she ran after him into the hall.

"Good-by, Corneel," she called softly.

His gruff voice responded from the front steps:

"'By, Sophy."

Then he was gone in the dusk of the street — and she realized that he hadn't returned her kiss. But resolutely, with all her old, dogged spirit, she repressed the stinging tears. At least, they had come nearer, nearer to that community of understanding which had flickered intermittently throughout the toilsome, early years. Perhaps, if she tried more earnestly, if she wasn't stupid, and served him faithfully and intelligently, perhaps — Well, it was a hope to cling to. And when the *Prometheus* put to sea next morning, towing a good-sized river steamer, the *Director*, and friends and business associates came to Washington Place to ask excitedly what had happened and where was the Commodore going, Sophia answered with gentle firmness that she didn't know. She suffered it to be circulated that her husband had gone off without saying good-by to her, which was not, technically, true; but the thought that she might be helping him, however slightly, stifled the ache in her heart, and helped to pass the time until she heard from him, three weeks later, via Aspinwall.

He was at Greytown, Nicaragua, as New York had suspected he must be so soon as investigation at the Custom House had revealed that the *Prometheus* had cleared for Havana and Aspinwall and intermediate points. But New York and Sophia and Phebe Hand knew nothing beyond this until Corneel steamed back North several months after his departure, thinner, his sun-tanned skin purply with *jigua* and mosquito bites, his temper more irascible, but the objective of his expedition attained.

How proud Sophia was of him as he came ashore from the steamer, and men thronged forward to shake his hand and congratulate him. She enjoyed his casually triumphant manner, the lordly condescension with which he accepted plaudits. And he kissed her — twice!

"I told 'em ye didn't even say good-by to me," she gasped into his stock.

He chuckled approvingly.

"Good gal! We're goin' up, Sophy."

A shiver wrenched her spine. Goin' up! It hadn't brought her much of happiness in the past.

"Far, deary?" she quavered.

"To the top," he answered confidently. "Don't ye worry."

"I — I won't," she promised.

But what was said afterward meant little to her. The words echoed emptily in her ears, disjointed phrases that popped out of the hubbub of voices — "millions in it," "sure, the Greasers were glad to have us," "build a hull fleet of steamers," "nineteen days to Frisco," "make them Panama fellers look silly." She merely nodded when Corneel parted from her at the door of her brougham.

"Goin' over to see Ma," he explained. "Be home later, Sophy."

Driving uptown she had a curious sick feeling. Goin' up! She knew what that implied. Mounting riches, ambition riding faster and faster, strained nerves, an overworked body, new interests, a mind that vaulted ahead of hers — and was impatient of pursuit. Was it worth while to keep on trying? Her plump fists balled so tightly that a silk glove split — she was never comfortable in gloves, she whose hands were stamped with the *imprimatur* of stove and laundry-tub. Scrutinizing the damage, she considered herself, corseted, gowned and shod — thanks to her daughters — as impeccably as Mrs. Brevoort, yet obviously out of part. Always out of part, these days. Ah, what was the use? Let the tears come; there was no one to see, for she had expected Corneel to ride home with her. And instead he was on his way to Staten Island to bask in the glow of her mother-in-law's approval.

Her tears ceased. She couldn't think of Phebe Hand, and weep. She knew too well the contempt such weakness would arouse in the redoubtable old woman. But she wasn't resentful of Phebe's hold on Corneel. That was something she had taken for granted all her life. The two, in her estimation, were in a class by themselves, not to be judged by ordinary standards. It was right and fitting that Corneel should respect his mother, but — Sophia scrubbed her damp cheeks with a handkerchief. She must strive to bear herself so as to suffer as little as possible by comparison with Phebe. That vein of stubborn Dutch courage, which characterized the Van Derbilt strain, came to her assistance. She might not be clever, but she needn't admit failure. Wasn't she Corneel's wife? Surely, as he grew older, he'd turn to her more. But would he ever grow older? No, she decided, with a strange flash of pride, he'd always be young in spirit, her Corneel. *Her* Corneel? Well, why not? Hadn't she done her share in the making of him? But — her Corneel?

A great, shattering sob wrenched her shoulders. No, not her Corneel, she admitted forlornly. In a sense, nobody's Corneel. She groped for a qualifying phrase, and abandoned the effort; egotist wasn't in her vocabulary. Nobody's Corneel, was her conclusion. And suddenly she felt so sorry for him that she leaned her head against the side of the carriage, and wept softly again into the soppy wad of her handkerchief.

V

New York chuckled admiringly at the tale of Corneel's exploits in Nicaragua. He had experienced no difficulty in obtaining from the government of the hour at Granada a supplementary charter, drawn in the name of the Accessory Transit Company, which provided that the grantee should carry on the purpose of the original American Atlantic and Pacific Ship Canal Company to construct a waterway between the oceans, if such an enterprise could be made practical, and that, pending the construction of a canal, it should maintain either a railroad or else a coach and steamboat line. In return for these privileges, and a monopoly of steam navigation, the company was to pay the Nicaraguan government a flat rental of $10,000 a year, until a canal was built, plus ten per cent of the profits of the Transit.

Naturally, there was no more intention in Corneel's mind to sink millions of capital in a railroad through 140 miles of trackless jungle than there was to commit himself to the superhuman task of digging a canal which must climb the Continental Divide. The coach and steamboat line would be inexpensive to launch, and relatively cheap to operate — providing steamboats could navigate the rocky course of the San Juan, intersected by three series of dangerous rapids. The engineers he brought with him in the *Prometheus*, however, spent a week trying to force the little *Director* upstream, and then returned to Greytown lagoon to report the river impassable. A boat might get by the Mico and the Valos rapids, they said; but the Machuca and the Castillo rocks would tear the bottom out of her.

Corneel was fit to be tied.

"Hell's delight," he howled. "I never see sech a passel of lazy, wuthless suckers. It's costin' me five thousand dollars a day to sit 'round here and smack the skeeters off. Now, I'll tell ye somethin', the lot of ye. Thar ain't goin' to be no more foolin'. We're goin' up that San Jew-on to the Lake, if I have to tow the *Director*, myself."

The engineers protested volubly. They didn't mind the fallen trees and the sand-bars and the inhospitable alligators; but it simply wasn't possible to pass the worst rapids. Of course, if the Commodore wished it, they could dig canals around the Machuca and —

"Canals, my eye," roared Corneel. "I'm through with canals. This is goin' to be a steamboat line. Fust ye steam up, and then ye steam down. That's all thar is to it. Git aboard, and I'll show ye how."

He embarked a crew of thirty men on the *Director*, borrowed plenty of stout cable from the *Prometheus*, and steamed into the San Juan, fuming and cussing. The men who accompanied him spoke of their experiences afterward with awe. Corneel, himself, in referring to the episode, was wont to remark placidly:

"No, thar wasn't much to it. I jest tied down the safety-valve, and jumped the damn rocks. The engineer fellers was skeered so they nigh puked. But we made it. Christ, I knew all it needed was guts."

But sometimes, even with Corneel at the wheel, the

Director couldn't jump "the damn rocks," and then they would get out the cables, and warp her up, using the trees on the river banks for snubbers and capstans. On the way, they made surveys, took soundings and plotted whatever channel there was, so that subsequently, with the aid of a little blasting-powder, the San Juan was readily navigable for moderate-sized river steamers, at least as high as the Castillo rapids. One other, and larger, steamer, the *Central America*, was sent up all the way to the Lake to supplement the *Director;* but as a rule, no attempt was made to pass the Castillo rapids. Passengers disembarked here, and after a short portage, resumed their journey in the Lake steamers. To this extent, the engineers were justified in their report that the San Juan was impassable. In sober truth, only a swaggering, belligerent egotist like Corneel would have cared to climb the Castillo rapids in a wooden-hulled boat. The river steamers *Clayton* and *Bulwer*, which he later sent down, were iron-hulled — said to be the first iron-hulled river boats built in America — and they used to clang merrily as they leaped from rock to rock of the ticklish stream.

Having reached the Lake, and as he expressed it, taught the engineers their business, Corneel was in his element. The Nicaraguans fêted him deferentially, impressed by his stature and his eagle-face. All classes, all parties, were overjoyed by the coming of *los Yanquis.* The country had been racked by revolution ever since the Captain-Generalcy of Guatemala threw off the yoke of Spain; first, the war for independence against Iturbide's Mexican Empire; then, the protracted struggle for a United States of Central America; lat-

terly, the internal strife which had succeeded the
break-up of the Federation. And with a confidence
pitiful in its ingenuous disregard of facts, this alien
people turned hopefully to their exploiters for a salva-
tion they had been unable to win for themselves. A
wonderful race, *los Yanquis*, miracle-workers, strong,
democratic, unselfish. Wherever they went, money
sprang up out of the ground. Their touch was golden.

And so it was. Nicaragua paid Corneel a million
dollars a year — but very, very little of it went into
Nicaraguan pockets. As for benefits, other than pe-
cuniary, they were negligible, and more than counter-
balanced by the plague of war Americans loosed on a
land, which, to be sure, already had pretty well ruined
itself. I wonder if Corneel would have gone into the
Nicaraguan venture if he had known what should flow
from it, all the suffering and the agony, the thousands
of lives sacrificed to no useful purpose, the bitter, lasting hatred. He wasn't, himself, directly to blame for
what followed; and probably, if he hadn't organized
the Accessory Transit Company another American
would have attempted it, and the same flood of consequences would have flowed from the same spring of
deeds. But I can't help wondering, for it was the Filibuster War in Nicaragua, and not, as most people suppose, the Mexican War, which earned the United States
the jealous fear of the lesser Latin-American countries.

No such thoughts were in Corneel's mind, of course,
when he reached the Lake, jeering profanely at his assistants. I am sure, too, there wasn't any particular concern for Nicaragua and the Nicaraguans in the plans he
furthered. Nicaraguans, to him, as to most other Amer-

icans "of the North," then and now, were Greasers,
more or less to be confused with niggers. He discovered
no more interest in them than in the superb scenery of
this raw, savage land, thinly veneered with an over-
layer of Spanish civilization, cloud-piercing volcanoes
and Indian ruins side by side with gorgeous cathedrals
and massive Moresque cities. The land was his chessboard, and the people on it his bishops, knights and
pawns. A million a year — that was Nicaragua to him.

A million a year! And time was money. Five thousand dollars a day this jaunt was costing him, you'll
remember. So he wasted no efforts on non-essentials.
Gruffly polite to the deferential, dark-skinned generals
and statesmen who waited upon him, he applied all the
driving power of his personality to settling the remaining problems of the Transit route. Aboard the *Director*,
he surveyed the Lake, chose a landing-place on the
western shore at Virgin Bay, gave orders for the erection of a wharf, storehouses and corrals, rejected all
the established ports on the Pacific coast as terminals
for his projected line of ocean steamers to San Francisco,
and instead selected an insignificant fishing village called
San Juan del Sur, which was only an open roadstead,
but possessed the advantage of being just twelve miles
distant from Virgin Bay. And with his hurricane energy
undiminished, he set in motion machinery to hire work-
gangs to improve the primitive mule-track, which was
the existing means of communication between Lake and
ocean.

This was all he could do at the time, and still swear-
ing and exhorting, he faced around, left the *Director* at
the mouth of the San Juan, and descended the river in

GRAPHIC STATUES, No. 1. THE COLOSSUS OF ROADS
The first of a series of cartoon covers from a contemporary periodical

a native *bongo*, supporting the inconvenience of quarters, food and insects better than any of his companions. Hurry, he snarled, at every interruption. Make them Greasers sweat. Time's money. How'm I goin' to run this Transit without I git me steamers built quick? And when, at last, he reached Greytown lagoon, and boarded the *Prometheus*, his first word to her skipper was Up-anchor. No steam? Hell, git it on. I'm goin' to be out of this stinkin' hole before night.

So, also, arrived in New York, he assailed the monumental task confronting him without consideration for himself or his associates. Eight more steamers he built, leviathans of two thousand tons and upwards: the *Webster*, the *Star of the West* and the *Northern Light* to ply with the *Prometheus* on the Atlantic side, and the *Independence*, *Pacific*, *North America*, *S. S. Lewis* and *Brother Jonathan* for the Pacific service. He ran a boat from New York every fortnight, and presently launched a service from New Orleans as well. A great terminal sprang up on Punta Arena opposite Greytown, and the first rough trail between Virgin Bay and San Juan del Sur was transformed into a metaled road, over which the passengers were conveyed in twenty-five stagecoaches, painted blue and white, the Nicaraguan colors. Two thousand travelers a month patronized the Transit's interlinking lines, and no small proportion of the bullion of California and the more expensive freight and mails went in Corneel's fleet.

The one advantage the operators of the Panama route had over him was the Government subsidies to the United States and Pacific Mail Steamship Companies. Corneel raged against this favoritism, as he saw it. He didn't say nothin' ag'in subsidies, if they was fair, but 'twasn't fair to give one feller a chance to stick his snout in the pork barrel, and keep out the next. But his raging didn't get him anywhere. Law, Aspinwall and their allies had taken the precaution to be first on the ground; their vessels had been built under government specifications for service as auxiliary cruisers in time of war, and were commanded by officers of the Navy on leave of absence. The Government was pledged to support them — as it was pledged to support the line recently established between New York and Liverpool by E. K. Collins, whose vessels were similarly built with an eye to use in war and carried amongst their watch-officers a required number of Navy men. Congress had gone so far. It refused to go farther. And the seed was sown for one of Corneel's most destructive campaigns, as will appear in due course. For the time being, he was enjoying himself too much, making money too easily, to do more than rare and cuss at the favored lines.

Indeed, it was an open question whether the Panama lines could be termed favored. Their traffic was falling off at a disastrous rate. They still obtained most of the bullion shipments because the Mint authorities at San Francisco were expected to give precedence to the subsidized steamers, and they had preference with the mails. But passengers and commercial agencies were attracted from them by Corneel's reduced rates. Exactly as he had predicted to Phebe Hand, he found he could make a handsome profit on first-class passages at $300, while the Panama lines charged $600 from New York to San Francisco.

Inevitably, the Panama lines had to meet his rates. Steerage fares, for instance, which had been $125, were cut to $35; and higher fares in proportion. But Corneel continued to hold the whip-hand over his rivals; his route was two days shorter. True, the journey across Nicaragua consumed more time than the four hours of the train ride across the Isthmus; but the Panama Railroad wasn't finished until 1855, and furthermore, it is questionable whether the completion of the railroad would have affected the Nicaragua Transit to any great extent. The Transit was closed, finally, for reasons of a political nature. To the end of its existence as a factor in the transportation scheme it held a decided advantage over Panama. What is more, to the end of its existence it served Corneel's advantage. It was another instance of his flair for making money selfishly out of competition which served the public interest.

He prospered as never before. His name was known in every state. The story of his rise to fortune, anecdotes which circulated the waterfront, his pugnacious methods, secured him popularity perhaps past his due. He was held up as a sample of what the plain American could accomplish. His difficulties were exaggerated; his defects glossed over; his virtues enhanced. And being a very human man, with all his crudities, he began to take himself more seriously — which was good for the community and good for himself, within limits. One symptom of this was the accentuation of his singularly naïve vanity, especially as to his wealth; although he maintained a bluffly non-committal attitude, he liked his friends to talk of it, on occasion would introduce the topic, indirectly.

"Who's the second-richest feller in the country?" he asked E. H. Carmick, one of his associates, during a visit to Washington in connection with the subsidy row in 1853. "I s'pose Astor comes fust."

Carmick, with a sense of humor, feigned not to accept the lead.

"Why, Stephen Whitney, I guess."

"Huh," said Corneel, disgruntled. "How much has he got?"

"About seven millions, Commodore."

Corneel's face lighted up in one of his very rare smiles.

"Hell," he observed, "Whitney'll have to git more'n that to be second-richest."

In this same year, '53, he boasted to another crony of his youth, Jake Van Pelt:

"Jake, I got $11,000,000 invested better'n any other $11,000,000 in the hull U. S. It's wuth twenty-five per cent a year, and no risk."

He must have been temporarily satisfied for the first time in his life, for he decided to take a vacation.

VI

PHEBE HAND had been failing. Her eyes were as bright as ever, and her wit was just as sparkling; but she was chary of moving around any more than was necessary, and the flesh of her face sagged unhealthily. Corneel was vaguely perturbed as he bent to kiss the wrinkled cheek she offered him.

"Not feelin' so good, Ma?"

"I'm eighty-five, son. Been livin' on borrered time fifteen years. But don't you talk. You're fifty-nine, yourself."

Corneel grinned boyishly — no one but his mother could summon that grin.

"Mebbe I am, but I don't feel it none," he returned. "Not much more'n ye do, I s'pose."

"I ain't so sure, Corneel," she snapped aggressively. "What's this the gals tell me 'bout you buildin' a steam-yacht big as a liner, and fixin' to gallivant all over Europe in her?"

"That's what I come to talk to ye 'bout," he answered. "I was wonderin' could ye come with us. We'll fix ye up fine, jest as comfortable as ye are here."

Phebe Hand cackled amusedly.

"I see myself! Why, you pesky young rascal, I've lived my life here in Staten Island, and I don't aim to lay my bones nowhar else. You cain't git me contrariwise, not with all the argufyin' in the world. But what's come over you? Ain't you satisfied at home? This yacht business'll cost you a fortune."

"I guess that's right, Ma," he admitted, shame-faced. "But I kin afford it — and I never had a vacation — not rightly speakin' — and the *North Star's* a good boat — I'm havin' her built 'special — I kin use her for passenger work afterward."

Those shrewd eyes of hers beat down his gaze.

"That ain't the reason," she asserted. "Oh, you'll figger in all that. But that ain't the reason. What's come over you? Want for everyone to believe money don't mean nothin' to you?"

"I'm goin' to show everyone what the name Cornelius Van Derbilt means," he flashed back. "Yes, and I'm goin' to show all them stuck-up Englishmen in London the power I've got. I tell ye, Ma, my name means somethin' right now; but its goin' to mean a lot more. I'm jest beginnin'."

"You're fifty-nine," she reminded him again.

He stood to the full height of his lean, nervous body.

"Years don't matter much, I guess," he said simply. "I feel like I could keep goin'." Shyness overcame him momentarily, then he blundered on: "I ain't done so badly, Ma. I'm the second-richest feller in the country. 'Ain't nobody but Astor got more — and his old man left it to him."

Phebe Hand's gaze wandered across to the clock of destiny that ticked on the mantel. She often looked at that clock when she thought of Corneel.

"No, you ain't done so badly," she conceded, and there was no edge to her voice, now — it was very soft, soft as it had been when it soothed the plaints of a tow-headed, blue-eyed baby in a cold, wet cradle of a winter's night. "No, you ain't done so badly. I dunno, Corneel — I dunno. Sometimes I've thought — mebbe you was nigh as — as big — as you thought you was."

A suspicion of a twinkle mocked the velvety tone, but Corneel purred amiably.

"I'm second-richest, Ma. Ye cain't git away from that. And as for power — "

He dismissed Mr. Astor to the limbo of impotence with a snap of his fingers.

The full, rich chuckle of his mother was a delight to the ear. No hint of age in it.

"I never seed the beat of you for downright conceit. But you do what you set out to do. I'll say that for you, son. And nobody but you would be buildin' an ocean liner for a yacht, jest to go to Europe in. I've had a heap of fun out of you — if nobody else has. And you've been a good son. I'll say that for you, too, Corneel. But you ain't ever been no great shakes as a husband — or a father."

He turned sulky.

"I'm takin' 'em all with me — 'cept that wuthless pup, Corneel. And if ye mean that time Sophy was crazy — "

"You know what I mean," retorted Phebe Hand. "But I allus calc'lated you couldn't help it. A body's what he is, and he cain't be no more. Leastways, not when he's forever thinkin' 'bout himself, like you. Well, talk don't mend sour memories, I say. You better run along. I'm gittin' tired."

"I didn't upset ye, Ma?"

His alarm was the more exaggerated because he

wasn't used to compunction. But she pulled one of his ears as he stooped over her.

"Land sakes, no! Only, I'm eighty-five — jest like you're fifty-nine."

And the suavely malicious mirth of her chuckle followed him from the room. She sank lower in her chair, and scrutinized again the imperturbable clock. So much to have come from so little! All those millions from one hundred dollars scraped together shilling by shilling. Suddenly, she chuckled anew.

"I'm blessed if I kin remember how I got that money! Ain't life funny?" she murmured to herself.

No one was there to answer her. But the clock recited primly: Tick-tock! Tick-tock! Or was its message: Buy stock, buy stock?

VII

If Corneel expected the cruise of the *North Star* to
cause a sensation he wasn't disappointed. The newspapers were agog over the enterprise, which seemed almost fabulous to a people who were only just emerging
from a frontier state of civilization and had no adequate
comprehension of what California's gold was going to
do to them. Nothing like it ever had happened in any
country, and sophisticated Europe was quite as interested as the provincial United States. There wasn't
in existence, at that time, a private yacht comparable
to the *North Star*, either in size or luxury. She was built,
expressly to Corneel's order and in part to his design,
by the Allaire Works, at the foot of Corlaers Street on the
East River shore. Like all American ocean steamers of
the period, she had a wooden hull. Her tonnage was
2,500; she was 270 feet long and of 38 feet beam; her
paddle-wheels, turned by two engines, gave her a speed
of twelve knots an hour, which was considered very
fast. She was rather superior to the contemporary
Cunarders, and not far behind the crack American
steamers of the new Collins Line. Her interior fittings
completely outclassed those of both British and American liners. People spoke of them with bated breath.
Her living quarters were heated by steam; the trim of
her spacious saloons was of satinwood and rosewood,
and their walls were covered with marble and granite,
the ceilings adorned with portrait medallions of Ameri-

can worthies; the staterooms were furnished as elaborately as bedrooms ashore.

She cost $1,500 a day to operate; the cruise, including the building of the vessel, herself, would consume half a million dollars, Corneel boasted to his friends. It was the one occasion of his life when he discarded restraint, and spent money regardless of his usual inhibitions. Nothing was too good. Sophia and the gals must have new bonnets and tippets and fripperies for the start. Afterward — why, there'd be Paris, and he guessed no wimmin could ever git by Paris without bustin' the old sock. A plentiful supply of ice was shipped, and the cupboards and store-closets of the galley were stocked with rare foods and wines. John Keefe, caterer to New York's fashionables, was signed as purser and steward. The waterfront was combed for tasty cooks. Captain Asa Eldridge, most notable of three notable seafaring brothers, master of the *Roscius* packet, of the Dramatic Line, and a year later to gain undying glory for his exploit in driving the clipper *Red Jacket* from Sandy Hook to Rock Light, Liverpool, in the record time of 13 days, 1 hour, was skipper. Dr. Jared Linsley, who had saved Corneel's life after the wreck on the Amboy Railroad twenty years past, was surgeon. The Rev. Dr. J. O. Choules, an Episcopal clergyman, of Newport, Rhode Island, was chaplain. The wives of all these gentry were invited to accompany them.

Oh, Corneel did it in style! Dr. Choules, I think, he asked with his tongue in his cheek, for not long after the party's return appeared a thick, prosy volume, the title page of which read: "The Cruise of the Steam Yacht *North Star;* a Narrative of the Excursion of

Mr. Vanderbilt's party to England, Russia, Denmark, France, Spain, Italy, Malta, Turkey, Madeira, etc., by the Rev. John Overton Choules, D.D., author of The History of Missions, Young Americans Abroad, etc. Boston: Gould & Lincoln; New York: Evans & Dickinson, 1854." I cordially recommend it to anyone with a sense of humor — not that it is an intentionally funny book. No, no! But the good doctor presents a very different picture of Corneel from that you will find in these pages. Yet perhaps I do him an injustice, for there can be no question that Corneel's attitude toward life was changing. I have spoken of this previously, and shall have occasion to speak of it again. This Corneel, hovering on the brink of sixty, the second-richest man in America, *was* a very different man from the blatantly ribald person we have known. He was prepared to make concessions to the conventions, must have grace said at every meal, and evening prayers at nine o'clock — but betweentimes he saw no objection to whatever cussin' might seem necessary. He was even prepared to eschew the company of the yacht's officers and Mr. Keefe for an occasional discussion of ethics, philosophy and religion with his chaplain and physician. And he was become the perfect family man, roughly attentive to Sophia and fond of heavy badinage with his daughters.

No doubt about it, Corneel was growing. Wealth and power were not trivial possessions to him. He didn't represent merely himself abroad, but the opportunity that America stood for in Europeans' minds. His vanity, his egotism, his medieval pride of name, were all recognizable instruments in his motivation; but there was an impersonal side to his nature, which had elements of grandeur. I don't believe he was always conscious of this. In his business affairs, especially, he was sometimes a partisan of the public interest, despite himself. Yet buried deep in his rugged soul was an integrity of purpose, which set him apart from the financial buccaneers of his generation. And it was this possibly subconscious integrity of purpose which moved him to employ the cruise of the *North Star* as an object-lesson to Europe of the opportunities afforded by intelligent democracy. It was an effective lesson, too. The London *Daily News*, then as now, the principal organ of Liberal thought in the British Isles, hailed him on June 4, 1853, in a lengthy editorial of which the following is a sliver:

"An American merchant has just arrived in Europe on a pleasure trip. He has come by train from Southampton, and left his private yacht behind him in dock at that port. This yacht is a monster steamer. Her saloon is described as larger and more magnificent than that of any ocean steamer afloat, and is said to surpass in splendor the Queen's yacht. Listening to the details of this new floating palace, it seems natural to think upon the riches of her owner, and to associate him with the Cosmo de Medicis, the Andrea Fuggers, the Jacques Cœurs, the Richard Whittingtons of the past, but this is wrong. Mr. Vanderbilt is a sign of the times. The medieval merchants just named stood out in bold relief from the great society of their day. Mr. Vanderbilt is a legitimate product of his country — the Medicis, Fuggers and others were exceptional cases in theirs. They were fortunate monopolists, who, by means of capital and crushing privileges, sucked up the wealth of the community. They were not a healthy growth, but a kind of enormous wen on the body politic. It took Florence nearly fifteen centuries to produce one Cosmo, and she never brought forth another. America was not known four centuries ago, yet she turns out her Vanderbilts, small and large, every year. America is the great arena in which the individual energies of man, uncramped by oppressive social institutions or absurd social traditions, have full play, and arrive at gigantic development. It is the tendency of American institutions to foster the general welfare, and to permit the unchecked powers of the highly gifted to occupy a place in the general framework of society which they can obtain nowhere else. The great feature to be noted in America is that all its citizens have full permission to run the race in which Mr. Vanderbilt has gained such immense prizes. In other countries, on the contrary, they are trammeled by a thousand restrictions."

So effective an object-lesson in democracy, however, was bound to make its exponent unpopular in aristocratic and conservative circles. The truth compels me to admit that fashionable England looked askance at Corneel and his party. The gals and their husbands, and Billy and his wife, were presentable enough; but Corneel and Sophia were rather difficult for English people of family to — ah — place. Mayfair regarded them very much as had Knickerbocker New York in the thirties. The Whiggery of Threadneedle Street, a stiff-necked breed, gasped an: Oh, my God! That impossible Yankee again; and hurriedly arranged a soirée at the Mansion House. We'll give 'em the Lord Mayor, and the Mace Bearer, and plenty of footmen. *All* savages like that kind of thing. At the last moment the City gentlemen threw in Mr. Carlyle, who, unfortunately, has left no record of his impressions of the most extraordinary character he ever met, whether he knew it or not.

Mr. Ingersoll, the American Minister, seems to have been no more anxious to sponsor his countrymen; he was content to invite them to one of his levees. It was George Foster Peabody, who saved the day for Corneel. Peabody, who was a whole Pilgrims Society and American Chamber of Commerce, rolled into one, gave a dinner, and provided boxes for a Command Evening at the Covent Garden opera — the nearest Corneel and Sophia came to meeting the "dear Queen" and Prince Albert. But the high spot of the visit to England was a dinner in Corneel's honor tendered by the Lord Mayor and Corporation of Southampton, who had a keen eye for the American trade and didn't like the way Liverpool was coming on. It was a love-feast, this dinner. Corneel made a speech, the only after-dinner speech of his on record; but I'm sure he didn't say what cold print declares. And His Worship, the Lord Mayor, toasted Corneel as a foe to monopoly and the possessor of "a large and interesting family" — at which Sophia, sitting in the gallery beside a flustered Lady Mayoress, must have beamed.

On the whole, the *North Star* departed from England in a blaze of glory; the common people really made a hero out of Corneel. And why not? He was what every common person dreams of becoming; and the *North Star* was so vivid an embodiment of the power of riches that the most ignorant Wessex peasant could comprehend the scope of the American's position. But all other circles breathed a sigh of relief to be rid of that terrible common, old Yankee, with the dumpy, little wife.

In Russia, for a contrast, the royal family offered the party marked attention. Czar Alexander II placed one of his carriages at the disposal of Corneel and Sophia, and the Grand Duke Constantine, the Czar's second son and Lord High Admiral, paid the *North Star* the compliment of a searching inspection and requested permission to have her lines drawn by his engineers. But in Paris the Van Derbilt clan were ignored by the Emperor Napoleon's tinsel Court, and the gals, who had hoped to examine the Empress Eugénie's trousseau at close hand, must be content with peeks across the stalwart shoulders of the Cent Gardes. Too bad! You might think that a man of destiny like Louis Napoleon would have enjoyed contact with the Western equivalent of himself. Not only that, some years previously, during his exile and imprisonment, the Emperor had devised a plan for a Nicaraguan canal, concerning which Corneel could have given him first-hand information. But this was on the eve of the Crimean War, and Louis Napoleon was busy evoking the shade of the Little Corporal to his assistance. No time for American millionaires, was the sign on the Tuileries.

The remainder of the summer was passed in the Mediterranean, where the *North Star* was a source of annoyance and misunderstanding in all the jealous countries aligning themselves to take advantage of the undercurrent of war. How could King Bomba of the Two Sicilies, or an intransigeant Austria, which still pretended to Italian domination, or rickety Greece, or fear-ridden Turkey, understand the *North Star* and her owner? But Corneel rather enjoyed being shadowed by Neapolitan *sbirri* and having Austrian men-o'-war anchored to bring their guns to bear upon his decks. These were new experiences for him, and like all men of exuberant vitality, he had an insatiable appetite for novelty. It was fun, too, when the suspicious foreigners reluctantly came to admit that he was only a mad American — and then had to be convinced that he was neither President nor First Minister. And all the time he was learning, asking questions, studying the traffic of ports, products, exports and imports, talking to American consuls and agents.

"If this war-skeer works to a head, I wouldn't be s'prised if a sight of business come to New York," he announced ultimately. "I guess we better start home."

It was September 23 when the *North Star* dropped anchor off Stapleton, and Corneel had a small boat lowered before the smoke of her saluting-guns had blown away.

"How's Ma?" he called to the neighbors who met him at the landing-pier.

"Purty well, Corneel," they answered kindly. "Not so spry most of the time, but she made 'em let her git into her chair when she heard you was comin' up the Bay."

He drew a deep breath, and released it very slowly.

"Fifteen years on borrered time," he muttered to himself. And aware of the expectant faces of the neighbors, managed to curb his feelings. "Thank'y, fellers. Had a fine trip. See ye later. I —"

They stepped aside with the native tact of country people, and he strode eagerly up the dusty road to Phebe Hand's gate — no longer Cornelius Van Derbilt, millionaire owner of fleets and argosies, but barefooted Corneel, come to render his mother the score of his scrapes and achievements.

In the doorway he hesitated doubtfully until her voice summoned him from the shadows of the kitchen.

"Well, well, son! Gittin' fat, hey? You better look out — fust thing you know you'll have a paunch on you like that sow Billy's allus cherishin'. What's the matter? Speak up! 'Tain't like you to be backward."

He fought for self-control, so weak that ironical voice, so sunken the pallid cheeks. Death had never interested him, except as something mysterious to scoff at, at need to fight. But now he was afraid, for the first time in his life, afraid.

"I — I — it's been four months, Ma," he stammered.

"Missed me, hey?" mocked Phebe Hand.

"Like — like hell," he answered, with a clairvoyant stab at the future.

Her worn features kindled in the sweetest smile he had ever seen on them.

"I guess you ain't such a bad boy, Corneel," she said. "Come, kiss your Ma."

He bent and touched her cheek, and she drew his great, silvery head down on her flat, old breast.

"'Ain't had you here since you was two," she whispered. "You never was much of a nurser — never one to come ahowlin' for every stub and bat. But I allus was proud of you, Corneel. More Hand in you than Van Derbilt. A bad boy — but I allus was proud of you."

He gulped.

"I'm — awful glad — Ma."

In three months Phebe Hand was laid beside that other Old Corneel — have you forgotten him already? — in the Moravian Cemetery.

BOOK SIX

NO QUARTER

I

BUSINESS troubles as well as personal sorrows darkened Corneel's homecoming. Before sailing in the *North Star* he had resigned the presidency of the Accessory Transit Company, and turned over its operation to a group headed by Charles Morgan, of New York, who succeeded him as president, and Cornelius K. Garrison, of San Francisco. During his absence Morgan and Garrison, who were also the chief partners in the great banking firm of Garrison, Morgan, Rolston & Fretz, of New York, Panama and San Francisco, had manipulated the business of the Transit and its allied steamship lines in such a way as to secure for themselves and their associates large sums of money from the violent fluctuations of its shares on the Stock Market. Corneel, however, thousands of miles away and out of touch, lost quite as much as they made, and likewise found himself for the time being dispossessed of control of the company.

It was the first time in his experience that he had been taken into camp on any considerable scale, and he was sore. He'd skin the dirty skunks. He'd l'arn 'em it didn't pay to steal Cornelius Van Derbilt's money. And he sat himself down straightway, and wrote — or, rather, his confidential clerk, Wardell, wrote from his blasphemous dictation — this trenchant declaration of hostilities:

"Gentlemen:

"You have undertaken to cheat me. I will not sue you because the law takes too long. I will ruin you.

"Sincerely yours,
"CORNELIUS VAN DERBILT."

But having announced his purpose he moved warily. It was one thing with Corneel to git mad. It was a hoss of a diff'runt color to let t'other feller ketch a holt of his temper. No, sirree. He guessed not. If ye had to fight, only way was to keep cool and play fur a good wrastlin' grip.

Wrestling was a familiar sport to Corneel, you remember. Once it had meant physical exercise. Now it connoted tussles for shares or bond-issues or grapples over rates and tariffs. So he maneuvered around, with a wary eye upon his opponents, to discover the best and safest way to regain his lost child, the Transit. Majority stock control was the one practicable course open to him, he decided regretfully, regretfully because it must take time to pick up the stock he needed in the open market, without giving his opponents chances to bid him up so high as to make the game hardly worth the candle. Of course, they'd soon hear he was after stock, but Corneel's idea, apparently, was to exploit quiet deals with gentry, who would be willing to surrender him their blocks in exchange for favors and alternative investments he was in a position to offer.

The plan worked excellently. Wily and aloof, Corneel passed over the annual meeting early in the new year, giving no indication of his strategy, He'd wait, b'God. And thinking of it, that spring, as men trickled into his office at No. 5 Bowling Green, with little packages and manila-paper envelopes which he stowed in the private safe of his inner office, he'd chuckle contentedly. When *his* lightnin' struck 'twas tarnal like a bolt out of Heaven. He became reconciled to his losses, and his temper improved. Sophia, dear soul, began to see more of him. He hadn't Phebe Hand to gab to, and he needed some woman he could trust. He even told her something of his plans, oh, nothing specific — and, of course, he never asked her advice. But she saw more of him than in years, and she was not disposed to quibble. Better a half-loaf than a crumby roll.

The trouble was that someone else was playing with lightnin'. This doctrine of Manifest Destiny, that had sprung up since the Mexican War, was taken at face-value by certain adventurous souls for whom California was become too tame. Why shouldn't they go down into those footless Latin lands below the Rio Grande, quell the recurrent revolutions with American rifles and then erect new states, in which the Yankee invaders would be a military, land-holding aristocracy — exactly after the fashion of the *conquistadores*, whose degenerate descendants it was proposed to supplant? Mostly, this was just barroom talk. All it needed, though, was a leader of personality and daring to be transposed into an incalculable social force. And such a man bobbed up in California, a man Corneel, and almost everyone else of consequence in the East, had never heard of. But for his own egotism, he might have changed the fate of this continent.

William Walker was four days short of being thirty when he sailed from San Francisco on May 4, 1855, aboard the brig *Vesta*, with fifty-eight companions, bound for Nicaragua. He was a Tennesseean by birth, a blond, tow-headed, little man, very quiet in manner, soft-spoken, courteous, his one distinguishing feature his gray eyes, luminous and possessed of a peculiar compelling power. In two previous helter-skelter filibustering expeditions he had earned a reputation for bravery and resource which had endeared him to the daredevils for whom Manifest Destiny was more than a pair of resounding words; and stay-at-home Californians respected him for his conduct on the dueling-field, and the sincerity of his political opinions. Already, he had acquired experience as a doctor, lawyer and journalist, and had studied for the Church.

No mountebank, this man. A visionary, perhaps. Certainly no statesman, as events should prove, yet a good, practical soldier, and a born leader of men. If he hadn't clashed with Corneel, if, instead, the two had worked together — But this is to anticipate the story.

Walker had a contract with the Liberal faction in Nicaragua to aid them in the current struggle with the Legitimists; his ulterior purpose, it goes without saying, was to provide an opportunity for Manifest Destiny to show what wonders it could perform. Into the morality or immorality of this I don't propose to go. The Nicaraguans hadn't up to that date, or, for that matter, haven't since, succeeded in governing themselves; but, as they contended against Walker, and later Americans who sought to emulate him, after all, it is their country, and if they want to govern it by revolution, in degradation and misery, haven't they a right to? Walker, with a good deal of moral courage, answered No to this question. No country, he asserted, has a right to misgovern itself to the disadvantage of its neighbors — which is a first-rate text for the Imperialists of any race.

He was the more inclined to be didactic, I suppose, because he was so immediately successful. His first move was to seize the port of San Juan del Sur, the Pacific terminus of the Transit. From this as a base, after he had been somewhat reinforced, he struck at Granada, the Legitimist capital, employing one of the Transit's lake steamers to convey his troops. Granada fell to him in one morning's fighting, and with it the brains of the hostile faction. He had Nicaragua in the hollow of his small, supple palm; and as word of what had happened seeped back North to San Francisco and New York, young men flocked to join him by every Transit steamer, Bowery boys, Irishmen from the Fire Companies, lads of the Knickerbocker families, youngsters from Harvard and Yale and Princeton, the reckless chivalry of the South, Texas rangers and riflemen from "Bleeding Kansas."

In a month, the whole United States was talking of Walker. Some people said the Knownothingers had sent him, in order to start another war to drain off the foreigners; some considered him a tool of the Slavers; some perceived the sinister touch of Business; some blamed him on the Administration. The truth was that Walker represented only that restless, discontented minority of adventurers, who weren't satisfied to see the race expand from ocean to ocean, but must push its rule south to Panama.

Corneel, stealthily occupied with his task of purchasing stock control of the Transit Corporation, gave the filibuster scarcely a thought. Walker was an American, and was keeping the Transit running. Moreover, he seemed to be in a fair way to restoring order in a country which had never known order, and an orderly Nicaragua might mean all kinds of by-products for Corneel — mines, cattle ranches; he'd heard tell thar was money in indigo and coffee and sugar, too. So he went on about his own affairs. By Fall of the year, 1855, he owned or could vote a majority of the Transit stock, and Morgan knew it, and very soon Garrison knew it in far-away San Francisco.

In the meantime emissaries arrived in New York from Walker. It seemed that the Nicaraguan government needed American recruits for the rifle battalions that were being raised. Why couldn't the Transit Company make a special rate for these men on their steamers? The company had never paid the government the ten per cent. on its profits from the overland route stipulated in the concession; its offer a year previous to compromise the claim for $30,000 had been refused by Nicaragua. Pending arbitration of this, Walker proposed, let the company transport recruits for $20 per man to Greytown, crediting the amount of fare over this figure to the debt owed by the company.

The Transit directors in New York very cannily put the proposition up to Corneel, who would soon be in control. And he had no reason to suspect any trouble should flow from his approval of the adjustment. The

THE CRUISE

OF THE

STEAM YACHT NORTH STAR;

A NARRATIVE OF THE

Excursion of Mr. Vanderbilt's Party

TO

ENGLAND, RUSSIA, DENMARK, FRANCE, SPAIN, ITALY, MALTA, TURKEY, MADEIRA, ETC.

BY THE

REV. JOHN OVERTON CHOULES, D. D.,

AUTHOR OF THE "HISTORY OF MISSIONS," "YOUNG AMERICANS ABROAD," ETC.

BOSTON:
GOULD AND LINCOLN.
NEW YORK:
EVANS AND DICKERSON.
1854.

THE TITLE PAGE FROM THE REVEREND JOHN OVERTON CHOULES'
ENCOMIASTIC TRAVELOGUE

Administration was raisin' hell over all this filibusterin', district attorneys wavin' indictments and sheriffs and marshals libelin' ships, but nobody keered a hoot for 'em all. As for the howls of t'other Central American countries, it'd be a good thing for the hull pack to git gobbled up. So the stream of recruits continued to flow south to Walker; a thousand went in two and a half months, after Corneel was consulted.

He had no misgivings. The first of the year came, and the stockholders' meeting, and Morgan and Garrison were chucked out of the board by the scruffs of their necks. Corneel was president again, with directors who would pitch the tune as he piped. The stock went up to 23 1/2, and wobbled between that figure and 22 1/2. Corneel sat back contentedly. A good job well done. He could look about now for something new to interest him. He was gittin' het up some over the North Atlantic trade. What with the Crimean War takin' so much English tonnage into the Mediterranean and the Black Sea, thar was fat pickin's. His ocean steamers were makin' good money. He'd half a notion —

And then a bombshell burst in his face. The steamer from Greytown that reached New York on March 14 brought word that Walker had persuaded the Nicaraguan government to rescind the Transit Company's charter, on the ground of its failure to render accounting of its debts to the Government, and grant a new charter to Morgan and Garrison. The "outs" of the Transit Company, with the backing of influential California politicians, had represented to the filibuster that the Transit would be more dependable for his purposes if it was operated by Westerners. And Walker, his vanity touched by

Van Derbilt's failure to notice him personally, had acquiesced.

Corneel was fooled ag'in. But he didn't intend to stay fooled any more than he had the fust time. The stock broke in four days to 13, and he made no effort to bolster it. Leave it be, he advised his friends. We'll choke these thieves to death. Mebbe Walker kin grab the Transit, but the ocean steamers are under the American flag, and they're mine. Thar won't another liner sail for Nicaraguey. I'll send a special messenger to Panama to charter a boat and go north, and head off the Frisco steamers, too.

He was completely successful in this, and Morgan and Garrison, whose plans had not been completed, were unable to obtain ocean steamers in a narrow market for six weeks, during which time Walker was entirely cut off from communication with the United States and the reinforcements and supplies of munitions he badly needed, with a fresh revolutionary movement staring him in the face. But when Corneel undertook to get the Federal Government to come to his aid, and brought suit in the courts against the new company for seizure of his property in Nicaragua, the officials laughed at him.

"You made your own bed, Van Derbilt, and you'll have to lie in it," they told him cheerfully. "Who was it used his lawyers to keep us from stopping the illicit traffic in men and arms with Greytown?"

Corneel cursed as proficiently as ever, and fought with all his might; but he had no illusions about the hole he was in. Got me for a dog-fall, he decided. Well, thar's more'n one kind of halter for a sorrel hoss.

And to those who came to him, either hypocritically or genuinely disturbed for his future, he snarled:

"If it takes my last dollar, I'm agoin' to ruin that cheap tin-sojer in Nicaraguey, and git my own back. You watch me!"

He hired every man he could find who was familiar with Central American politics, and poured money into the capitals of the small countries neighboring Nicaragua, urging them to unite against Walker. Some of his friends remonstrated with him. After all, Van Derbilt, this Walker's a white man, like us. If he can hold the country we'll all have a look-in yet. But Corneel shook his head ferociously. No, sirree, I don't call a feller a white man that done what he done to me. I played square with him; and he give me a kick in the backside for pay, All right. Him and me are enemies. If he cain't git me, I'll git him.

Walker, unfortunately for the dreams of empire that had animated his picturesque campaign, played directly into Corneel's hands. The filibuster roused the Central Americans to an hysteria of race hatred by having himself elected President of Nicaragua in the early summer of 1856. Troops from Costa Rica, Honduras and Guatemala, and hordes of Nicaraguan revolutionaries, converged upon the slender garrisons of American riflemen holding the cities and posts adjacent to the Transit. Corneel, never slow to comprehend an opportunity, shipped rifles and ammunition to the filibuster's opponents. But fighting with splendid gameness and aggressive determination — fighting with the tactics Corneel, himself, would have employed in the same situation — Walker beat back his enemies, pounded them unmercifully, and by the end of the summer had concentrated his troops in stronger positions than he had formerly held. Several thousand additional recruits were ready to join him as rapidly as they could be accommodated on the Morgan and Garrison steamers.

"Huh," Corneel grunted disgustedly. "I guess I got to teach these Greasers how to fight besides payin' 'em and findin' guns for 'em."

So, in the fall of the year, he received into his pay a quaint pair of desperadoes, who had come to him recently with a plan, the shrewdness of which he had perceived as soon as a map was spread before him. They were the Hon. W. R. C. Webster, an Englishman of uncertain antecedents, who had lived for years in Central America, and Sylvanus H. Spencer, an American. Spencer claimed to be a son of John Canfield Spencer, Secretary of War under Tyler and a brother of Midshipman Philip Spencer, who was hung for mutiny at the yardarm of the *Somers* brig-of-war. A roving sort of rascal, typical ne'er-do-weel of a good family, Spencer had been an engineer on one of the Transit boats, had inherited a portion of the company's stock and hated Walker desperately. He and Webster were apt tools for Corneel.

They went to Costa Rica, with letters of introduction, and were allotted a small force of native troops, whom they embarked upon rafts on the San Carlos river, which they descended to the San Juan, entirely unheralded. One by one, then, they surprised and captured the American river-posts and the river and lake steamers. By January 1, 1857, the Transit was in the hands of Walker's enemies, and he was more effectively cut off from his supporters in the United States than ever. Corneel had him in a trap. The end was only a question of time. And on May 1, 1857, he surrendered the handful of men remaining to him to Commander Davis of the U. S. S. *St. Mary's*. Actually, Walker had defeated all the attempts of the besieging Central American forces, but Corneel was able to focus against him finally the opposition of the new Buchanan Administration at Washington. Davis told the filibuster that even if he defeated the Central Americans, he would not be permitted to transport his own troops by sea, and without that facility it would be impossible to reestablish himself, especially since Morgan and Garrison, financially exhausted by their contest with Corneel, had been obliged to abandon him.

Corneel had won the most amazing, chancy, melodramatic of all his struggles. He had annihilated the Morgan and Garrison group that had twice tricked the Transit away from him. But he hadn't, by any means, annihilated Walker. And he was as far as ever from holding the Transit in fee simple once more.

II

WALKER'S expulsion from Nicaragua didn't serve to clear Corneel's title to the Transit. To begin with, Costa Rica, recently Nicaragua's ally and would-be deliverer, claimed the line of the San Juan river as the rightful frontier between the two countries, and insisted that the franchise must revert to her. Morgan and Garrison stepped forward promptly with the assertion of their de facto ownership of the most recent charter issued in Nicaragua, an assertion which naturally stirred the resentment of the Nicaraguans, who looked upon the successors of Van Derbilt as no more than creatures of the hated Walker. Finally, to complicate the issue further, H. G. Stebbins, a well-known New York merchant, and Joseph G. White, who formerly had been one of Corneel's attorneys, acquired control of the old American Atlantic and Pacific Ship Canal Company, which, in a manner of speaking, had spawned the Transit, and by virtue of its overriding privileges contended that *they* were the lawful owners of the concession.

But Corneel didn't keer a cuss for all the pickpockets and confidence men in Wall Street. To hell 'n blazes with the lot of 'em! One more fight wasn't no more'n mustard on his ham to him. The Panic of '57 was in full swing, and he had far-reaching plans under way in the North Atlantic — I'll come back to these later — but I think he really enjoyed the extension of the scrap over Nicaragua. It helped him to forget Phebe Hand. Perhaps that is the key to the feverish activity, the tigerish belligerence, he showed in the years that elapsed from the date of her death up to the opening of the Civil War. Always a fighter, he was never, at any period of his life, so constantly and variously engaged in hostilities as during this interval of seven years. He seemed to be searching for chances to fight, and wherever the fight was offered, and under whatever terms, he'd couch lance in rest and ride the barrier, with that chill fury which made him more feared in old age than any American capitalist of his own or subsequent generations, including the elder Pierpont Morgan.

Despite the demands upon him, he continued to spend money judiciously in Nicaragua, winning the *politicos* to his interest. His agents were active in Greytown, in Granada and Managua, in San José de Costa Rica, yes, and in Washington. When Walker, brave but ill-advised, mustered a second expedition in the fall of '57, and captured Greytown and the Eastern half of the Transit, Corneel had so far redressed his prestige with the Administration at Washington that he was able to cause an overwhelming concentration of men-o'-war against the filibuster. Commodore Paulding, holding the Caribbean command, acting on his own responsibility, landed marines, disarmed Walker's force and compelled their embarkation for the United States; and Walker's last opportunity of empire in Central America was gone, irretrievably gone, although this greatest of the filibusters, as dauntless as the enemy he was never to meet, refused to admit defeat, and died miserably several years later under the rifles of a file of Honduran *soldados* on the outskirts of Truxillo.

If the fiasco at Greytown did Walker no good, it served to clear the air for Corneel. The Nicaraguan *politicos* were frightened to the depths of their abject souls by this recurrence of the specter of the apostle of Manifest Destiny. And they were impressed by Corneel's omniscience. Whatever he set out to do he did. They had seen it happen again and again. So, they reasoned, it was better to end this uncertainty and give the Transit to him. They could be sure he'd protect them against Walker, at any rate. And they had some hopes, after what had happened, that he'd remember the ten per cent clause in figuring the corporation's annual revenue.

But Corneel had no intention to commit himself once more to active operation of the Transit. He had thought up a much shrewder scheme, one not particularly to his credit, a slip in his long record of competition. But Jiminy Jesus, what was a feller to do? Here he was, holdin' things together all through '57, what with them damnfool railroaders losin' thar shirts, and fixin' to give folks a crackerjack line to Europe and bust thatair hellish subsidy. He jest had to have money. And anyways, didn't he pay out of his own pocket to smash that tin-sojer Walker? Well, he guessed he had a bit comin' to him, now, and if it come easy, who's business was it but his'n?

The Transit was definitely transferred to him on March 8, 1858, and the first thing he did was to go bluntly to the officers of the Pacific Mail and spread his hand before them.

Engraved on wood from a photograph by Brady

THE LATE COLONEL JAMES FISK, JR.

"I got the Transit, and I got the ships to hook up with it. What's she wuth to ye, if I leave her be, hey? Travelin's purty good to Californy, hey? Thought ye might like to have the punkin all to yourselves."

Nobody like Corneel to leer knowingly, as he rolled his cigar between long, mobile lips.

Marsh Roberts and the other fellers in the Pacific Mail were every bit as interested as he'd expected. Surprised, too. Mutterin' to each other behind their hands — I'll be damned! The old robber! Say, that's the coolest even the Commodore ever pulled.

They hemmed and hawed to gain a little time, and inquired politely if Commodore Van Derbilt had any definite ideas on the — ah — subject. Corneel rolled his cigar to the other side of his mouth.

"Well, with all the business ye'll git, with no competition, ye oughter have another steamer, hey?" he suggested. "Might let ye have my *North Star*. Sightly boat. I kind of hate to part with her, but I ain't goin' to Europe ag'in very soon, and she's a mite smallish for the North Atlantic, the way Collins 'n Cunard are buildin' ships. But she'd ought to do fine for your trade. Tell ye what. Let ye have her for $400,000."

That was rather a stiff price, but the Pacific Mail people plucked up courage. The *North Star* was a good boat, and if they could buy off Corneel for $400,000 they'd soon make up the outgo from increased rates.

"Why, certainly, Commodore," they said. "Glad to have the *North Star*. We know you built her yourself. Very nice of you to think of us."

Corneel grinned.

"We're agreed, then. But that ain't all. I'm goin' to

lose a chunk of income if I leave the Transit lie fallow. I've took better'n a million a year out of her — for myself. Not countin' what others made. I guess ye'll have to sweeten the loss for me, hey?"

"Why — ah — what would you suggest, Commodore?"

"Forty thousand dollars a month," snapped Corneel.

"Oh, but now see here, Van Derbilt —"

"Take it or leave it. She'll never go down, but she may go up."

They argued and debated, pleaded poverty and hard times; but he wouldn't budge a dollar, and rose from his seat with their undertaking to pay him his blood-money. Within a month the Pacific Mail jumped the price of steerage tickets to California to $125. And presently, when Corneel became dissatisfied with the bargain he had made, or at least said he was dissatisfied, and talked of reopening the Transit, the Pacific Mail meekly raised his bribe to $56,000 a month.

Including the price of the *North Star*, he must have rooked the Pacific Mail for better than a million dollars. Consequently, there was general surprise when he abruptly terminated his bargain in the fall of 1859, and announced that he would reopen the Transit. It was even rumored that he intended to employ filibusters, if he had trouble with the Nicaraguan authorities, who were disposed to be jealous of any American intrusion, in view of Walker's repeated attempts to launch expeditions from the Gulf states. Certainly, one of Corneel's steamers, the *Philadelphia*, loaded a cargo of arms at New York and went around to pick up a company of

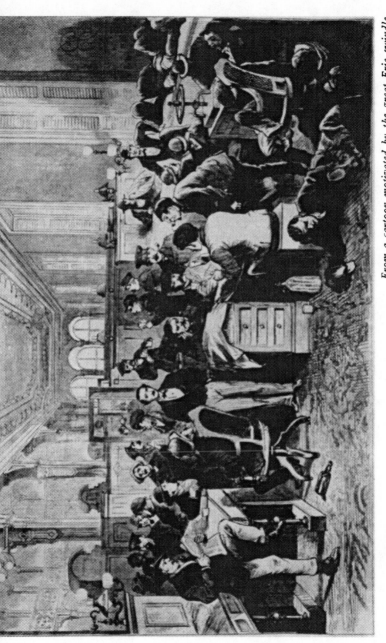

From a cartoon motivated by the great Erie swindle

NEW YORK CITY — THE ERIE WAR — JAY GOULD'S BODY-GUARD ENCAMPED FOR THE NIGHT IN THE OFFICES OF THE COMPANY IN THE GRAND OPERA HOUSE BUILDING

filibusters at New Orleans, where she was seized by the Federal officers on a charge of violating the neutrality laws. "Liveoak George" was mixed up in this affair, and there is some mystery as to the precise degree of Corneel's complicity. He and Law may have formed a filibustering partnership, or he may have been using Law for a catspaw, or Law may have been trying to use him — this last hypothesis is very unlikely. Anyway, the expedition came to nothing, and about the same time Corneel abandoned his half-formed plans for reestablishing the Nicaraguan route to California. The Transit stations lapsed into the jungle, and Nicaragua continued placidly upon her routine of revolutions, *pronunciamentos* and fusillades.

It is to be doubted, however, that Corneel abandoned the Transit because he was loath to resort to force. The most credible explanation is to be found in his simultaneous decision to withdraw from all his ocean shipping interests.

III

To understand Corneel's reason for deciding definately to abandon the Transit and withdraw gradually from all his ocean shipping interests, it is necessary to go back several years and take up the thread of the story of his fight against shipping subsidies — or, to be strictly accurate, his fight against preferential shipping subsidies. He had no disposition to be inimical to the principle of subsidies, but he did object strongly to the payment of subsidies to individual favored lines. If Collins and the Pacific Mail were subsidized by the Federal Government, then Cornelius Van Derbilt had the same kind of treatment comin' to him.

His first contact with the subsidy system came in 1850 when he was establishing the Accessory Transit, with its allied steamship lines. The Pacific Mail, and its subsidiary, the United States Mail, were paid subsidies aggregating $900,000 a year; but notwithstanding this advantage, as has been shown, Corneel's lines more than held their own, partly because of their initial advantage in offering a trip two days shorter, partly because of their more reasonable rates, partly because they were more efficiently run, and partly because the public instinctively supported the attempt to break the stranglehold of a monopolistic enterprise. He made an effort in 1853 to secure Congressional action readjusting the Pacific Mail's subsidy and granting Government support to his own lines; but the Administration was deaf to his appeal, and he seems to have relinquished the fight in disgust. His excursion to Europe diverted his attention, of course, and he had the consolation of knowing that the Transit lines were more profitable than the Pacific Mail, with the advantage of being entirely free from Government control.

His European trip, however, and the Crimean War determined him to enter the North Atlantic field, and this brought him into collision with E. K. Collins, of the Collins Line. Collins was a Cape Cod man, from Truro, bred in the tradition of the sea, who had been extremely successful with the Dramatic Line of sailing packets, on the Liverpool run, and also owned a line to New Orleans. The tremendous expansion in American commerce, consequent upon the gold discoveries in California, led to a demand for a line of high-class American passenger steamers to compete with the English Cunarders, and Collins was selected to organize it. In return for the subsidies, the steamers were to be built according to specifications of the Navy Department, so that they could be used as auxiliary cruisers, and were to carry a number of Navy men as watch-officers. The original subsidy was $385,000 a year for twenty voyages, or $19,250 a voyage. The Cunard Line was receiving from the Admiralty at this time, 1850, $30,000 a voyage.

The brief story of the Collins Line is a bright chapter in the history of the American merchant marine, and however economically right Corneel may have been in his attempt to compete with it, no American who believes in the policy of maintaining the flag at sea can be enthusiastic over the dire results of competition plus sectional and political animosity. Collins built three steamers, the *Arctic*, the *Atlantic* and the *Pacific*, of 3,000 tons each, nearly twice the size of the Cunarders in operation. Their hulls were of seasoned oak and hard pine, the frames strapped with iron. They were side-wheelers, and capable of steaming 316 miles a day. George Steers, who designed the yacht *America*, supervised their construction. There was nothing like them afloat. They cost the huge sum of $675,000 apiece. Each could accommodate 250 passengers and 2,000 tons of cargo.

The purpose of the Collins Line — that is, the Government policy which sponsored it: to break the Cunard Line's monopoly of the high-class passenger trade and fast freights, and conversely, to stimulate American interest in ocean steamers — was attained from the start. Within a few months after the *Arctic* sailed for Liverpool on April 27, 1850, the Cunard Line had cut its freight rates from £7 10s to £4. The effect of American competition on passenger traffic is indicated by the fact that between the months of January and November, 1852, after the Collins Line was fairly recognized, it carried 4,306 passengers to the Cunard's 2,968. The Collins liners, on the average, beat the Cunarders more than a day each way on all voyages. But to maintain such relatively high speed, with more expensive crews and the greater overhead of a new business, cost a fortune — Collins testified before a Congressional Committee that merely to reduce the running time of the steamers a day on each trip cost $1,000,000 a year. In recognition of all this, and of Collins's achievements, Congress, in 1852, increased the subsidy to $858,000 a year for twenty-six voyages, or $33,000 a voyage, slightly more than the Cunarders were getting.

So far, all had gone well with Collins. And the worst trouble he encountered in the ensuing year or so was the onslaught of Corneel upon his preferential subsidy. The Crimean War, which was a boon to all American business and shipping, likewise benefited the Collins liners, which, after the Cunarders were commandeered by the Admiralty for trooping to the Black Sea, had a taste of monopoly for themselves. American ocean steamers were coming ahead fast. They increased from a tonnage of 20,870 in 1849 to 115,045 in 1855. In New York City alone during these years 10,000 men were employed in shipbuilding, an extraordinary figure, and a considerable percentage of this total were engaged in the yards, foundries and engineering works which produced steam tonnage. Corneel, as I have said, licked his chops, and cast an envious eye upon the rich trade that went to Collins. It give him the itch to see a feller gittin' chances he didn't know what to do with. Takes a steamship man to run steamships. Oh, Ed Collins is all right, but he's been in sail too long. Figgers ye kin drive steamers like ye do packets. All of which criticism had enough truth in it to be worth remembering.

Corneel needn't have been so uppity, though, for Collins had reached the end of his luck. On September 27, 1854, the *Arctic* was in collision with the French ship *Vesta*, and presently sank, with a loss of 232 lives, including those of Collins's wife and children. Corneel, who liked a game man and scorned to take advantage of an injured foe, promptly offered the loan of the *North Star*, the only American ocean steamer afloat fast enough to maintain the Collins Line schedule. Collins refused; the *North Star* was sufficiently fast, but she lacked passenger accommodations, designed, as she had been, for a private yacht. Instead, Collins ordered immediate construction of a new liner, the *Adriatic*, 4,144 tons, at a cost of $1,100,000.

But overnight misfortune befell him again. The subsidy system was devised by Southern politicians in President Polk's last Congress; Senator King, of Georgia, and Senator Rusk, of Texas, had been its originators, and handled the first subsidy bill. Now, in 1855, the South turned upon its own creation. The rage of the slavery interests over the Kansas-Nebraska squabble, following the admission of California as a free state, precipitated a revival of factional jealousy. Whatever measures were helpful to Northern business and prosperity the Slave party wished to destroy. And the subsidy stimulated commerce out of all proportion to the amount of money the Government sank in it. The agricultural interests of the West were as willing then as they are now to believe the worst of the manufacturing and commercial Northeast, and joined ranks with the Slavocracy's representatives at the session of 1856 to reduce the subsidy to its first figure of $385,000 for twenty voyages.

This was a sorry blow for Collins, but it wasn't the sole one that evil year dealt him. In January the *Pacific* had sailed from Liverpool, under command of Captain Asa Eldridge, who had been master of the *North Star*. She was never heard of again, and Collins was left with the *Atlantic* and the *Adriatic* to carry out his government mail contracts. He hired steamers, and

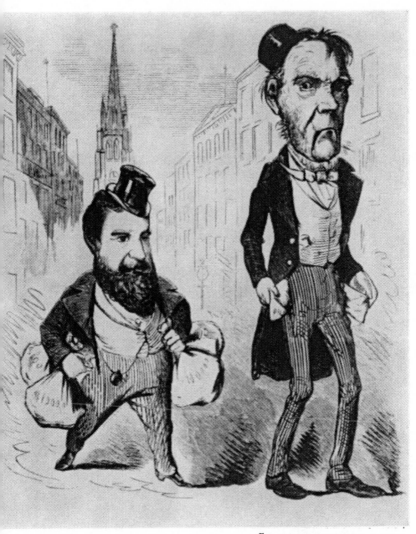

From a contemporary cartoon

THE LONG AND THE SHORT OF IT

The little man, Jay,
who was short ——— of stock

The big man, Daniel,
who was too long ——— of stock

struggled on as best he could, for with the reduction of subsidy it was impossible to think of building a new steamer. He was put to it, as it was, to make both ends meet. His company had never paid a dividend, putting back all its revenue into improvements or to offset the loss of the two steamers. And to accentuate his difficulties, Corneel was hammering him relentlessly again.

"Tommyrot, Collins," Corneel had barked. "Ye'd oughter be able to git by with $16,000 a v'yage."

"I could never make it pay," denied Collins.

"Huh, then ye're in the wrong business," Corneel retorted gruffly. "I could do it easy."

They appear to have conducted some unofficial negotiations, looking toward a compromise of their differences. Corneel, with dubious virtue, contended that Collins was gittin' too much from the Government. Collins, probably distracted by difficulties, offered to back Van Derbilt in a bid for Congressional support for a subsidy equivalent to what he was getting, but he wouldn't undertake to support a request from Corneel for $16,000 a voyage. That would be to confess his own incapacity, which was the point Corneel was driving for with the ruthlessness of conscious ability. So Collins employed whatever influence he had left at Washington to defeat Corneel's subsidy legislation.

"All right," said Corneel the next time they met. "I'm goin' to build me some steamers, Collins, and I'll run 'em ag'in ye without a subsidy. I didn't need one to Nicaraguey, and b'God, I won't need one to Europe."

As good as his word, he set afoot plans for the construction of the greatest of all his steamships, the *Vanderbilt*, of 5,000 tons. He built also a smaller racer, the *Ariel*, and a slower steamer, the *Harvest Queen*. And while his project was simmering, the Slavers in Congress struck Collins a final devastating blow. They rescinded the subsidy altogether, and left him nothing but the inland and sea postage, about $346,000 a year. His only assured advantage over the Cunarders was that they were restricted to the sea postage on mail of American origin. The utter unreason of the politicians who brought this about, the appalling disloyalty of men to whom the Union apparently had ceased to mean anything, is revealed in the debates, which, along with Corneel's competition, caused Collins's ruin.

"I see no reason why," said Jefferson Davis, "if we can get our mails carried in British vessels across the Atlantic, we should establish a line of American vessels merely that we may compete with them in a race across the Atlantic."

And Senator Tombs, of Georgia, declared:

"I would as soon have my letters carried in British as in American bottoms, and I would prefer that they should carry them, if they did it cheaper."

In January, 1859, Collins sent out his last vessel. He went into bankruptcy, and Brown Brothers, as holders of the mortgage on the *Adriatic* and the *Atlantic*, sold them to the highest bidders. The mighty *Adriatic* was bought by the British, and for several years was the record holder on the Liverpool run; the *Atlantic*, more fortunate, was purchased by the Pacific Mail.

Corneel already had established his own service, in dogged determination to make good his boast that he didn't need no subsidy to beat furrin steamers. It was a good service, too. The *Vanderbilt* and the *Ariel*, on a Southampton, Havre and Bremen schedule, beat the Collins liners nine out of ten times on the transatlantic passage, and were correspondingly ahead of the Cunarders. But Corneel soon learned that Collins had been neither ignorant nor incompetent. It was one thing to operate the Nicaraguan lines without a subsidy, and something very different to compete with English and French lines that paid lower wages to the crews and were guaranteed against loss by their governments, while all the assistance his country gave him was to allow the "postage" on the mails he carried.

The last straw for him was an Internal Revenue tax of two per cent on the hulls of vessels and of three per cent (afterward five per cent) on engines. This tax, which was not repealed until 1868, may be said to have sounded the knell of American steam shipping in the Atlantic. Nor was it the only burden devised by an ignorant Congress to ruin the nation's hard-won admiralty; there were similar taxes upon iron, steel, copper, lead, spars, sails, paints and cordage. It was as if the Government called before it Corneel and every other shipping merchant, and ordered harshly:

"See here, my men, we've had enough of this foolishness. Get off the sea, and stay off. Haven't we got plenty of dry land for you to amuse yourselves with?"

That was how it seemed to Corneel, at least, and he quit the sea in disgust, as soon as he could make arrangements to dispose of his fleet. The Civil War clinched his determination.

"What's this I hear tell ye ain't agoin' to run steamships anymore, Corneel?" asked Sophia.

"Thar ain't no sense in steamships," he growled.

"Why, honey, ye made a heap of money —"

"And I don't aim to lose what I made. I'm sellin' my boats to Allen & Garrison. Goin' to give me $3,000,000 cash for 'em — 'cept the *Vanderbilt*."

A tinge of sorrow in his voice directed Sophia's gaze to his frosty eyes.

"Goin' to keep her?" she inquired.

"Nope." His long, flexible lips snapped shut. "Goin' to lend her to the Government. I paid $800,000 for her, and I put all I knew 'bout ships into buildin' her, and I'm damned if I'll give her to anybody."

He hesitated, plumbing forgotten memories of his turbulent past.

"I guess I've built a hundred steamships and steamboats," he ruminated. "Never lost one of 'em while I owned her — barrin' the old *Andrew Jackson* that blew up under Jake on the River. And I never paid a dollar of insurance, neither. Good vessels and good masters — that's the best kind of insurance. Why should I pay somebody else to carry my risks?"

Outside in Washington Place a newsboy was shouting the latest intelligence from the Potomac.

"Mebbe thar's been another battle," said Sophia placidly. "What ye goin' to do, now, Corneel?"

"I guess I'll try railroadin'."

"My lands," she protested. "We got enough money, ain't we? Why don't ye lay off — and live like a gentleman?"

Corneel grinned.

"No, Sophy, we ain't got enough money yet," he answered slowly. "And I ain't what toney folks 'd call a gentleman, neither."

"But ye're gittin' on for seventy," she cried.

"Huh! Don't feel it," he grunted. And then, more to himself than to her: "I ain't satisfied with this steamship business. Got to do something wuth while. Might be railroads. Yes, might be railroads." He looked up at Sophia. "A feller's remembered by what he leaves behind him, gal. If I died today thar wouldn't be anything wuth a damn to call up Cornelius Van Derbilt to mind."

"Thar's your steamship," she exclaimed.

"What's a steamship?" he scowled. "No, I made money out of steamships but the lines I started are gone — all gone in a leettle more'n ten years. Why, folks won't remember they ever *was* in another ten years. I guess I got to begin all over again."

Sophia sighed.

"Ye allus was so restless, Corneel. Gittin' on for seventy, and ye might be a colt with a burdock in his tail."

BOOK SEVEN
SPOOKS AND VISIONS

I

WHEN the Civil War started Corneel was sixty-seven. He was worth about $15,000,000, and, probably, was the most powerful individual figure in American finance; but it seemed to those who knew him that he was at the peak of his career, his achievements behind him. The terrible panic of '57, the Western Blizzard, as it was called, had thrown to the front of affairs an entirely new type of speculator-financier, young, reckless fellows, who patterned their tactics after the school of Daniel Drew. Jim Fisk and Jay Gould, who, presently, will make their appearance in these pages in the rôles, respectively, of comic and heavy villain, were legitimate examples of this type, although they did not figure on the stage of Wall Street until a decade after the panic blew to pieces the whole fabric of American business.

Perhaps there is no more valid tribute to Corneel's shrewdness than his success in weathering the storm of '57. The explanation, I take it, lies in his unwillingness at that time to commit his capital to the mushroom growth of railroad corporations. In the West, especially, railroads were being built at a rate, and under financial conditions, out of all proportion to the country's resources. A perfect mania of speculation had developed, in itself a direct consequence of the vast increase in credit facilities caused by California's gold — which, obviously, like all of fortune's favors, was a curse as well as a blessing. It must be remembered, too, that there was no organization for checking and controlling speculation. Banking was conducted in a hit-or-miss fashion, the Treasury Department was little more than a tax-collecting agency and the natural laws regulating the ebb and flow of credit were imperfectly understood. When once public confidence was shaken panic reigned unchecked; whatever was unsound went by the board.

Corneel, and men like him, whose money was in shipping and conservative manufacturing enterprises, escaped that blast of destruction with nothing worse than a few bad debts. But here again is an example of his uncanny sense of the drift of popular interest. While there was money in shipping, he stuck to shipping. So soon as factionalism at home, the trend from wooden to iron construction abroad and the Civil War became threats to shipping profits, he unloaded his steamers and looked about for some more profitable investment. And being devoid of prejudice when the question of investment was concerned, he saw, even in the midst of war, that railroads were to be the great speculative opportunity of the future.

But speculation to Corneel connoted something very different from what it did to Daniel Drew, who was to be his arch-enemy in the battles of ensuing years. Corneel, let me repeat, was a builder. Whether consciously or unconsciously, he sought to serve the public. His one failure to adhere to this standard was his recent coup with the Pacific Mail. Otherwise, throughout his life, he was always building or fighting for something which would redound to the public's advantage. Not unselfishly, let me repeat once more. He was the essence of selfishness. But his peculiar genius informed him there was more money in stimulating competition for the public's interest than in rooking the small fry of Wall Street, driving corporations into bankruptcy and unsettling business. It isn't accurate to say, as has been said in the past, that Corneel was a Bull and Drew a Bear. Corneel could be either a Bull or a Bear, at need. Fundamentally, he was a builder, and Drew was a wrecker. It wasn't an accident that Corneel consolidated and built the most valuable trunkline of his generation and founded a financial dynasty, and that Drew died ruined, hated, all but forgotten, leaving nothing but a questionable odor of sanctity.

No, this gaunt, dyspeptic, foul-mouthed, egotistical, old man had a genuine gift of vision, a gift that wasn't the less genuine because it was attended by an almost incredible degree of superstition. He could focus those cold, blue eyes of his upon the chaos of the Civil War and the turmoil of the years that followed, and through all the welter of graft, animosity, hatred, bigotry, dishonesty, misdirected energy and honest endeavor, he could *see* that the day of the railroad was at hand. A country racked by internal strife, enormously expanded, must span its imperial distances with rails or else crumble apart from the dead-weight of its size. Being a New Yorker, his thoughts centered about his native state; he dreamed of a great railroad, which should run from end to end, paralleling the Erie Canal, transport-

From contemporary newspaper wood engravings
Victoria C. Woodhull

Tennie C. Claflin

ing the products of the West from the Lake ports to tidewater.

And from a vision such as this he could turn to spiritualistic séances, confabulations by dim lights with spooks who professed to impart the present condition and views of Phebe Hand. Just when he took up spiritualism, mesmerism and clairvoyance is uncertain, except that it was after his mother's death; but his predilection for it was strengthened by the death of his third son, and youngest child, George, during the war. George was the handsomest and sturdiest of the Van Derbilt boys, his father's favorite, the only one of the children, indeed, for whom Corneel manifested any sentimental feeling. He was sent to West Point, graduated in time to join the Army in the West, broke down from exposure in the field before Corinth and was invalided home, to die a few months later in Paris. This was a great shock to Corneel. After Phebe Hand, I suppose, George was the one human being he really loved. With both of them gone, his interest in the spirit world drew him frequently to the home of a Mrs. Tufts, in Tompkinsville, Staten Island, whose contact with the hereafter he seems to have relied on. There were other mediums and spiritualistic advisers, clairvoyants and magnetic "rubbers" on his list, a couple of whom you will meet later; but I gather that Mrs. Tufts enjoyed preference. She was patronized by several of his daughters, who entertained beliefs similar to his own.

After all, however, there is nothing particularly odd to modern eyes in the spectacle of a hard-headed man becoming addicted to conversations with the dead. It happens more frequently in our day than it did in Corneel's. But if his own children are to be credited, and there is no adequate reason to doubt them, his spiritualism was of an unusually catholic brand. He likewise believed that diseases could be inspired through the medium of spells applied to a miniature representation of an individual or by means of a lock of hair, and cured in the same manner; he thought that some clairvoyants could see the interior of the human body, and its ills; he believed in the efficacy of the touch of mesmerists, considered that he derived supernatural assistance from such treatment. Once, at least, his family physicians threatened to withdraw from a case in his household because he and one of his daughters desired to use a prescription from Mrs. Tufts.

He came close to believing in witchcraft, judging by these enumerated superstitions; but I don't see that as a reason for doubting his sanity. He was simply an ignorant, old man, with almost no education or knowledge of natural science, the product of a group of peasants, whose nearness to a city did not make them any more intelligent or well-informed than the other country folk of eighteenth-century America. If it hadn't been for that strange knack of his which enabled him to *feel* the social undercurrents before they were outwardly perceptible, he would have lived and died a coastwise sailor or ferryman. While he could make money, and was familiar with the machinery of commerce, he had no conception whatsoever of economics as an abstract subject. He never heard the name of Adam Smith. He knew nothing of philosophy or history. The only book he ever read was *Pilgrim's Progress*, which he encountered at seventy-five, and read and reread the rest of his life, delighted with its atmosphere of conflict and the crude symbolism of Bunyan's child-mind.

Humanly, I think, there is a very appealing quality in this spectacle of a man endowed with so extraordinary a gift of vision, who could swallow eagerly the claptrap of cabinet spookery. If it doesn't prove anything else, it proves the spontaneity of his genius. For there could be nothing labored or artificial about the mentality of such a contradictory figure. He improved river steamers, engineered competitive combinations, threaded the Transit across Nicaraguey, made his bid for the North Atlantic trade, switched his energies to railroads, not as a result of any conscious analysis of impending factors, but quite automatically, instinctively, directed blindly by that inner force, which, to be sure, was himself.

A strange, perhaps an unanswerable, problem in personality. He was very chary of discussing his spiritualistic views, and few rumors of them ever reached the public until after his death. So we shall never know for certain whether any of his decisions, which meant so much to the country's development, were the result of tips passed to him by Phebe Hand from the Beyond. Personally, I don't believe they were. I can't see Corneel accepting tips from any spook. Advice as to his or Sophia's health, yes. Suggestions, say, of sal hepatica for rheumatiz'. But no spook, not even Phebe Hand's spook, could have imposed upon that grim, chisel-edged mentality any line of conduct which might have exposed him to the tender mercies of Dan'l Drew, Marsh Roberts or George Law, let alone them hellions Fisk and Gould. Sooner than credit that, I'll throw over all the spook evidence in his past. But that's unnecessary because he never did let his foot slip on the dividing line between vision and spookery.

In fact, I suspect — it's nothing but suspicion, mind — that Corneel's brand of spiritualism was simply a rather harmless kind of mental dissipation for a very busy, old man, whose wrists were becoming a little too weak for long sessions with fast trotters and who found whist tiresome as a steady diet.

II

You will search far to find an old age as unusual as
Corneel's. The Civil War, which turned the country
topsy-turvy, had as profound an influence upon him as
upon younger men. He grew in mental stature, in
character, very much as he had grown, despite himself,
after attainment of wealth had sobered and steadied
him. The creative kink in his brain, the itch to build up,
to fight all attempts at destruction, made him a last-
ditch Union man. He was a good friend to the Federal
Government, a mighty force for victory, one of Lincoln's biggest assets — how big, is difficult to say. At
a moderate estimate, though, his steady pressure for
stability, his prompt reaction against the market raids
of Drew's clique, his unswerving belligerence, had as
much to do with ultimate victory as Grant's stolid
determination.

In fact, the Civil War, like all wars, was as much of
an economic as a military struggle, and the North's
preponderance of economic strength was what shattered the will of the South. It was California's gold,
which had aggravated the rivalry between the states,
and so brought on the war, which also had built up the
factories and railroads of the North, and so permitted
the physical plant of the North to outlast the physical
plant of the South. Lee's army in Virginia was starving
during his last two campaigns, not because there was
any lack of food in Confederate territory, but because

the railroads had collapsed under the augmented strain of war, and there were no facilities for repairing them properly.

It was Corneel and the other Union men in Wall Street who kept the wheels of commerce revolving while the armies were fighting, who made provision of the money, munitions and supplies required by the Government at Washington. Of course, they didn't do it all themselves. Providence and the country's good name helped. By a stroke of luck, the years 1861, '62 and '63 produced bumper crops, especially in the Western states, when Europe's were below average as a result of severe droughts. This combination of Europe's need with an American surplus of foodstuffs enabled the country to offset in large part the loss of the cotton crop, which had constituted two-thirds of our exports. In 1861 and '62 Europe took $200,000,000 of our exports, and England alone sent us $60,000,000 in gold.

What was equally important was the continuance of the stream of immigration. Eight hundred thousand aliens landed on our shores during the war, and took the places of citizens at the front, yes, and many of them signified their loyalty to their new country by enlisting before they could well understand the orders of the drill-sergeant. But either on the farm or in the factory or under arms, these 800,000, men and women, helped to replace the drainage of war. They were, as a whole, very nearly equivalent to the fighting man-power of the South.

One of Corneel's principal contributions to the cause of the Union was his loan of the *Vanderbilt* to the Navy, and hitched to that is an amusing anecdote. As he told

Sophia, his purpose was to *lend* the *Vanderbilt*. You haven't comprehended his disposition, if you suppose that he was ever inclined to *give* anything to anybody. In this case, he saw no need at all of presenting the steamer as an outright gift. The Navy fellers could use her, and afterward give her back. They wouldn't need her, come peace. But the Government didn't understand the transaction that way. They gratefully accepted the *Vanderbilt*, fitted her out to catch the *Alabama* — she was the fastest American steamer afloat — and turned her loose. She came near catching the *Alabama*, too. Missed her prey by only three days at Capetown. Thereafter she was used in one capacity or another until the end of hostilities, when Congress passed a resolution conferring upon Corneel a gold medal and the thanks of the nation for his gift of the *Vanderbilt*.

If there were any cuss-words he didn't shower publicly upon the heads of Congress, he didn't know them.

"The damn, dirty thieves," he exploded. "What 'n hell do I want with their twenty-five dollar gold medal? What's a medal, anyway? I want my steamer! I never said I'd give 'em the *Vanderbilt*. They took her. They stole her, the —"

It didn't do him any good. What the Nation taketh, Congress keepeth. Corneel was out one ocean steamer, 5,000 tons, costing $800,000. If it was any consolation to him, he was in a good deal of valuable publicity, which he wasn't bashful about accepting — or even exploiting. There is one story of how he came to deliver the *Vanderbilt* to the Navy, which he appears to have encouraged, himself, but as to which I am inclined to be dubious. It recites that after the *Merrimac* had ravaged Hampton Roads, Washington appealed to Corneel for assistance; and straightway he embarked in the *Vanderbilt*, steamed down to Fortress Monroe, and to the officer who boarded him there issued stern orders to "cl'ar the way for him." He was goin' to ram the *Merrimac* when she come out! Tut-tut, I just don't believe it. He was too hard-headed, was Corneel. And if he ever had said such a thing, it would have been in the history-books. It *must* have gotten into the history-books. What else are history-books for?

A possible reason for the action of Congress in blandly insisting the *Vanderbilt* was a gift is that Stanton appointed him agent for the War Department to buy, rent and equip vessels for the military authorities, and if the researches of muck-rakers are to be read at face-value this job was a prolific source of graft. I am bound to say, however, that Corneel doesn't seem to have been the kind of man to indulge in petty peculations. Many general and vague charges have been leveled against him, but none has ever been proved. Why should he have been a grafter? He worked on too big a scale. The stakes he played for were the stakes of empire. He left it for others to graft on himself, as they surely did occasionally. But graft, personally? Not he! If for no other reason than that he was too impatient, too unmindful of side issues. I nearly said that he was too intelligent, and while that seems contradictory after previous statements, it is true in that his simply wasn't a grafter's mind.

But where there was so much smoke there must have been a spark or two. He delegated the work for Stanton to one T. J. Southard, who exacted from owners of craft commissions of from five to ten per cent for approving sales, which, it is fair to assume, went into Southard's pocket. There was also an exaggeration of values placed upon vessels. Senator Grim, of Iowa, in one of the debates, harped at length upon the fact that vessels were being rented to the Government at prices eighty per cent over what the Government previously had paid for the same vessels. But some of this represented the universal upward trend in living costs. Corneel, personally, was too busy to keep track of everything that went on. Probably, he should have done so, but he didn't; and I can't find that the graft in steamships was any more iniquitous than the graft in every other article, big or small, purchased by the Government. That was a period of widespread dishonesty. The best-known men in business were charged again and again with dishonorable bargains. Of them all I do not believe one was as little concerned with Government money as Corneel — although it is quite possible Congress thought differently. Many of the Congressmen were no better than the other rascals who regarded the war as an opportunity for profit, and they would have judged him by their own standards.

The war, as a war, meant very little to Corneel after George's death. It was a disagreeable task to be ploughed through as rapidly as possible. He hadn't any doubt the North would win. He wouldn't permit himself to doubt it. Fight! Ye got to fight. If a feller's got guts he kin allus win. We got the money, we got the men. All we want is guts — and b'God we ain't goin' to quit for want of 'em.

He was, now, more than ever, a dominant figure, someone to be referred to, to be consulted. "Oh, we'll have to see the Commodore," men said, if there was a new loan to be taken up or arrangements in refinancing to be considered. Nothing was undertaken in Wall Street without his endorsement. When Drew and the rest of the Bear raiders launched selling epidemics after Confederate victories or gossip of peace negotiations, Corneel was the first man in to steady the market. "Never sell short," he used to say. And another favorite remark was: "When ye buy, buy for investment." When Daniel Drew urged him to sell a stock which had sustained a considerable rise, he answered: "She'll hit par some day, Dan'l. What's the use in lettin' her go?"

Nothing more clearly establishes the position he had acquired than an incident which occurred in February, 1863. Lincoln telegraphed to Thurlow Weed, the journalist and politician, on the eighteenth, asking him to come to Washington at once. Weed reached Washington the following morning, and went direct to the White House.

"Mr. Weed," said the President, "we are in a tight place. Money for legitimate purposes is needed immediately; but there is no appropriation from which it can be lawfully taken. I didn't know how to raise it, and so I sent for you."

"How much is required, Mr. President?" inquired Weed.

"Fifteen thousand dollars. Can you get it?"

"If you must have it at once, give me two lines to that effect."

Lincoln scribbled hastily on a slip of paper:

"Washington, Feb. 19, '63.

"Mr. Weed:

"The Matters I spoke to you about are important. I hope you will not neglect them.

"Truly yours,

"A. Lincoln."

Weed caught the first train back to New York, and by five o'clock that afternoon he had appended to that paper this list of signatures, with amounts pledged:

Charles Knapp	$1,000	Novelty Iron Works. Horace Allen, Pres.	$1,000
Marshall O. Roberts	1,000	James T. Sanford	1,000
Alexander T. Stewart	1,000	Spofford & Tileston	1,000
Isaac Bell	1,000	J. F. Winslow	1,000
W. H. Aspinwall	1,000	Secor & Co.	1,000
C. Van Derbilt	1,000	P. S. Forbes	1,000
James Mitchell	1,000	Russell Sturges Henry W Hubbell	1,000
H. B. Cromwell	1,000		

That is a fairly complete roster of the men who really mattered in New York's business affairs during the war. Weed nor any of them ever knew what the money was for, but it went to Mr. Lincoln and was spent.

III

In the midst of the flurry and excitement of the war Corneel never lost sight of his main objective: acquisition of a coherent railroad system. But he moved deliberately, cautiously, a step at a time. His single predetermined policy was to buy weak, run-down roads, which could be built up and linked together, an idea, I think, which was inspired originally by the success of thatair fool Billy in reconstituting the wreck of the Staten Island Railroad, a miniature property thirteen miles long, which had gone to the wall in the preliminary pangs of the panic of '57. Billy, you will recall, had never enjoyed his father's confidence. A sickly feller, Corneel would fume, no good for nothin' but farmin'. And when Billy came to him, after the Staten Island road had acknowledged bankruptcy, and asked his influence to be made receiver, Corneel first blinked mildly, then abruptly decided to give his footless son a chance.

"Ye never amounted to a hoot in hell, Bill," he said gruffly. "Hadn't been for me to look after ye, I dunno but what ye'd be loafin' on the ferry-dock, barefoot."

Billy, grown to be a silent, thoughtful, cynical man, and as keen a judge of human nature as Corneel himself, flushed slightly.

"I don't know as that's altogether true, father," he objected. "I've made my farm pay. It brings in $12,000 a year."

"Twelve thousand dollars!" scoffed Corneel. "Dear God! When I was your age — Well, go ahead. Ain't no use argyin'. I'll speak to the creditors; see what kin be done. If they're agreeable, I'll git ye named receiver. But if ye botch it —"

"I won't," asserted Billy, mildly.

And to Corneel's amazement, he didn't. The stock had been worth practically nothing when he stepped in. He pruned expenses, but not wastefully, speeded up operation, repaired the rolling-stock, and in five years had the shares selling at $175.

Corneel was more than amazed. Watching Billy's performance during the years of his preoccupation with ocean shipping, the thought recurred to him often that the same tactics might profitably be employed upon a larger scale. All about him he saw railroads, hastily built, scandalously financed, hovering on the verge of receiverships, notwithstanding the rich territories they traversed. He studied such roads covertly, keeping his plans to himself, and, as has been told, so soon as the opportunity offered he hauled out of shipping, and commenced quietly to buy control of the New York and Harlem, a line in wretched condition, but possessing the advantage of direct entry into New York City.

When he commenced buying Harlem, in the fall of 1862, the stock was at $9. It had been as low as $3 in '57. Under the impetus of his purchases it rose steadily to $30 early in 1863, and reached $50 in April, after he assumed control. On April 21 he accomplished another coup by inducing the Common Council of the city to pass an ordinance permitting him to extend his right of way in Fourth Avenue, where the Harlem's terminal was situated, by street-car tracks down Broadway to the Battery. A clause in the original charter of the Harlem provided that this might be done at any time with the city's consent. Corneel's ancient enemy, "Live-oak George" Law, had entertained a similar project, and at that very moment was lobbying energetically with the Legislature at Albany for the grant of a street-railroad franchise in Broadway. But Corneel, through the influence of Boss Tweed, succeeded in persuading Governor Seymour to veto Law's franchise; and having had comparatively slight acquaintance with politics, fancied he had complied with all the requirements of the situation, and put his work gangs into Broadway to dig up the street and lay rails. In the meantime, however, the members of the Common Council, as arrant a pack of rogues as existed outside the halls of the Legislature, with some advice and encouragement from Daniel Drew, mapped out what seemed to them a perfectly feasible project for hanging Corneel from a hickory limb and shaking loose the contents of his pockets. The stock had continued to rise. It went to $75 on the announcement of the approval of the city ordinance, and Corneel's election to the presidency of the road boosted the shares to $100 on May 19. What would be easier, the politicians whispered, than to sell Harlem short, then rescind the ordinance, and proceed to pound the stock down to $50 or $60 before buying in for their deliveries?

So, with Drew's astute aid, they dumped thousands of shares on the market, rescinded the ordinance, and when Corneel scornfully refused to heed their action, secured an injunction from Judge Brady, in the Court of Common Pleas, restraining the laying of tracks in Broadway. Harlem sagged in a nightmare market to $72, but below that point it could not be forced. Corneel took every share offered, and when, at last, the short-sellers became worried, and decided they had better cover, there was a rocketing leap in the price. Harlem raced back to par, skipped it and soared to $179. For Corneel owned, not only all the 110,000 shares of Harlem actually issued, but thousands of imaginary shares the shorts had plucked out of the smoke-laden air of the Exchange. He forced settlements on his terms, and the city politicians were ruined. Drew, with the tobacco-juice dribbling down his chin, whined and pleaded and prayed and reminded Corneel of how we wuz both pore boys, Van Derbilt, and ye hadn't oughter be so rough on a feller as growed up on the river with ye. And Corneel cussed and threatened and relented, as he always did when Drew was concerned.

"Damn ye, Dan'l," he'd growl. "I dunno why I ease up on ye. 'Tain't 'cause ye deserve it, and 'tain't 'cause I hope ye'll ever turn honest. Mebbe I'm jest cur'ous to see what deviltry ye'll try next."

Having secured Harlem, he made Billy. vice-president and general manager in charge of the reconstruction of the road. To his increasing surprise, he was finding his son a good man to lean upon.

"Beats me, that feller does," he confided to Sophia. "Allus figgered he didn't have the sense he was born with — kind of pindlin' and no-account — reg'lar soft pup."

"He's your own son," returned Sophia, gently disturbed. "Ye hadn't oughter talk so 'bout him."

"I dunno," continued Corneel, heedless of her rebuke. "I ain't so sure 'bout him. Never says much, but he seems to git to what he's after. He beats me. Too soft. Allus did what I told him to. 'Tain't right. No, sirree, 'tain't right! But he does seem to know his mind."

"Course he does," flamed Sophia. "Ye talk like ye was the Lord Almighty, Corneel. Don't ye never make mistakes?"

He grinned. It was seldom Sophia pecked at him.

"Not often, I don't," he answered. "Can't afford to. Too many folks kin do it better 'n me."

"Well, ye'll give Bill a chance, won't ye?" Sophia asked anxiously. "He's awfully set on railroadin', Maria says."

"Yes, I guess I'll keep him on," Corneel assented. "He'll do what I tell him to, anyway. Got to have someone I kin trust."

He paused.

"And he named that oldest younker of his Cornelius. I'm goin' to watch that younker, Sophy. Thar ought to be a Cornelius Van Derbilt after me."

Sophia winced. Motherwise, she had a corner in her heart for her prodigal, who was the bane of his father's life.

"Thar's our Corneel —"

"Don't ye mention his name to me," Corneel bade her fiercely. "He ain't my son. I ain't responsible for him. He's — he's — dirt."

"Oh, ye hadn't oughter talk so!"

"How else kin I talk?" he rounded on her. "I got to have *someone* to carry on my name. I got to have *someone* to keep up my work." His face contorted, as it

From a contemporary cartoon

Men of the Avenue — Cornelius Vanderbilt

did in moments of tense feeling. "I tell ye, gal, if I'd died a few years ago I wouldn't have mattered. Folks 'd have forgot me quick. But Van Derbilt's goin' to stand for something, 'fore I git through."

Sophia twitched uneasily.

"Oh, ye say that all the time," she protested.

"I mean it," he retorted. "Where'd ye all be, if 'twasn't for me, hey? What could the lot of ye do without me?"

"Not much," she admitted wearily. "But we done what we could, Corneel. I — I done all I could. Mebbe — mebbe I won't live to see this grand fortune ye talk about. I'm gittin' old."

"Thar ye go, talkin' weak," scowled Corneel. "Stiffen your back, gal. Age don't bother me!"

IV

HAVING a safe clutch on the Harlem, Corneel decided as his second step to obtain control of the New York and Hudson River, another decrepit carrier which never had paid the interest on the moneys invested in it. For years, in fact, ever since they were built, the Hudson and the Harlem had been engaged in fruitless competition, with the net result up to this time of hamstringing each other. Corneel planned to combine them, reduce overhead and by combination rates boost business and traffic. And he made no secret of his intention.

"Hell, everyone knows I ain't goin' to stop with Harlem," he growled in response to representations from Billy. "Buy in the open market, boy, buy in the open market."

This was in the fall of 1863, a year after he opened his campaign to control Harlem. Hudson stock was at $25. He had no difficulty in acquiring a majority interest, and when the Legislature convened after the first of the New Year he went to Albany, and bent the whole force of his powerful personality to the task of obtaining authorization for the union of the roads. Tweed and other agents helped him, and considering the spirit of the times and the prevailing corruption in New York politics, there can be no doubt that bribes were paid. It was the only way in which corporations could secure privileges, however legal or desirable such privileges might be; and inasmuch as Corneel was a practical man, and had no time to waste, he would scarcely have winced at the dictates of custom.

At any rate, what between a carpet-bag of green-backs and the gaunt majesty of his presence, the legis-lators were acquiescent. The pledges of a safe majority were given, and Corneel departed for New York in February. Hudson stock had reached $150. Wall Street was amused and exhilarated. The Commodore had done it again.

But underneath the surface slimy and sinister in-fluences were at work. That unmitigated hypocrite Dan'l Drew nearly swallowed his cud of tobacco every time he reck'lected how Van Derbilt had trimmed the hide off'n him, and there were plenty of legislators whose pocketbooks still ached from the extraction of their Harlem losses. Drew and these sour-bellies put their heads together and confabulated over a projeck to git back their own. Van Derbilt couldn't allus win.

They agreed, undeterred by past experience, to repeat the trickery of the Common Council. The Legis-lature, having been pledged to pass the Hudson-Harlem consolidation bill, should defeat it. Pending this result, the legislators, through Drew's agency in the Street, would sell Hudson short. They couldn't fail, Drew de-clared. Jest waren't nothin' to it, 'cept fixin' on a figger to buy in at. Oughter bump Hudson down to $50. Clean up millions, boys. We'll give Van Derbilt a lesson in speckelatin'. Mebbe he'll be drawed from his ungodly ways, and git to know grace.

The plans of the conspirators worked according to schedule. They sold short thousands of shares of Hudson, then defeated the consolidation bill and dumped more thousands of shares on a weak and wobbly market. Hudson slumped under terrific hammering, to $90, but below $90 it could not be driven. Corneel, mobilizing every dollar he controlled and assisted by some of the keenest operators in the Street — men like Tom Tobin, who had been a gate-tender in the early days of the Staten Island ferry; the Schells, Dick and Gus; and Leonard Jerome, a young New Yorker of connections as aristocratic as Corneel's were plebeian — was able to take everything offered, and sustained the market, resisting all advice from the timid.

"I'm goin' to bust them thieves," he said. "All I got is in this. And I'll take all they'll give me."

He did. He bought 27,000 more shares than the Hudson Railroad had issued, and panic assailed the tricksters. It seemed impossible to intimidate the savage, harsh-voiced, old man, whose hearty curses resounded from his office windows. The panic spread. Orders to buy Hudson flooded the market — and were unanswered. The price rose, slowly, then rapidly, finally by leaps and bounds. Back to $100, to $110, to $125, to $150, to $200, to $285. Whooppee! Wall Street howled and wept. Dan'l Drew lost the cud out of his mouth as he bent over order-slips. There were tears in his rheumy eyes; his falsetto voice cracked on a whine of self-pity. He was bombarded with threats and denunciations from the legislators he had duped. Appeals for mercy began to be heard, but Corneel was implacable.

"Put her up to $1,000," he ordered.

Finally, Jerome and Tobin came to him, and begged forbearance.

"My God, Commodore," exclaimed Jerome, "if we keep on we'll break every house in the Street."

"All right," said Corneel briefly. "We'll stop her here. But she stays here, remember, you fellers."

Next day contracts for 15,000 shares matured, and settlement was made at the top of $285. Corneel had a fine time.

"Nothin' like trimmin' a bunch of thieves," he used to say of it. "We busted the hull Legislature. Some of the honorable gentlemen didn't have money to pay thar board bills up to Albany."

Drew came to Washington Place, and fawned on Corneel with oily indecency.

"Guess I made a leettle mistake, Van Derbilt. But you know as well as me 'tain't good jedgment to squeeze a customer, jest 'cause ye got him in a corner."

"That's your reg'lar rule, hey, Drew?" Corneel returned drily.

"I'm a marciful man," asserted Uncle Dan'l. "And a God-fearin' man. 'Cordin' to my lights, I aim to live —"

"I ain't interested in your religion, but your money," snapped Corneel.

Drew lifted a trembling claw to wipe a stain of tobacco-juice from his yellow chin.

"Ye hadn't oughter talk like that to an old friend," he pleaded. "Didn't I name my boy after your boy, William Henry?"

"Hell," rasped Corneel. "What's that got to do with tryin' to corner me? Ye wuthless skinflint, if ye'd busted Hudson to $50, like ye tried, where'd I be? And what'd ye be doin' to me, hey? Pay up or shet up!"

Drew protested, and made threats by innuendo. Thar was the law. And a stock-delivery contrack says the buyer kin *call*, but it don't say the seller's got to *deliver*, and —"

"Pay up or shet up, Drew," interrupted Corneel. "I'm busy."

A few days later Uncle Dan'l made the best of a very poor bargain, and accepted a settlement, which cost him around a million dollars. He had lost half a million in the Harlem corner, and you might suppose had had his fingers burnt sufficiently, but of all the social parasites who have infested Wall Street, and blighted the country's prosperity, he, the earliest of the type, was probably the most indefatigable. There was no reforming, no teaching, Dan'l Drew. He was immune alike to shame or misgiving. After each piece of rascality he had only to present money to another charity, or donate to a new chapel, to be convinced that he had achieved a perfection of grace, while those who denounced him were miserable sinners wandering in the muck-heaps of perdition. Uriah Heep was a Christian gentleman beside this product of misdirected Methodism.

Corneel, who, despite the assertions of various biographers and friends, scarcely deserves the title of a formal Christian, yet contrived to live a far more Christian life than many of the pious rich men of the same period; and with all his faults and shortcomings, with his ignorance and superstition and lack of sensibility, he seems sympathetic, great-hearted, generous, besides such malformed souls as Daniel Drew. Whatever else may be said against him, he was a builder. This trait cannot be overemphasized. It is the key to his character. It was what made him loom above his contemporaries. It is what makes him today deserving of membership in the limited ranks of the group of Americans who may truthfully be called empire-builders.

He didn't buy railroads for speckilashun, like Drew and Jay Gould. He bought them to improve, to make them capable of better service, and thereby, of course, capable of greater earning power. He never wrecked any corporation wantonly. His competition with Collins was inspired by very natural resentment against the favoritism of the subsidy system as practiced, and even in this instance, it must appear obvious that he, personally, was not responsible for the collapse of Collins — notwithstanding that he liked to fancy he was — which came about through a complex of reasons, as I have narrated.

In the present case of the Harlem and Hudson railroads his purpose was eminently constructive. Denied consolidation, he proceeded to unite their service and interests as thoroughly as was possible, short of absolute legal permission, and into the battered fabric of the Hudson he poured fresh capital from his recent winnings, so that within several months of the corner the road was netting him a profit.

V

THE acquisition of the Harlem and Hudson lines gave Corneel control of the traffic in the region lying between the east bank of the Hudson and the Conneticut border and Long Island Sound, and extending upstate as far as Albany, where the Hudson's tracks terminated. Whatever through Western traffic the road received came to it via the New York Central, which was a third ramshackle line, running from Albany, on the West bank of the Hudson, up to Buffalo. Corneel's vision of empire involved the acquisition of the Central to supplement the Hudson and the Harlem and supply him with a continuous trunkline of rails, extending from tidewater to the Lakes; and so soon as he had disposed of Drew and the disgruntled legislators, and established Billy in the offices of the Hudson to restore its dilapidated plant, he started deliberately to buy a majority interest in the Central.

Here, however, he met with determined and organized opposition. The Central was controlled by a group at the head of which were his old opponents of steamboat days on the Hudson, Dean Richmond and Peter Cagger, who were likewise the surviving partners in the Albany Regency, heirs to the Democratic state machine of ex-President Van Buren. They were not lightly to be displaced. Their first step was to form an alliance with Daniel Drew, who scrambled for any chance to strike back at the man who had refused to condone his rascality. Drew still owned the steamboat line between Albany and New York, and the Central arranged to turn over to him all its through freight, besides selling through tickets to and from New York via the river boats, instead of the Hudson River Railroad.

As a result, the Hudson road lost practically all its through traffic from the West and much of the west-bound traffic originating in New York; but Corneel didn't hesitate to strike back, although he had to wait for his opening. When winter came, and the river froze over, Drew's steamboats couldn't be operated. The Central officials, without thinking, blithely ordered the through traffic to be diverted to the Hudson road again — and suddenly discovered that the Hudson Railroad's trains were being halted a mile east of Albany on the opposite side of the river. Here, regardless of protests, freight was dumped out in the open, and passengers were unloaded to tramp across the river to the Central's station in Albany.

Great excitement followed; charges flew back and forth; the politicians, who all hated Corneel, orated lustily — and what was more to the point, New York Central stock sank fifteen per cent in value. This man Van Derbilt was becoming a menace. It was time he was taught that he owed some respect to the rights of the public. So the Legislature appointed a committee to investigate his refusal to make connections with the Central, and apply the requisite chastisement.

"Why didn't you run your trains to the river, Commodore Van Derbilt?" questioned the committee's counsel, when Corneel had been subpœnaed and sworn.

"I wasn't thar," replied Corneel.

"Not there, eh? Well, where were you?"

"I was home."

"And what were you doing?"

Corneel pondered the question.

"I was playin' a rubber of whist," he answered while the hearing room hung on his words. "And ye know, gentlemen," he continued confidentially, "I never allow anything to interfere with me when I'm playin' cards. Ye got to keep your attention fixed on the game."

There was a roar of laughter. Not a very auspicious opening for the attempt to bait him. But the committee were undiscouraged. Their counsel resumed his cross-examination, and Corneel, in a bored, leisurely way, took a law-book from one of his attending lawyers, opened it and pointed to a marked page.

"Tell ye what, gentlemen," he said, in that confidential manner he had assumed, "the real trouble is thishere law ye passed."

"Law? What law, Commodore?"

"Why, thishere one. 'Cordin' to it, the Hudson River Railroad is forbid to run trains across the river."

The committee were flabbergasted. A hasty consultation was held, and it was discovered that the old law in question, regarded as a dead letter for years, had been passed at the behest of the Central in an earlier effort to cripple the Hudson.

The case against Corneel collapsed right there, and he resumed his attitude of refusing to receive the Central's traffic, except upon a basis of equality with the Hudson. He put $2,000,000 of his winnings in the Hudson corner into Central stock in 1864 alone, but the powerful political influences behind its directorate were able to prolong the battle until November, 1867, when a committee representing a majority of the directors compelled Richmond and Cagger to surrender. On December 11 of that year a single ballot elected thirteen new directors, with Corneel as president and Billy as vice-president, to represent the $18,000,000 of Central stock the Van Derbilt interests had bought. The first thing Corneel did was to have his engineers, under Billy's supervision, conduct a painstaking examination of the Central's rolling-stock and right of way. At his orders, most of the old cars were burned, defective engines were sold, new rails and ties were laid. He advanced $2,000,000 of his own money to buy new equipment to replace the old, and the Central increased its revenue in the same ratio as the Hudson and the Harlem.

In the fall of 1869 he finally secured the passage of a consolidation act, permitting him to unite the three roads into one system, seven years after he had launched his campaign to obtain a trunkline railroad. The stock, which had varied between $75 and $120 in recent years after the mania of speculation died down, now touched $200, and taking advantage of the terms of the consolidation act, he increased drastically the capitalization of the three constituent corporations, from $44,000,000 to $86,000,000. This is one of the classic examples of stock-watering, and for it Corneel has been severely attacked by one school of economists, who quote the statement of Charles F. Adams that "$50,000 of 'absolute water' was poured out for every mile of track between New York and Buffalo," and contend the public was swindled to this extent.

I cannot endorse the contention. Corneel not only added to the value of the physical plant of each section of his system, but — and this was most important — by combining them in one continuous line, and cutting out wasteful competition and reducing overhead, he transformed three weak, unprofitable enterprises into a single giant of industry. The mere increase in value of the stock, coupled with the sustained revenues which were earned, proves this to the satisfaction of any unbiased student. Of course, the author of so radical a plan profited enormously, and whether you approve of such profits in business is a question of individual viewpoint and interpretation of social justice. It may be said that no man deserved to receive $6,000,000 in cash and $20,000,000 of new stock as his "fiat" profit, as Corneel did; but to say this is to oppose the whole American conception of business as an affair of personal enterprise.

What Corneel did with the Harlem, the Hudson River and the Central did not hurt the public. On the contrary, it was of substantial benefit to the public. Transportation was made cheaper and more comfortable. The development of the West, the stimulation of New York's upper counties, was facilitated to a degree difficult of comprehension. And the fact that all this was done through the initiative of a man, who was actuated primarily by a desire to make money for himself and erect a dynasty of endeavor, scarcely vitiates the actual good accomplished.

One of the wickedest lies ever perpetrated by American journalism was the assignment to Billy, years after Corneel's death, of the phrase "the public be damned" as the watchword of the New York Central Lines. Billy didn't say that, and if he had said it it wouldn't have mattered, because it was never the slogan of the Van Derbilts — or Vanderbilts, as they called themselves then. If there is one fact that protrudes from every important undertaking Corneel was connected with, it is that, unconsciously, mechanically, quite selfishly, he worked for the public, never consciously against the public. Nor would he lend himself to advance the projects of others who opposed the public. He was too instinctively shrewd. Serve the public, and ye make money. Fool the public, and ye git to be like Dan'l Drew. 'Tain't sense to steal.

VI

So Corneel became a railroad magnate, the greatest single factor in the destinies of his State and probably the richest man in the America of that day. Seventy-four when his dream was realized, still hale and strong and virile. Ruthless toward his enemies, short-spoken with his friends, domineering, narrow-minded, enormously selfish, sceptical and credulous. What a character he is, this man of spooks and visions! He would go from a directors' meeting to Mrs. Tufts or Mrs. Clark or some other medium, and gawk and goggle as the sepulchral tones echoed through the darkened room — "Is Corneel there? I have a message for Corneel. His other name is Van Something. Van Derbilt — is that right? Well, Corneel, your mother says to tell you she's very happy in the Beyond, and so's George. They often meet and talk about you. And she says you can't do nothin' better than rubbing for dyspepsia and internal complaint, but a dram of licker won't hurt now and then, and flannel on the ab-*do*men is good in damp weather."

He might have come straight out of the Middle Ages. The London *Daily News* likened him to the Fuggers and the Medicis, and, indeed, there is a flavor of the Renaissance about him. Such as he was must have been the first generation of coarse, ignorant, superstitious merchants of any great trading family. And the odd corollary to this is that he was essentially American, as American as Andrew Jackson or Horace Greeley or Abraham Lincoln. Perhaps we aren't so far removed from the past as we like to think.

New York was rather proud of him. He was a variation from the precise, aristocratically self-conscious merchants of the early nineteenth century, a product of the people, tangy of the soil. But he was just as conservative and moderate in his views as the survivors of the gentry who had been invited to Philip Hone's dinners or were considered eligible for the Brevoorts' balls. His influence was a healthy restraint upon the mad debauch of speculation which succeeded the war. Nobody was disposed to sneer at his lack of grammar or appreciation of so-called higher knowledge. What he needed to know he knew better than anyone else, and if his table-manners were somewhat faulty, why, he made no pretense to culture. You must take him as you found him, and the Knickerbocker swells, indulgently disposed towards such refulgent success, spoke of him as "that quaint Mr. Van Derbilt" and "the delightful old Commodore."

People were even kind to Sophia. Her children were very nice, and quite socially eligible, you know. And she was a harmless creature, kindly and all that. But Sophia was less disposed to sample Society than ever, and Corneel, too, for that matter, no longer worried about being asked to the dinner-tables of the men he dealt with in the business world. Dinners bored him. He didn't feel at ease in a mixed company. People were allus watchin' him. Couldn't take aholt of his fork without someone 'd watch to see if 'twas the right one. Not that he cared, you understand. It just irked him.

The trouble, he had discovered, wasn't worth the bother. If he wanted company he preferred a rubber of whist with a select group of cronies. His rubbers became as famous as himself; it was considered an honor to be invited to join the Commodore's parties — Chester W. Chapin, Joseph Harper, C. K. Garrison (Corneel's opponent in the Nicaraguan battles, who was restored to intimacy in the twilight wrangles of life), Andrew Boody, and a dozen or so more. At the old Racket Club or the Manhattan Club or in Saratoga, during the summer, there were tables sacred to Corneel's whist-parties, and when he was playing a respectful circle would stand at gaze, watching the fall of the cards. A tribute to his personality, since the play was never high — seldom more than $60 bid on a hand.

Sometimes Sophia went to Saratoga. More often she didn't, and this was increasingly so as she grew older. Strange people bothered her. As for Corneel, she had given up trying to understand him. Simply and genuinely religious, I fancy his toying with spiritualism and witchcraft was a source of constant worry to her. As much of a worry as had been his occasional interest in other women, his unremitting pursuit of wealth, his remorseless abuse of his own body and intellect. But her nerves had been too blunted by the hardships and sufferings she had known for her to experience more than a dazed unease of mind. Life was become a hazy procession of familiar faces, children and grandchildren and poor relations, notched with pictures from bygone years: that night of moonshine on the Ferry Road when Corneel asked her to marry him, her first day at Bellona Hall, the little, old gentleman who had been polite to her the evening they came back to New York, baby Francis before he died. Memories, sorry and glad.

She was always very tired, now. She wanted only to sit, and doze. She wondered if Phebe Hand had felt like this. Things mattered so little. Should she wear her black bombazine or the purple silk Ethelinda had helped her choose at Mr. Stewart's store? Corneel hadn't liked one of them — she couldn't remember which. Well, it didn't matter. Nothing mattered. Up in the morning, to bed at night, a little wearier the next day. . . . So this was age. Not for Corneel, true. He refused to bow to age. . . . But she wasn't Corneel. . . . Only Corneel's wife. . . . Tired. . . . So tired.

The summer of 1868 Corneel went to Saratoga as usual. He was inclined to be self-indulgent; he felt he deserved it. His railroad empire was won; he and Billy were whipping the roads into shape, and it was only a question of time before the Legislature would authorize their consolidation. So, in a moment of expansion, he suggested to Sophia that she accompany him. She'd never trouble him, he knew. All she'd ask would be a secluded corner of the hotel porch to rock on. But to his surprise she refused his invitation. She guessed she'd stay on Staten Island with the gals. Too many folks at Saratoga. It kind of stunned her, the talkin' and the flutterin'.

"Suit yourself," he answered shortly, and tooted off in his private car at the head of a retinue of friends and attendants.

He was enjoying himself, when, in the dog-days of August, a telegram summoned him home. Sophia was very ill. To do him justice, Corneel left Saratoga as fast as an engine could haul his train, and in the days that followed, the few, short days, he lent the entire strength of that iron will of his to keep her alive. But there were limits to what his will could accomplish, he learned. Or perhaps it was just that Sophia didn't want to live. Perhaps she shrank from the struggle of deciding whether she'd put on the bombazine or the purple silk. Life is like that sometimes for the Sophias, not worth the effort of keeping the flame alight. . . . She lay limply on her bed while they fought over her, and Corneel sent for doctor after doctor and ordered them curtly to spend all ye need, money don't count — and in the midst of their efforts she died.

A great many people grieved for her. I think she would have been surprised, vaguely disturbed, too, if she had known. Why hadn't they made more fuss over her, alive? But at any rate there was an impressive funeral, with Mr. Stewart and Mr. Greeley and other prominent men as pall-bearers. And her children and sons-in-law mourned her very sincerely. And some thirty grand-children were appalled, amazed, interested or disturbed, in accordance with their several ages and dispositions. And Corneel donned black, and looked a trifle more grim than usual — and when he sought the cabinet spooks, very pointedly didn't request communication with Sophia amongst those who had Passed Over.

BOOK EIGHT

HONOR AMONGST THIEVES

I

YOU might suppose Corneel's appetite for rail-roads would have been satisfied by his three recent acquisitions. But not at all. So soon as he was assured of control of the New York Central and had charged Billy with the reorganization of its plant and service, he switched his attention to a fourth broken-down road. Bankrupt in 1859, the Erie had fallen into the clutches of Daniel Drew, who had succeeded in having himself elected treasurer. Since then it had been his toy, the speculative football of Wall Street. Nobody owned it, nobody was sufficiently interested in its fortunes to oust Uncle Dan'l's pernicious influence. Its equipment was rusting away; a burden of debt smothered any chance of profits. Wall Street's conception of the situation was summed up in a saying current in the brokerage offices:

Dan'l says up — Erie goes up.

Dan'l says down — Erie goes down.

Dan'l says wiggle-waggle — Erie bobs both ways.

Yet there were possibilities in the road. Under efficient management it might prove a dangerous rival to the New York Central system which Corneel was welding together, and this factor undoubtedly entered into his calculations. Another motive was his resentment at the spectacle of a valuable property being ruined by a financial reprobate like Drew. Say what you will about Corneel, remember he was a builder; it rasped his sensibilities to see a road, which could be used to develop the country it traversed and to create new business, employed as an excuse for stock-jobbery. He guessed he'd skin the hide off o' Drew. Such fellers was pests — oughter be run out of town. No better'n thieves.

He wasn't so inclined to be lenient these days in his judgment of Drew's rascalities. Owning railroads seemed to strengthen that disposition to conservatism in his character. He sensed in a blind, incoherent fashion that a man who owned a railroad owned an obligation to the community. That is, if the community didn't prosper, the railroad didn't prosper. It was proper self-interest to be honest. You made more in the long run. So he'd git aholt of the Erie, and have Billy shine up the injines and fix things so's the trains could keep a schedule.

But Drew was a wily enemy, and was entrenched behind barricades of stock wrung from a gullible directorate. In the preliminary skirmish between the two he won. Corneel had anticipated this, however, and executed a flank attack. There was another railroad, the Boston, Hartford and Erie, which owned two hundred and forty miles of single track linking Boston with Fishkill on the east bank of the Hudson; its main reason for being was that it connected by ferry with the Erie's terminus at Newburgh. The owners of this road, mostly New Englanders, conceived the idea of unloading it on the Erie, and with that object in view, invested heavily in Erie stock. Corneel heard of their plan, and suggested they combine forces with him, his principal stipulation being that Drew was to be barred from the new directorate of the Erie; in return for their help, he wouid agree to an arrangement whereby the Erie guaranteed the interest on $4,000,000 of their bonds, nearly half the amount of the mortagages on the line.

On these terms a bargain was struck. It didn't give Corneel control of the Erie, by any means; but it did provide him with a substantial footing in Erie affairs — and it promised to assure the removal of Drew's influence and a chance to lift the road to a paying basis. If he played his hand skilfully he had a right to expect a very considerable extension of his power. It was probable that another year or two would witness his ascendancy in the Erie's board, without the expense of a prolonged stock-buying campaign such as had won his other roads. But he deliberately threw away the advantage he had obtained by one of the most inexplicable acts of his career.

Uncle Dan'l came to Washington Place again, the moment the news of the Erie coup was abroad. Uncle Dan'l's eyes watered, his voice quavered on its falsetto key, tobacco-juice dribbled down his chin. This here was a fine way for a feller to treat a friend, Corneel! Why, you'n me have fed out of the same manger nigh on forty year.

"Hell's bells," roared Corneel. "Don't I know it? I oughter have had more sense. 'Tain't in nature for a man to feed with a hog."

But Uncle Dan'l wouldn't take offense. He leaned on his rickety, old cane that had been the ferrule of his umbrella, and his hands trembled in time with his voice.

"You're a mighty hard man, Corneel. A hard man, and sinful."

"I ain't a God-damned hypocrite!"

"That's blasphemy! Oh, take a miser'ble sinner's advice —"

"If I want advice, I'll go to an honest man."

"But takin' the Lord's name in vain! Oh, my dear friend —"

"I ain't your friend."

"Yes, you be," retorted Uncle Dan'l, undiscouraged. "Course, you be. Forty year we've knowed each other, Corneel. Fust on the river. And then railroadin'. Why, I helped you back in the war days when you give up steamships, and —"

Corneel shouted with laughter.

"Ye helped me! Ye sway-backed, interferin', old scoundrel, ye've helped yerself to anything ye could *take* from me."

Uncle Dan'l sighed indulgently.

"Say whatever ye please —"

"Ye bet I will!"

"— And cuss me all you want, Corneel. I'll forgive you. I'll forgive you for the old days. I couldn't quarrel with you. We been friends too long. And we're 'bout the only fellers in the Street as don't put on airs."

"Humph!" Corneel ejaculated uneasily.

Uncle Dan'l blinked slyly, then whined on:

"Why, it makes me happy every time I think of how we both of us come up purty nigh the same way. It takes something in a man, Corneel, to git to count his millions when he started off a drover or a ferryman."

"Millions ain't no use if ye steal 'em," growled Corneel.

"You'll be sorry for them words," Uncle Dan'l responded with dignity. "The Lord's had His share in my business. My partner I call Him. And I couldn't afford to steal for Him. But a man can't succeed, and not make enemies. You'd oughter know that, Corneel. Some fellers say ter'ble things 'bout you."

Corneel cleared his throat.

"I s'pose so. But there ain't no use talkin', Dan'l. I've agreed with that Boston gang your name ain't goin' on the new directors' ticket."

"I ain't askin' that it should," returned Uncle Dan'l.

"No? Then what 'n hell ye jawin' 'bout?"

The sly look in Uncle Dan'l's eye became a leer.

"Ye don't need to elect me on the new ticket, Corneel. Put a feller on who'll resign next day, and then elect me in his place."

"I'll be damned," exploded Corneel. "A dummy, hey? But why should I? Ye'd betray me like ye did afore."

Uncle Dan'l stumbled to his feet.

"Well, I won't hold it ag'in you," he said meekly. "Only when you feel the need of a feller beside you to trust, jest you recklect I offered to help."

A slow grin lighted up Corneel's weathered face.

"A feller to trust," he repeated. "Damn ye, Drew, if I ain't got a mind to try ye once more! But if ye reckon to fool me, I'll smash ye so's thar won't be a piece left big enough to tell ye by."

Uncle Dan'l let his head droop forlornly to hide the exultation in his watery eyes.

"You won't be sorry, Corneel," he quavered. "But I could wish you'd spoke with more grace. A friendly act oughter be friendly meant."

"Don't ye worry for that," Corneel responded grimly. "I'm friendly. As friendly as ye let me be. Christ! Ain't I goin' back on all I said I'd do to ye?"

"But unjustly," interposed Uncle Dan'l. "Words uttered in wrath is words uttered unjustly. And anyhow," he added more practically, "there ain't nobody knows the Erie like I do."

"I guess that's gospel," assented Corneel. "Know where every dollar went, don't ye? Sluiced 'em into your own bucket, hey? Well, that's ended. I'll be watchin' ye, Dan'l, I'll be watchin' ye."

Uncle Dan'l's mouth jerked open so quickly that a slimy, black gout of tobacco-juice dripped over the untidy, gray bristles on his chin.

"Got to have your joke, ain't you, Van Derbilt?" he snarled. "But I don't mind. If a man's conscience is clear he kin laugh at jeers."

Corneel leveled an admonitory forefinger.

"I ain't figgerin' on your conscience. I'm figgerin' on your eye for profits. Ye know the Erie finances, and if ye're honest she oughter make a sight of money. If ye ain't, she'll go plumb to hell — and ye'll go 'long with her. No, I ain't threatenin'. I'm warnin' ye. A man kin play monkeyshines up to a p'int, but if he pushes past it, he's a goner. All I ask of ye, now, is honesty. Do I git it?"

Uncle Dan'l wiped a scrawny hand across his nose, so that the tigerish set of his lips was disguised.

"You'll git it, Corneel. Sure, you will. I'm a man of my word, a God-fearin' man. You leave the Erie to me. I'll make her pay."

"I'll see that ye do," amended Corneel.

From a contemporary cartoon

A WELL—MERITED RECOGNITION

PICKPOCKET: " Allow me, Mr. Vanderbilt, to thank you, in the name of my whole pro-
fession, for the admirable manner in which you conduct your Fourth Avenue Railroad.
In the struggling crowds with which your cars are packed we can operate with facility,
and thus earn a comfortable livelihood. Good morning, Sir."

II

THE new deal in Erie was executed at the annual meeting on October 8, 1867. Drew was not on the ticket, but, as he had suggested, a dummy nominated in his place withdrew afterward, and the ex-drover was substituted, and resumed the office of treasurer. Aside from this, the election of directors was notable chiefly for two of the names on the ticket, James Fisk, Jr., and Jay Gould, a pair of young men who were to make themselves synonymous with all that was wicked, selfish and ugly in Wall Street. This was their first appearance in what might be called the Big Time of finance. Fisk, a stout, genial sensualist, with an adroit and cynical mind, was probably nominated through the interest of Eben D. Jordan, a Boston merchant, who formerly had employed him. Gould's friend at court is uncertain. The dark, pasty, timid, little man had come from upstate, with a mouse-trap, invented by himself, to sell, and gathering a few dollars by devious means, had accumulated sufficient funds in the feverish war market to obtain a partnership in a Stock Exchange house.

They seem to have gravitated together on the Erie board through the operation of the psychic law known as the attraction of opposites. Two men couldn't have been more unlike. Fisk was big, brassy, tremendously virile, a high liver. Gould was small, retiring, cautious, afraid of life. But both were greedy and unscrupulous, and they made an admirable team, each complementing the other's defects. Their rise, facilitated by Corneel's misguided weakness for Drew, was to be rapid and destructive. That was an extraordinary era in American history. The country was still suffering from war shock; the South was convulsed by the attempt at reconstruction; President Johnson was being impeached by the radical Republican element in Congress; politics was at a low ebb, morally, and the same might be said of business. Perhaps never have our people presented a more repellent picture. Hypocrisy walked hand-in-hand with cant; injustice was handmaiden to crime. In New York City, Boss Tweed methodically was looting the municipal funds; the State Legislature had reached the absolute depths of corruption; the judiciary was rotten. And in the upper ranks of society a pretense of virtue masked the tenets of debauchery widely practiced in a man-made world. New York was prim, proper and inwardly putrid — and in this respect no different from the rest of the country, save, perhaps, in the matter of degree.

The Brownstone Era was at hand. The warm, homely, red-brick city, with a lingering aroma of eighteenth-century dignity, was gradually disappearing before the march of a very questionable progress. St. John's Park no longer represented the acme of social prestige. Washington Square was "downtown"; Gramercy Park and Madison Square were the fashionable centers. People were vastly interested in the new Central Park. The distribution of wealth had increased tremendously, but so had the prevalence of poverty. On the lower East Side, centering about the Five Points, were slums equaling in horror and depravity any contained in the centuries-old cities of Europe, where hordes of miserable immigrants, mostly Irish and German, spawned and groveled, themselves hating the rich and by the rich hated and despised.

Here was a new radicalism in America, the radicalism of discontented alien citizens, who had fled across the Atlantic to escape exploitation, and quite naturally became enraged when they discovered — as they thought — that in the Land of Liberty they were the tools of corrupt politics and a selfish economic policy. The Gentile ghetto in which they dwelt was subject to spontaneous eruptions of hate, seizing upon any chance political or religious excuse, and when this happened — as in the Astor Place Riot of 1849, the Draft Riots of 1863 and the Orange Riot of 1871 — men of substance obtained an idea of the seething unrest beneath the city's foundations. But people soon forgot. There was so much else to think about. And a man who had money could have such a good time in the gaudy gambling palaces and sporting houses on East Fourteenth Street and West Twenty-third Street and many other streets, where champagne popped continuously and the choicest assortment of girls in the universe strove to provide their patrons with a change from the dull formality of the domestic life of the generation.

I suppose that only under such conditions, in a time of social bewilderment, following a period of intense idealistic absorption, could two knaves of the stripe of Fisk and Gould have found the opportunity for the program of chicanery to which they devoted their natural talents. They were, it is true, the pupils of Dan'l Drew, and the tactics they developed were simply

Dan'l's carried further by minds shrewder and more enterprising; but they would have had short shrift in a time of honest law and order. Fisk, certainly, would have been a petty magnate, under such conditions, possibly a theatrical producer — he was always the showman in everything he did. Gould it isn't so easy to relegate to failure. He had a good mind. But it is to be doubted whether in our day, for instance, the means by which he amassed a fortune would have earned him great wealth. Like Fisk, he succeeded by exploiting the lawlessness of the time.

Indeed, the most illuminating fact about these two freebooters is their first alliance with Drew; they were products of his peculiar school of economics, and by that they deserve to be judged. They were as unlike Corneel, and all he stood for, as the history of the Gould fortune has been unlike the history of the Vanderbilt fortune — Fisk, poor devil, left nothing behind him to speak of but the stench of an evil reputation and the memory of a few merrily cynical gasconades.

It was he, by the way, who established contact for the team with Uncle Dan'l. Drew wanted to sell his Stonington Line of steamers, in order to accumulate capital for his projected effort to secure definite control of the Erie, and Fisk handled this sale so cleverly for him as to prompt an offer of alliance. Fisk took the occasion to recommend Gould to Drew, and before long the three had their heads together plotting how to shake off Corneel — or the Commodore, as everyone called him. Corneel was buying all the Erie stock that was offered in the open market, and Uncle Dan'l was worried. There wasn't, as yet, a breach between the two, but their relations had become strained in the few months since the annual election of directors. Not that Corneel had any right to complain. He had invited trouble when he yielded to Uncle Dan'l's plea for mercy, and trouble was piling up for him exactly as he should have known it must, with Uncle Dan'l's treacherous spirit at work on the directors.

I am afraid, too, that Corneel didn't have as much influence with the board as he had anticipated. It was very easy for Uncle Dan'l, with the help of his lieutenants, to go from one director to another, whispering warnings against this feller Van Derbilt. All he wants is to cripple us so's we can't compete with his roads. I tell you what, we got to take a strong line with him.

Drew distinctly outmaneuvered Corneel in these passages. He put the Commodore in a hole again when he induced the directors to authorize an issue of $10,000,000 of convertible bonds to finance the replacement of the road's worn-out iron rails with steel rails, and likewise, the laying of a third rail, so that trains of standard-gage roads could be operated over the Erie's six-foot right of way. Corneel didn't realize the importance of those convertible bonds in Drew's plans for the future, but he did know that the third rail would enable the Erie to make a working agreement with the Michigan Central and the Canada Southern, which would give it entry into Chicago and ensure direct communication between the rising metropolis of the Middle West and New York City. This was an advantage for the Erie over the New York Central, which was standard-gage, to be sure, but had no direct connection west of Buffalo. At the same time, Corneel couldn't place himself in the position of refusing to allow the Erie to repair its dangerous road-bed.

But Uncle Dan'l had no intention of spending $10,000,000 for new rails. He locked up the resolution authorizing the bonds, and ordered his repair gangs to turn the old iron rails inside out, so as to present an unworn edge to the car-wheels. Of course, these old rails were soft and rather out of shape, but they would do for a while, and anyhow, he had other uses for $10,000,000 in unissued bonds — convertible bonds, at that. As for the third rail, Corneel need not have worried; it wasn't laid. That, too, would have cost money.

Corneel, buying Erie stock with undiminished zest, heard of Uncle Dan'l's trick, and with his usual aggressiveness flew to action. He'd be damned and etc., etc., etc., if any mangy skinflint could steal the money of a road he was director of; and he went to his friend, Bill Tweed, with whom, you may be sure, his relations were not exactly innocent, and Bill Tweed's judge, Barnard, issued an injunction restraining Drew from acting as treasurer of the Erie and prohibiting the issuing of any more stock or bonds. The point of this order was to vitiate those convertible bonds, which Uncle Dan'l had never intended to sell as bonds. What he wanted was more stock to load onto Corneel, and since the Erie charter forbade the issuing of any more stock, the only recourse he had was to issue convertible bonds, in other words, bonds convertible into stock, a quibbling difference, yet, nevertheless, in the eyes of the law, a difference.

But in those days an injunction wasn't an insuperable obstacle. As I have said, the country was thor-

oughly disorganized, and public morals at the nadir of
our history. Drew, with Fisk and Gould, took their
authorization of $10,000,000 of convertible bonds to a
printer, and had him strike off 100,000 stock certificates,
meanwhile selling shares for future delivery as fast as
the Van Derbilt interests would absorb them. The
certificates, damp from the press, were sent over to the
Erie office on West Street, where Drew and Fisk and
Gould tied them in neat packages. When everything
was ready Fisk disappeared, and Uncle Dan'l summoned an office-boy.

"Here, sonny," he whined, "you take these packages over to the Transfer Office in Pine Street — and
don't you be no longer 'n you kin help."

And Uncle Dan'l winked at Gould, who was nervously tearing up strips of paper. The boy took the
packages, and walked out the door. A few seconds later
he popped in again.

"Oh, Mr. Drew," he wailed, "a man swiped them
packages."

"Dear me, now, sonny," exclaimed Uncle Dan'l.
"That couldn't never be!"

"Yessir, right outside in the hall here."

"You better call the secretary," advised Gould.
"We'll have to look into this."

The secretary, to whom Judge Barnard's order was
directed, entered the office rubbing his hands together,
an oily smirk on his features.

"Here's a funny business," said Uncle Dan'l. "This
boy says them convertible bonds was stole from him —
and right outside in the hall, too."

"Dear, dear," said the secretary, rubbing his hands
a little harder. "That's too bad."

"Did you see him, boy?" spoke up Gould.

The boy hesitated.

"Now, don't you be afraid, sonny," advised Uncle Dan'l. "Jest you tell us what he looked like."

"Well, he was awful big — and he had a yaller moustache — and a lot o' shirtfront."

"Dressed kind of tony?" inquired Uncle Dan'l.

"Yessir," grinned the boy.

"Might almost be Jim Fisk," remarked Gould drily.

The secretary guffawed, but Uncle Dan'l was shocked.

"Oh, I wouldn't say sech things, Jay," he remonstrated. "Whatever would Jim steal them bonds for?"

"Whatever?" echoed Gould.

III

STRANGE as it may seem, 100,000 shares of freshly issued Erie stock, late convertible bonds, turned up in the offices of Fisk, Belden and Company, brokers for the Erie cabal, next morning, and were dumped on the floor of the Exchange the minute the gong sounded for trading to begin. Corneel's brokers, acting under general instructions, took the first offerings of one thousand, two thousand and three thousand share lots, with comparative equanimity, but when five thousand share lots commenced to hurtle at them they sent to him for confirmatory orders. Hell's broke loose, Commodore. The bottom's out in Erie.

Corneel rolled a cigar between tight lips, and snapped:

"Tell them fellers to support the market."

More messengers came. The Schells, Jake Little, Jerome, Tom Tobin, all were frightened. Close to fifty thousand shares, Commodore. How are we going to carry it?

"Support the market," returned Corneel, and rallied every banker on whom he had the shadow of a claim — they were many.

Erie fluttered under this pounding, but so prompt were Corneel's purchases that it never dropped very far. Back and forth swung the quotations, wilder grew the excitement, men shouting and cursing on the floor, the streets jammed with interested crowds. Uncle Dan'l's chin was one smear of tobacco-juice. Gould tore up strip after strip of paper. Jim Fisk kept everyone in a ripple of laughter with the smutty stories that crackled tirelessly off his tongue. And Corneel smoked placidly, and swore at the calamity howlers. Keep your shirts on. They're tryin' to stampede us.

Then the Drew faction launched their final offensive. They unloaded a second 50,000 shares in one crashing deluge of printer's ink and barefaced chicanery. The market went crazy, and Erie sagged abruptly from 83 to 71. Corneel's brokers stormed off the floor, one at a time, dripping with sweat despite the cold of the March day, wringing their hands, pop-eyed. They've got us on the run, Commodore. You never saw such a sweep. *And they're making deliveries!*

"Been workin' the printin'-press overtime, I guess," remarked Corneel. "Have to see what Jedge Barnard has to say to that, hey?"

"But what are we going to do?"

"Buy Erie. Buy every God-damn share of Erie that's offered."

"But how are we going to pay for it?"

"You leave that to me."

He ended the day with some $9,000,000 of freshly printed Erie stock, and his bankers called on him, anxiously pleading that he should sell a portion of it — you can't handle such a wad, Commodore.

"I kin handle this, and more," he retorted. "Stand behind me, and I'll be all right."

When Dick Schell came to him, lugubrious of countenance, and reported certain banks were refusing to loan money on the collateral offered, largely Erie shares, Corneel answered:

"You tell 'em if they try to hang me up I'll start sellin' New York Central at 50 tomorrow — and bust half the Street."

He got his loans, and that afternoon drove home as usual, a tall, imposing figure in fur coat and silk hat, managing the trotters easily, for all his seventy-three years. Billy and his army of brokers and hangers-on were concerned, but he was cool and undisturbed, although he had been obliged to raise and transfer to his opponents $4,000,000 in greenbacks, besides securities, in payment for the more or less worthless stock they had showered on him.

"If thar's any law we'll git them fellers," he asserted confidently. "It takes a bigger man than Dan'l Drew to bust Cornelius Van Derbilt."

In the morning he scored. Judge Barnard issued warrants for the arrest of the offending Erie directors for contempt of court; and Uncle Dan'l, Gould and Fisk, gathering up their spoil, $7,000,000 in greenbacks and securities, together with the Erie books and records, fled across the Hudson to Jersey City, where they opened new headquarters in the Taylor House, fortified with gangs of armed plug-uglies and cannon to resist any possible attempt by Corneel to kidnap them back into the jurisdiction of New York.

The market still seethed and boiled, with Erie the featured star on the playbill; both sides employed all the machinery of the law, and intrigued for political support. Court orders, injunctions and processes for contempt dazed the public and clouded the issues. Uncle Dan'l and his promising young men were able to induce the New Jersey Legislature to pass an act legalizing their $10,000,000 issue of convertible bonds by holding out the inducement of a promise to transfer the Erie's main offices to Jersey City permanently. And of course, there were other, more personal, considerations for the acquiescent legislators.

Spurred on by this success, the fugitives agreed that Gould should go to Albany, and attempt the same thing with the New York Legislature. You see, Corneel and the Stock Exchange and the machinery of finance were all in New York, and they couldn't be sure of their plunder until they had secured a favorable ruling superior to Judge Barnard's injunction which they had defied. The crux of the whole case was the question of the legality of that $10,000,000 issue of bonds that weren't bonds. So Gould drew $500,000 from the $4,000,000 in cash they had brought with them from New York, and slipped off to Albany, covering his trail by a story that he was bound West to settle the long-pending treaty of the Erie with the roads that would afford it entry to Chicago. But his presence in Albany soon became known, and Barnard sent a court officer to arrest him — a sordid farce, for Gould, supposedly by bribery, persuaded the officer to give him free rein, refused to present himself in New York City, and when he was quite ready, slipped out of the state again.

In Albany he had great luck. Boss Tweed, who had been working in Corneel's behalf up to this time, had been rewarded with a block of $180,000 of Erie stock. Naturally, being so large a stockholder in the road, he had interests in common with Gould, and when

Gould disclosed himself as being equipped with ammunition infinitely more potent than stock of a run-down railroad, it was scarcely surprising that Tweed should find himself disposed to change sides. Nearly ten years later, the boss told a Special Investigation Committee of the Board of Aldermen of New York that "it was impossible to do anything then without paying for it. Money had to be raised for the passing of all bills. In 1868 Mr. Gould carried up a satchel containing $500,000 in greenbacks to be distributed to a block of thirty Democratic and Republican legislators. These were known as the 'Black Horse Cavalry.' They were to vote as paid."

As much as $20,000 was paid for crucial votes, sometimes to men who had accepted almost as large sums from the opposing faction. Gould paid most, and won. The bill authorizing as legal the issue of $10,000,000 of convertible bonds, bonds that weren't bonds, passed triumphantly, and under the law of the state Corneel was obligated to accept them as valid securities. He was, to tell the truth, purty sick of the hull business. Not licked, you understand. Anything but. What bothered him most was the repercussion of this raid upon general conditions. His own Central stock, the apple of his eye, had dropped from 132 to 109 in a scary, nervous market. It would be cheaper, he decided, to compromise than to waste more energy. His position was strong, notwithstanding the extent to which he had been rooked. His resources were larger than his opponents'; his standing in the community had been enhanced by his conduct in the Erie War, as it was beginning to be called. And what was more important, his holdings of Erie stock were a menace to control of the road by the Drew faction.

Uncle Dan'l, he knew, was as weary of the fight as himself, and with the craftiness which he could employ at need he smuggled a short note to the old scoundrel who had tricked him. I got nobody to blame but myself, he told Billy. Oughter have known better. Thar ain't a straight bone in that damned, old hoss-leach's body — which is what I'm figgerin' on now. He's done me for all he kin, and he knows it. What he's after next is to do Fisk 'n Gould out of the plunder. You watch, boy! I'm tellin' him it's time we git on two sides of a desk and work out a settlement. He'll come to me like a fly trailin' a sugar-spill.

Good psychology. Uncle Dan'l evaded his partners, and sneaked across the Hudson on a Sunday when process-servers weren't working. He wasn't exactly humble, but he made it plain that his only concern was for himself. As for Corneel, he was equally blunt.

"This paper I'm stuck with ain't wuth the ink on it to me. I doubt if it's good to anyone. Same time, I kin make a heap of trouble for ye with it, and if —"

"Don't let's talk of trouble, Corneel," whined Uncle Dan'l. "You 'n me are agittin' too old for trouble. We'd oughter fix our thoughts on the bright days acomin' — Over Jordan. A man ain't more 'n a maggot on the footstool 'less 'n he has grace."

"To hell with you and your religion," bellowed Corneel. "I'm here to talk business. What 'bout that stock ye loaded onto me? If ye want peace, ye got to take it off my hands."

"How'm I goin' to git money to take over all that

stock?" complained Uncle Dan'l. "I'm a poor man,
Corneel. I ain't rich like you be."

"Oh, ain't ye?" inquired Corneel. "Huh! Well, I
don't keer where ye git the money, but ye git it — that's
flat. And good day to ye. Next time we meet talk business."

Next time, alas, Uncle Dan'l thought he had evaded
Fisk and Gould again; but they were no fools, and their
agents kept the ancient reprobate under constant es-
pionage. So, when Uncle Dan'l met Corneel at the house
of Judge Pierrepont for a final interview, his partners
weren't far behind him. They walked into the Judge's
parlor while he was in the act of proposing to take the
money required to buy Corneel's stock from the Erie
treasury — 'cause I'm a mortal poor man, Corneel, but
anything for peace, I say.

Corneel received the two minor conspirators with
cool indifference.

"Might as well have everyone here," he said, grin-
ning. "Then thar cain't be no misunderstandin'. Drew
says he'll agree to take my Erie, and pay for it out of
the Erie treasury. Got any objections?"

"Holy Moses!" cried Fisk. "I'm no saint, but that's
a little steep, I'd say. It comes close to robbery."

Gould was more savage in his tone.

"All right," he snapped, almost as forcefully as
Corneel. "Let Drew use the Erie treasury, instead of
his own profits; but he gets out of Erie, and stays out."

Uncle Dan'l started to protest, his chin wobbling
earnestly.

"Why, that ain't no way for you to do, Jay. I put
you fellers in right in Erie. I allus aimed to take you in

on my accountin' with Corneel, but 'twasn't no use to tell you till —"

"What a dirty, old liar you are!" hooted Fisk. "I believe you'd sell out this Lord of yours you're forever talking about. I'm with Jay. We'll run the Erie, without you. Speaking for myself, I don't like to have to worry every day over what my friends may be doing to me."

Uncle Dan'l appealed to Corneel.

"Ain't that a heartless way for two boys to treat an old feller that took 'em into Wall Street, and showed 'em the way 'round?"

"It's what you deserve," growled Corneel. "But I ain't interested in your affairs. Git to the p'int! What terms are you offerin' me, the three of you?"

The upshot of their negotiations was that Corneel was to be relieved at once of 50,000 shares at 70 — he received $2,500,000, and $1,250,000 in Boston, Hartford and Erie bonds at 80. In addition, he was given $1,000,000 for the privilege of calling upon him for the other 50,000 shares he held at 70, the call to be exercised within six months. Erie eased up to 72 1/2 on the news of the settlement of the feud which had been distracting the Street, but Fisk and Gould, who immediately made good their threat to squeeze out Uncle Dan'l, had no intention of permitting Corneel to benefit by the higher price. They straightway repeated their former tactics, sold 100,000 shares short, with the effect of breaking the price to 35, and then, employing the spoils wrung from Corneel, bought in sufficient shares at the low price to assure them absolute control. Corneel was glad to settle at 40 for his remaining 50,000 shares, when the raiders exercised their call.

THE MODERN COLOSSUS OF (RAIL) ROADS

From an old caricature in *Puck* picturing Commodore Vanderbilt, C. W. Field and Jay Gould

This meant that all told he had obtained from them by way of restitution $6,500,000. He had held 100,000 shares, or rather less, but he hadn't bought this at par. On the whole, I am inclined to agree with his own contention that his net loss on the series of transactions was $2,000,000. It was the one time in his career that he was taken into camp on a generous scale. Himself, he made no bones about admitting it.

"Cain't beat a printin'-press, and if the law ain't honest a feller has to git from under. I don't reckon on playin' with thieves any oftener 'n I have to."

To his contemporaries there was an element of comedy in his attempt to annex a fourth railroad and the sinuous devices which procured his defeat. Mingled with this was a feeling of relief, for there can be little question that the acquisition of the Erie by him would have tended to erect a drastic monopoly of transportation. The Legislature of New York reflected the prevailing sentiment of the state in the following year when it enacted a law forbidding the combination of the Erie and the New York Central Lines. Yet it is probable that had Corneel won, and brought the Erie into his system, the curse upon the road would have been lifted. Instead of being looted by Gould and other harpies, it would have been reorganized and improved, according to the methods Billy had evolved for roads no less decrepit.

IV

CORNEEL was through with railroads for the present. His chief purpose was to steady financial conditions against the insanely dishonest wave of speculation loosed by the operators whose leaders now were Fisk and Gould. Uncle Dan'l had been relegated to a subordinate position in the ranks of shysters, welchers and thieves; he lied and cheated as pertinaciously as ever, but the day was at hand when, as Fisk had predicted, he'd "sell out this Lord of yours" — renig on the subscriptions he had made to the seminary which bore his name. A disturbing influence Drew always was, but he was no longer head devil in the inferno he and his kind made of the Stock Exchange. That questionable honor was confered upon Jay Gould, with Jim Fisk laboring cheerfully for second place.

In the midst of these conditions Corneel was a stalwart supporter of honesty in business. Without him, the harm wrought by the Drews, the Goulds and the Fisks would have reached infinitely greater proportions; there would have been several other panics, perhaps a cataclysmic collapse of credit. Let it be said to his honor that he never wavered. Bluff, ignorant, selfish as he was, he had a broader conception of business than any leader of his day. He worked for progress and stability; he was everlastingly a Bull in a predominantly Bear market; he fought, tooth and nail, hip and thigh, the raiders whose intent was to pick bare the bones of any valuable property, and then discard it for posterity to worry over.

I don't wish to be hypocritical about Corneel. He was as far from being a hypocrite, himself, as a man could be. He wasn't nice in his personal tastes and habits; he wasn't a man of sensibility, let alone a gentleman. He was superstitious, as well as ignorant. He fought his enemies with whatever weapons they used. If they bribed aldermen, he bribed aldermen. If they tried to buy up the Legislature, he tried to buy up the Legislature. If they attempted legal trickery, he countered in kind. But he never preferred dishonesty; he was too intelligent. It didn't pay to be dishonest. Fellers that stole had somethin' to hide. And personally, I find significance in the fact that whenever he descended to questionable practices he seems to have run into trouble. He wasn't apt at chicanery. How could he have been? First and foremost, he was a builder.

It was as a builder that he shone in the five years between 1868 and 1873, the most fruitful years of his life for his country, although his accomplishments were rather in the way of preventing his opponents from tearing down than in building on his own initiative. When that precious pair, Fisk and Gould — or Gould and Fisk; they were on all fours in knavery — cornered greenbacks a few months after the Erie settlement, it was Corneel who led in supporting a market that had tumbled thirty points under money stringency. An amazing stunt, this was, not original with Gould's agile brain, however, for three years previously, a young broker named Dimock had tried it successfully, but was so appalled by the first reactions of his plan that he abandoned it forthwith. Briefly, it was predicated upon the limited supply of available currency, and the requirement of the banks to maintain a reserve equal to twenty-five per cent of their deposits. Gould and Fisk put up $10,000,000, between them, then patched up peace with Uncle Dan'l, and took him into their pool to the tune of $4,000,000 more. This gave them a total of $14,000,000 to play with. They deposited it in a number of banks, and drew certified checks against the whole amount. The certified checks they used as collateral upon which they borrowed greenbacks — which they withdrew from circulation.

The result was automatic. The withdrawal of $14,000,000 in currency affected credit to four times that figure, thus compelling the banks to call their loans for $56,000,000, which withdrew an equivalent amount of greenbacks from circulation, making, with the $14,000,000 in the possession of the pool, $70,000,000. So violent a contraction of the currency, coming in the season of crop movements from the West — Gould had timed his stroke with exact appreciation of his opportunity! — precipitated a miniature panic. Loan rates skied, margins were called, hundreds of thousands of shares poured into the market, and Gould, Fisk and Drew, who had been selling short for weeks, stuffed millions in dirty profits into their pockets. Without Corneel, the market would have been stampeded. He and his supporters amongst the Bulls dammed the flood of sales in time to avert a chain of failures such as creates a nation-wide panic.

A year afterward, in the fall of 1869, he had to step forward again and buoy up a falling market. Fisk and

Gould, having discarded Uncle Dan'l once more, engineered the most audacious wholesale robbery of the public that even they undertook. Gold since the war had been selling at a premium, and they planned to corner it. This involved a political intrigue, which embraced in its slimy web the person of Austin Corbin, brother-in-law of President Grant, through whom the reckless conspirators obtained assurance that the President would permit the gold market to take care of itself. Working on this assurance, they pushed gold up to 162, when, without warning, the Government intervened and commenced to sell gold from the Treasury — bona fide gold, not what Jim Fisk euphemistically styled "phantom gold." Crash! The bottom fell out of the corner. In a few minutes gold was down to 135, and a reaction set in on the Stock Market, which was held within bounds mainly by the exertions of Corneel, who heaved a million dollars into the turmoil to sustain prices, and by his personal endeavors and assumption of confidence inspired others with confidence, even after Gould and Fisk, relying rightly upon their control of the Tammany judiciary, through Boss Tweed, welched on their own commitments.

The Street looked to Corneel more than ever. He seldom appeared in public, never had anything to say; but everyone knew which side his influence would be on. He might have his little peccadillos. Who cared? He was the apostle of sanity in business; his railroads offered good investments; that rough, windy voice of his stilled the fears of many an uneasy bank president.

"We'd better send for the Commodore," was the decision of almost any vexed conference.

"It's pretty late. Guess he's left Washington Place."

"Yes, he's probably at Dick Schell's."

"No, somebody said he went down to Woodhull and Claflin's an hour ago."

"Haw, haw, haw," laughed the staid and grave directors surrounding that particular table. "Dropped in to see Tennie, eh? Well, maybe we ought to give him time."

"Give him time, that's right."

"He's got to have his fun, like the rest of us."

"The rest of us aren't seventy-five."

"Neither's Tennie."

"Haw, haw, haw!"

Which leads up to the most bizarre of all the bizarre episodes in Corneel's unconventional life.

V

Victoria Woodhull and her younger sister, Tennie C. Claflin, came to New York from Pittsburgh in 1868 while the Erie War was at its height. They were notable for several reasons, but especially as prominent members of the first generation of feminists and social radicals. For the ensuing six or seven years they shocked, amused and entertained the city, and incidentally piled up a small fortune apiece. Victoria was the thinker, the strategist, of the combination; Tennie, who in later life turned her first name and middle initial into the more euphonious Tennessee, was the salesman. I gather that Tennie had what our film experts term "IT"; she was dainty in figure, peppy in her speech and attractive to look at. She specialized in men of mature years. Victoria, on the contrary, who had been married and divorced, was temperamental and odd, a spiritualist, with bobbed hair.

According to a brief biography of Victoria, written by Theodore Tilton, who sued Henry Ward Beecher for alienation of his wife's affections, after charging her seduction by the preacher, Victoria was as partial to spooks as Corneel.

"I must let out a secret," Mr. Tilton confesses archly. "She acquired her studies, performed her work, lived her life, by the aid (as she believed) of heavenly spirits."

She entertained them, not unawares, from her third year, and they served to lighten the burdens of a childhood harassed by cruel parents. In her tenth year while she was rocking the cradle of a sick sister, two angels entered the room, pushed her away gently and fanned the little one with their white hands until its cheeks were rosy. A fact, I assure you. Mr. Tilton says so, and he ought to know — Victoria publicly professed most intimate relations with him.

The angels, however, did nothing for Victoria, herself. From a distressed childhood, she passed, while still a child, into marriage with a drunkard, Dr. Canning Woodhull, nephew of a Mayor of New York, a man of excellent family, whose family had cast him off. With Woodhull Victoria remained until 1863 — she was just twenty-five, then, and Tennie was eighteen — when she left him, and with Tennie's assistance launched a sanitarium at Ottawa, Illinois, where they professed to practice an infallible system of cure-alls. If spiritualism couldn't help you, why, then, yarbs should. They did very well for several years, but an unfortunate attempt to cure a cancer with mustard-plaster precipitated them from Ottawa to Cincinnati, then the riotous headquarters of the Whiskey Ring, which was run by disreputable friends of General Grant. The whiskey kings took a fancy to the Claflin sisters, and they had a grand time until the funds they had saved from the sanitarium venture ran low. They decided to move to Pittsburgh, and search for a new occupation; but nothing offered, and they were menaced by poverty, when, again according to Tilton, one of Victoria's pet angels appeared and notified her that a house was all ready and waiting for

A view of New York and environs in 1868, illustrating graphically the a

her, furnished and coal in the grates, at 17 Great Jones Street, New York City.

What angel could have been kinder? Of course, it was time, considering all the hardships Victoria had suffered, but she doesn't seem to have cherished any resentment. Which goes to prove that she was a philosopher. At any rate, she and Tennie packed up their dwindling wardrobes and set off to conquer the Sodom and Gomorrah that was Gotham. Whether the angel told them to or not, their object from the first was to fish in the troubled waters of speculation, and nobody was cleverer at it than they were.

You see, they made so many friends. There were dozens of rich gentlemen who wanted to give them tips, and show them how to ride the market and when to sell short and when to stay on the long side. Really, it was embarrassing the way men swarmed around Tennie, and women, even the properest of the bluestockings and intellectuals, were won by Victoria's suffrage arguments and her denunciation of the double standard. Victoria was born fifty years ahead of her time, although she would have been regarded as radical even today.

When they first reached New York they opened an office in the Hoffman House, but shortly moved downtown to 44 Broad Street. Woodhull and Claflin, brokers and bankers, was the firm name. Some people whispered that that old rip Commodore Van Derbilt was financing 'em. I don't know whether it was true. Nobody does. If it was true, it was to Corneel's credit, for it reveals a humanness, an accessibility to new ideas, not typical of the times. And whether true or not, the fact remains that Corneel was very friendly with Woodhull and Claflin, with Claflin more than with Woodhull, to be sure. He was often seen at their offices. There was a story told by some of his children that he was on quite intimate terms with the lady bankers, as they were called. It was actually reported that Tennie used to slap him on the back of an afternoon, and cry:

"Wake up, old boy!"

He went to the house in Great Jones Street, too, which the angel had so nicely selected. And he guided them safely amidst the pitfalls of speculation in Erie, and cautioned Tennie to beware of that showy feller, Jim Fisk. He ain't the kind of feller for a nice, young gal to git in with. A whoremaster, that's what he is, Tennie. Take all the rope he kin git. At which Tennie would tap his shoulder gently — the slap being reserved for more uproarious moments — and assure him that the Jim Fisks of this world were welcome to all the rope they could pull out of her very capable hands. No Jim Fisk ever lured or fooled Tennie. She was as hard-boiled and sure of herself as a flapper fresh from finishing school.

"The Princesses of Erie," Wall Street christened Woodhull and Claflin. In six weeks, during the winter of 1869–70, they claimed to have cleaned up $750,000. But don't get the idea that there was anything hoydenish or undignified about them. Quite the contrary. On the door of their private office was a conspicuous sign:

ALL GENTLEMEN
WILL STATE THEIR BUSINESS
AND
THEN RETIRE AT ONCE

They might be hail-fellow-well-met with Corneel, the most powerful financier on the continent, but none of the small fry of the Street tried familiarity with them. Woodhull and Claflin were ladies of perspicuity and resource. And if Corneel proposed marriage to Tennie, as was alleged, you may rely upon it that she refused him. She had other fish to fry. Marry a man old enough to be her grandfather? Not she! Why should she, indeed? She had never experienced difficulty in earning a good living. That mustard-plaster in Ottawa was a misstep long since forgotten, although the lesson conveyed by it was not. On the whole, I believe Corneel did want to marry her, and that for a very sufficient reason — he married another young woman, not long after he made acquaintance with Tennie. But marriage could make no difference in his friendship. There was something in the Claflin sisters that appealed to his horny, battered, old soul. He liked their picaresque daring, their self-confidence, their contempt for opposition, their ability to think independently.

How he enjoyed the roll of their exploits! Not content with being bankers and brokers, they started *Woodhull & Claflin's Weekly*, a magazine which did not always appear weekly, but which attained a circulation of 50,000 and was the most talked-of publication in the United States while it lasted. In its columns they printed the story which caused the Beecher-Tilton trial. For a similar attack upon a well-known broker they were arrested on a charge of sending improper matter through the mails, but after they had been detained six weeks in jail the case against them collapsed. Victoria, having married a second husband, Captain J. H. Blood, managing editor of the *Weekly*, scandalized the town by receiving back into the house in Great Jones Street her first husband, who was sick and penniless. Tennie, when Mr. Charles Delmonico protested that he couldn't possibly permit a female, unescorted, to enter his restaurant, triumphantly hailed in her cab-driver, and dined in the jehu's company.

Victoria was a drawing-card at Cooper Union, and made the principal address for the Women's Rights Association before the Judiciary Committee of the House in Washington. One of her addresses on "The Naked Truth" — which was very naked — led her into Ludlow Street Jail. She and Tennie were at the head of the Twelfth Section of the International Workers' Party, and raised a demonstration of 50,000 people to protest against the deaths of Flourens and Dombrowski in the Paris Commune. Yet they were not pacifists, for Tennie was offered the colonelcy of the Ninth Regiment of the National Guard after Jim Fisk was shot by Edward S. Stokes on the stairs of the Broadway Central Hotel, and refused it to accept command of the Sixty-first, a poor, ill-equipped organization, which she drilled and uniformed properly at her own expense.

The sisters were exotic figures in the drab, prim, narrowly hidebound life of New York. They believed in birth control, and that women should share equally with men the privileges as well as the burdens of existence! They thought that capitalism should be curbed, and that workers deserved leisure in reason! And they weren't afraid to say what they thought or to put their theories to the test. Small wonder that the New York of the sixties and seventies regarded them as hussies and bad wimmin and no better 'n they oughter be. Small wonder that gossips gabbled busily whenever Corneel was seen in the office at 44 Broad Street or the house at 17 Great Jones Street. An old feller like him cavortin' 'round with an impudent slut like that Claflin girl! It was a wonder the banks didn't call his loans. His family should have him committed.

There were nasty stories told, which some of his children apparently believed. I don't. After looking over the evidence, such as it is, I think that Corneel, struggling fiercely against the slow approach of that Shadow which had so recently engulfed Sophia, developed an insatiate appetite for youth. It made him feel younger to have someone young and bright to associate with. It helped him to forget the Shadow. It roused his sluggish blood to spurts of such volcanic energy as the ferryman had known. It helped him to fight off the savage onslaughts of the Bears, who kept dinning it into the ears of Wall Street that the Commodore was a goner, a mossback. And so he went often to see Tennie, who refused to take him seriously, clapped him on the back and pulled his whiskers, or to talk with Victoria, of the throaty, resonant voice, about that spirit world which was real to him, if, by chance, it wasn't to her. After all, too, he liked a fighter — and these women were as fearless, level-headed, come-and-be-damned-to-you fighters as he ever met.

In exchange for their friendship he offered tips on the market, which they had the ability to utilize profitably. They certainly had some one besides the angel of the Great Jones Street house to guide them in their early days in the Street, for they were quite ignorant of the inside aspects of the market, even though they may have tried long-distance speculating in Cincinnati and Pittsburgh, as is possible. But if Tennie wanted to marry him, she bungled the job, which wasn't a habit of hers. The sisters were adepts at handling the brute man; their common sense was as marked as their temerity.

They had an uncanny facility at falling on their feet. When they finally wearied of the *gauche* hostility of New York society they went to England. Victoria had dispossessed herself of Captain Blood, and she presently married Mr. John Biddulph Martin, a wealthy banker. Tennie, now yclept Tennessee, became Lady Cook and Marchioness of Montserrat in Portugal. Both were distinguished by good works and social rectitude. Both lived to sample the satisfaction of a pleasant, useful old age. Victoria died only the other day, her passing serving to remind a generation able to comprehend her theories of life that she had once been a candidate for the Presidency of the United States, and had blazed the trail for the emancipation of her sex. Tennie survived until 1923, and being a person of infinite humor, she must often have chuckled to herself as she surveyed the perspective of the years. I'd give much for her opinion of Corneel. She seems to have been the one woman, except Phebe Hand, who could bridle his arrogance.

BOOK NINE

IN THE SHADOW

I

CORNEEL was lonesome after Sophia died. He had never made companions of his children; and as they grew older resentment was mingled with the awe which had ruled them in youth. Billy was closer to him than the others, closer to him than any of his family; but Billy was not a companion. Father and son were fundamentally antipathetical: Billy, slow, cautious, analytical; Corneel, swift and instinctive in all his moods. The nearest the pair came to an understanding was when Corneel realized his son's ability as an executive. After that their community of business interests was established; Billy was no longer referred to as a sucker and a putterin' farmer. But they remained two separate souls, two foreign intellects. They were master and apprentice, not father and son. Billy was always, to the very last, a little afraid of his father, an affliction he shared with the generality of those whose ways crossed Corneel's.

It was this lonesomeness which impelled Corneel to develop his friendship with Tennie Claflin and Victoria Woodhull. They were young, daring, vigorous. They reminded him, indirectly, of the traits that had endeared his mother to him. They diverted his mind from the

Shadow which was mantling his head, the Shadow which had engulfed successively the three people whose lives meant most to him: Phebe Hand; George, the one child he deeply loved; and Sophia — poor, work-worn Sophia, who seemed more desirable dead than she had living. But Tennie laughed at his suit. Marriage? Now, now, Commodore! I'm not the bird for your cage. We'd scratch each other's eyes out in a month. All right, you can hold my hand, if you want to, but what are you doing in the market tomorrow?

That was as far as he got with Tennie, and being lonesome and old and secretly fearful of the Shadow, he went from her to the only other young woman he knew, who possessed the qualities which attracted him. Frank A. Crawford was a Southern girl. She had come North with her mother from Mobile, Alabama, after the war, ruined like the rest of the Southern aristocracy. They had called on the Van Derbilts, and maintained a nominal acquaintance, because one of Frank's great grandfathers was Samuel Hand, a brother of Phebe Hand. For several years Corneel must have been meeting Frank Crawford off and on, in his own house and in the houses of his daughters; but he seems not to have been attracted by her until the summer after Sophia's death when he encountered her — accidentally, on his part — at Saratoga.

She is described as a tall, handsome young woman, no child, rather older than Tennie, undeniably a gentlewoman. One of her father's relations had been the late Senator Crawford of Georgia, Democratic candidate for President in 1824. She was intelligent, also, and perhaps more refined than any woman with whom

The old Terminal of the New York Central on the northwest corner of Forty-Second Street and Fourth Avenue

Corneel had been familiar. Cool, dignified, very religious. On the whole, a strange mate for him to pick, except that she was young. Younger than any of his children, no older than some of his thirty-odd grandchildren. A startling contrast to Sophia, whose grave in the Moravian Cemetery was only recently green.

Whatever the attraction she had for him, they eloped from Saratoga to London, Ontario, in the summer of 1869, and were properly married in the presence of Gus Schell and one other of Corneel's cronies. And Billy and the gals found a new mistress at 10 Washington Place when they paid their duty-calls. It was irksome, although none of them dreamed of saying so. Corneel's word was law in his tribe. He held the purse-strings. But, of course, that was the rub. What was the stepmother going to be able to do in the way of loosening his grasp? The answer, instantly rendered, was: nothing. And to do her justice, she conducted herself in a difficult situation with diplomacy and aplomb. To do Corneel justice, likewise, he wasn't, then or at any time, in his dotage. He knew what disposition he wished to make of his fortune, and he made it, regardless of whose feelings were hurt. All he asked of his wife was companionship and the stimulus of youth.

She gave him what he wanted, and without curbing his restless spirit, she contrived to tame his ruthless intolerance and ween him from spiritualism. He gave over spooks and spells from the day she entered his home. Instead of communing with Phebe Hand and George through a medium, he prayed for them. When he was sick, she made him confine himself to Dr. Linsley's ministrations, which is probably one reason why he lived to be eighty-two. She never got him to church, but she did succeed in introducing a clergyman as a regular visitor to the household and ultimately made this person, Rev. Charles F. Deems, his intimate adviser. Her greatest achievement, probably, was in persuading him to reverse his dictum against charity — Hell! What's the use in givin' folks money? Them as wants it kin git it. It's the lazy ones beg — and make several princely gifts for public purposes.

Dr. Deems is usually credited with inducing him to make this departure from his lifelong rule, but Mrs. Frank must have been the silent mainspring of the kindly conspiracy. Surely, Corneel would never have given $50,000 to buy the Church of the Strangers for Deems without suggestions having been made in the home circle. And while it is true that Deems brought him in touch with Southern clergymen who were agitating the educational needs of their war-torn region, his wife's descriptions of the South's sufferings were certainly a factor in carrying him to the point of giving $1,000,000 to found and endow Vanderbilt University. However you regard it, Mrs. Frank was a force to be reckoned with. If she lacked the shrewd and pungent personality of Phebe Hand and the self-effacing devotion of Sophia, she nursed and tended a crotchety, fierce, old man, who was dreaded in his periodic rages by all who must approach him, and gentled him into paths of humility he had never trod before.

She deserves her place in the small gallery of women who molded his character.

II

THE last seven years of Corneel's life were as fruitful as any which had preceded them. They constituted a period of consolidation. He sat back, and with Billy's assistance reorganized and developed the properties he owned. Conservatism was his watchword. There was no more reckless plunging such as had marked his conduct during the Erie War. He was content with what he had. Whatever moves he made were calculated for the purpose of strengthening his fortune, never with an eye to expanding his existing holdings. Yet even so, he could not avoid the purchase of additional roads required to round out his New York Central system. Destiny, of which he had been a tool, made sport of his determination to halt his railroad empire at Buffalo.

"We've gone far enough," he said to Billy after the Erie War. "Buffalo's my limit. If we go on west to Chicago, we might as well go clear to Frisco and China."

Acting on this belief, his energies were directed to the logical development of the Central and the Harlem. After the New York Legislature had authorized the consolidation of his roads in 1869 — as a set-off to this concession, previously refused, debarring in perpetuity any combination of the Central lines with the Erie — he bought from New York City the area of St. John's Park, in the lower end of the Greenwich Village district on the West Side, and erected on this site a huge freight terminal, the first adequate terminal within the city limits. It sheds light on his character to learn that he paid $250,000 for an immense bronze bas-relief of Industry to be placed on the terminal's façade, and saw to it that the contract for the job went to a young sculptor who was a son of one of his former ship-captains. The result was a monumental horror, dominated by a stiff caricature of Corneel, himself, the only statue of him in the city. But he was entirely satisfied, and nobody criticized it to his face.

Gradually, however, it became evident to him that arbitrary designation of Buffalo as their western terminus must cripple the Central lines in competition with roads having direct entry into Chicago. Billy had been alive to this from the days of the Erie War, when Drew and Gould were threatening to negotiate a treaty with roads owning Chicago terminals, but he had a difficult job in convincing his father that they should stretch westward. As it was, Corneel bought in the Lake Shore and Michigan Southern simply because if he hadn't it must have gone to rival interests. And this unprecedented vein of conservatism which characterized his old age led him to hold off from purchasing the Canada Southern and Michigan Central until a couple of years prior to his death.

It is fair to say that the Central's rails were pushed to Chicago against his stubborn opposition. After it was accomplished, he was as proud of the increased area of his empire as Billy, yes, prouder. He liked to study the maps which traced the steel track 978 miles from the seaboard to Lake Michigan, and boast to his intimates of the advantages it assured to his family and the country. Frankly, he thought more of his family than of his country, and therein, probably, lies the clue to this contradictory hesitance to adopt measures obviously sound and desirable. His name had become something approaching an obsession to him. Cornelius Van Derbilt! B'God, that meant something today, just as he'd told Ma and Sophy it would. Richest man in America. Biggest, too. Where'd ye find another feller owned 978 miles of railroad acrosst the richest land in the nation? Huh, ye'd hunt far!

The Van Derbilt system, folks called it. The Van Derbilt railroads. The Van Derbilt fortune. His tired, shrunken heart, which was beginning to falter now and then, pumped faster whenever he read or heard one of those phrases. A name hitched to a railroad nigh a thousand miles from terminal to terminal wasn't likely to be forgot.

"Doctor," he told his old friend and physician, Linsley, "if I'd died in Jersey in that wreck in '33 or when I was sick in '36 or that time in '54, who'd remember me? Why, the world wouldn't have known I ever lived! But I was spared, and I figger I wasn't spared accident'ly. No, I was spared to do a great work that'll last and remain after I'm gone."

His one objective was to ensure the New York Central's permanent identification with the Van Derbilt name. It must always be the Van Derbilt railroad. Van Derbilts must always run it. He must be careful to make no false step which might cripple his fortune or endanger its ability to thrive and exist, generation after generation. Hence, his extreme caution, so unlike the attitude he had maintained for over seventy years. Hence, his iron resistance to all Bear speculations in the market. Hence, his consistent policy of upholding business against the guerrilla raiders who strove to capitalize the abnormal conditions prevailing throughout Grant's administrations. It was selfishness, pure and simple, but intelligent selfishness. You might call that the keynote of Corneel's life: intelligent selfishness. As it happened, what was profitable to him usually was profitable to the country.

He was as selfish in his attitude toward his family as in his attitude toward the general public. In making his will he had but the one aim in view: perpetuation of the power of the Van Derbilt name. All else was secondary to that. And power, as he saw it, involved centralization of the family fortune in one pair of hands. Spread his millions fairly amongst a dozen children and two score grandchildren and great grandchildren, and the stock necessary to command the fate of his railroads would be dispersed beyond recall.

Billy was the favored heir, Billy who had proved capability by humility and service, who had snatched a cigar from his mouth and thrown it away at his father's snarled command. Billy, the farmer and blatherskite! Billy, whose patience and plugging determination overcame executive problems Corneel would never have tackled personally, who, denied the gift of vision, yet perceived that without a Chicago terminus the New York Central was a stub-end, isolated and incomplete. Billy, who never argued with his father, never refused him anything, but somehow contrived to twist him to his will. Billy, who for thirty years had planned and schemed to stand in his father's shoes. No slouch, Billy. Unattractive personally, a dour, saturnine man, prone to

Courtesy of New York Central R. R.

E New York Central Locomotive "Commodore Vandfrbilt" from a photograph taken in the seventies. Note the Commodore's portrait on the headlight

+ HE + WAS + WORTHY + FOR + HE +

ERECTED
To the glory of GOD
And in MEMORY of
CORNELIUS VANDERBILT
BY THE
CHURCH OF THE
STRANGERS
'74
A.D
'77

HATH

BUILT

+ US + A + SYNAGOGUE +

Memorial Tablet Erected to the Late Commodore Vanderbilt in the Church of the Strangers, New York City

lip-service, and persuaded thereby all men were alert to deceive and make use of him; but withal, a worker, a doer, a builder. Without him, I doubt if the fortune Corneel acquired could have been as solidly fortified as it was, for Corneel had no tolerance for details, and subordinates couldn't have reorganized the New York Central with the painstaking care he practiced.

Next to his father, he was probably the greatest of the Van Derbilts. But he had no flair for popularity. He was never liked, and the public distrusted him, although he was not a whit more selfish than his father. Where Corneel was picturesque, magnetic, a symbol of the spiritual forces which drove the country forward, he was plain, negative, unappealing. An excellent hand at analyzing statistics and plotting freight rates, he hadn't, as a rule, the ability to see over the hills into unexplored regions. He could never have entered the stock market, as his father did, and in three swift, dramatic campaigns conquered the railroads which composed the backbone of the Van Derbilt empire; but he could, and did, conceive the means for knitting these disjointed roads into one profitable whole.

And he had no such flaming pride of name as animated Corneel. The millions he inherited were merely millions to him, security against want to be passed on to his children. He hadn't won them; they had come to him. Perhaps he had a distaste for them. He never seemed to enjoy them, and the cares they entailed wore him out years before his time. I can't help wondering whether the slights he suffered from his terrible father, the contempt with which he was treated, didn't sour any joys their possession might have conveyed. Surely, his manhood and his self-respect must have ached whenever he thought back to the day he condoned his mother's commitment to the asylum in Flushing; and the recollection of every incident of subordination to dogmatic and contemptuous authority was a scar upon his vanity.

From this distance he is a pitiful figure. The only thing he is remembered by is a misquotation by a mendacious reporter: "The public be damned." And ironically enough, most people believe that it was Corneel who said it!

III

THE biggest single achievement of Corneel's latter years was his bull-headed stand against the panic of 1873, one of the two or three most disastrous financial upheavals in the country's history. His stand was purely defensive; the panic was beyond any individual's restraint, as it was the product of no particular individual or group. Jay Gould and Dan'l Drew were leaders of the speculative maniacs, who, in turn, led the American people into a debauch of railroad-building, overstraining the slight and inelastic currency system which was the foundation of the toppling pyramid of credit; but if they had not led, some other perverted geniuses would have emerged from the thoughtless horde of Wall Street as Lords of Misrule to jangle cap and bells in the face of economic fact. It happened to be Gould and Drew, that's all — Fisk, wretched clown, was long since dead of Stokes's bullet, forgotten by his comrades in crime as by every Mistress Loosegirdle who had graced his seraglio in West Twenty-third Street.

To Corneel it was an old story. He had seen the same phenomena in '57: the same abuse of prosperity, the same overextension of credit, the same wild speculation in railroads reacting upon all other branches of industry. As in '57, he pulled in his horns, mobilized his resources and sat tight. To those who asked his opinion he gave it; otherwise, he kept his mouth shut. He didn't believe in publicity, didn't like newspapers when they interfered with him. He had two maxims with which he responded to any request for an explanation of his success:

"All ye have to do is attend to your own business, then go ahead."

"I never tell what I'm goin' to do till I've done it."

They are a fair summation of his philosophy of business. He was no talker, no apostle. He didn't approve of the way the country was going, but it never entered his head to say so — and if it had entered his head, he'd have kept quiet, on the theory that what he knew was nobody else's business. As a deterrent force, then, he helped only to the extent of setting an example of conservatism. But when the storm crashed out of the West on the morning of September 18, with the announcement of the suspension of Jay Cook and Company, financiers of the Northern Pacific, he put his shoulder to the wheel, and worked as silently as before to keep the catastrophe within the narrowest possible bounds. He couldn't do much, but without him and other men of his type, who had refused to succumb to the furore of speculation, the country would have been worse off than it was — which is saying more than any American of this generation can comprehend.

We don't know what a real panic is. In all likelihood, we never shall know because the Federal Reserve system provides machinery for absorbing the shock of periodic depressions and mustering vast reserves of credit at threatened points. In Corneel's lifetime a panic was as devastating as a war, leaving behind it a swath of bankruptcies and failures, defalcations, suicides, wrecked homes, poverty, starvation. It is doubtful if any panic was more harmful than the panic of '73, yet, thanks to the sobering influence of that river of gold which had flowed East from California, there was very little radicalism; it wasn't necessary, as in '35, to call out troops to guard the banks. People complained and threatened, starved and shivered, suffered and died — and those that survived hung on until times had changed for the better a year or so later, and jobs were once more available.

Easy to talk about, now. But to Corneel, nearly eighty years old, with hundreds of men of substance leaning upon his advice, it must have been a nightmare. He seldom went downtown, making his headquarters in a one-room office in Fourth Street, behind his home at 10 Washington Place, and here he was besieged by an army of bankers and brokers and merchants, seeking credit or advice. And grimly, unflinchingly, he told them what he thought.

"Ever drive a hoss? Ever have him git his head, make a break for it, hey? Well, 'tain't no use to haul him in right away. Jest keep aholt of the reins, feel him, pull him in slow. If he don't pitch ye out, ye'll purty soon have him trottin' ag'in."

And to those who wrung their hands and sobbed:

"If ye got to go, ye got to go. Might as well make the best of it. I'm doin' all I kin for ye. 'Twon't help none to pull me down with ye."

He gave one interview during this tense month.

"Good morning, Commodore," said the reporter. "What do you think of the panic?"

"I don't think about it at all," he growled.

"What do you intend to do about it, then?" pressed the reporter.

"I don't intend to do anything at all."

"Well, haven't you got anything to say about it?"

"Not a word."

The reporter, crestfallen, started to walk out past the table where Lambert Wardell sat answering Corneel's mail. As he reached the doorway, Corneel relented, and called after him:

"Say, sonny, lookahere. Let me give ye a word of advice. Pay ready money for everything ye buy, and never sell anything ye don't own. Good morning, sonny."

But if he wasn't talking, he was acting — or, rather, preparing to act. In that initial swirl of failures he saw several of the brokerage houses he employed go under — Dick Schell's, Jake Little's — but he stood aloof. He had no intention of being caught up in the whirlpool, himself, and engulfed with the rest of the ruined. What spare capital he could raise went to support those whose positions were basically sound; he'd waste no money on any man, however much he liked him, unless he was certain the man could be saved. Money expended for sentiment was money flung haphazard into the whirlpool.

Level-headed, clear-eyed, he saw the Union Trust, the Bank of the Commonwealth, the National Trust, Henry Clews and Company and a score of reputable brokerage houses in New York City suspend. He saw the blight overrunning the whole country. He saw Gould's raid on Western Union, one of the immediate contributory causes of the panic, reach a point where the stock couldn't be sold at 45, half its value, and Gould, himself, temporarily frightened by the consequences of protracted short-selling. He saw the Stock Exchange closed *sine die* on the twentieth, in a frantic attempt to stop the *débâcle*, which continued to spread notwithstanding, an inchoate, amorphous thing sired by Fear on Ignorance. He saw the Exchange reopened on the thirtieth, and an unbroken stream of failures resumed.

Those first two weeks of October took the hearts out of iron-willed men who had kept their nerve through all the turmoil of September. It seemed to most people that the country was tobogganing to destruction. But Corneel detected signs of improvement. The most obvious indication on the bright side was a diminution in the numbers of failures. True, business was dreadfully depressed, stores empty, sales dwindled to almost nothing. But this, he knew, was inevitable. Panics, which came in cycles, moved through cycles, themselves. First, the wrecking of securities' values; next, the reaction on dealers in securities and credit; last, the consequent prostration of business. Conditions seemed to be at their worst. Therefore, the right fillip at the right time would start the pendulum moving slowly in the opposite direction.

On October 14, there was a wild, crazy market, marked by heavy selling stimulated by another Bear raid, under Gould's leadership, upon Western Union. This stock, which had climbed back to a figure approximating its normal value, was abruptly depressed again to 49. A few more failures were announced, and men went home that night distraught and uneasy. Would the panic never end? Was anyone safe? Had they lasted through four weeks of hell for nothing? If there was any power in thought, Jay Gould must have writhed in his bed that night, for millions damned him, husbands to wives, mothers to children, the religious to their God. He loomed over broad America, a little, pasty, bearded man, nervous, shifty-eyed, forever fidgeting with his fingers, the incarnation of Evil. Corneel, who stood across from him, old, gaunt, flint-hearted, was seldom in the thoughts of the common folk, and was unconcerned for that. Like Gould, he fought for his own hand, but his hand was the country's hand. If Gould represented Evil, Destruction, Misrule, he represented Progress, Order, Justice. Or you might say that he was the spirit incarnate of California's gold. He was Property. Let a sneaky rat of a gambler steal the millions he had piled up to perpetuate a dynasty under his name? Not by a jugful!

On October 15, he judged the moment had arrived to strike back, and he struck — in his own way. It was announced that the New York Central was paying $3,600,000 in dividends. Not much as we regard money. Not a great deal in that day. But it came at a time when dividends were being passed, and when railroads were peculiarly discredited as investments. And here was the New York Central finding the cash to meet its stockholders' needs.

There was a prompt reaction. Van Derbilt's all right, men said. The Commodore's safe. Yes, and his road. Guess things 'll be easier.

There were more failures, and few dividends were paid. Millions of men were out of work, and that winter the poor must be fed by charity. But the awful pall of fear which had oppressed the nation was cast aside.

Men could hope. The ruined set themselves to building anew. Business lifted a bludgeoned head. Corneel furnished an example. He launched a campaign to secure from the Legislature a charter for a Grand Central Depot on Forty-second Street, in New York City, with a wide area for trainyards and the use of a cut in Park Avenue to Harlem. Next year he was granted it. Quite typically, he saw to it that there was included in the charter a provision "allowing" the city to contribute one-half of the expense of the cut. Wasn't it a civic improvement? Wasn't it to the city's advantage to remove the trains from the streets? Very well, then, let the city pay its share. The contracts would foot up to $6,500,000, and that, with the depot building, would supply work for idle laborers.

Intelligently selfish!

IV

THE Shadow lowered nearer, but Corneel refused to be daunted by it. He was as tenacious of life as of property. Dreading death, he didn't fear it. Rather, he challenged its inevitable might. Take me, if ye kin ketch me, he said in effect, and cudgeled his will to resist the processes of dissolution. He *wanted* so to live. He didn't like to think of the day when his bleak frown would no longer quell a mutinous director, when another owner's hand would rub the sleek flanks of his trotters or tool Postboy or Mountaineer through the new driveways in Central Park, when his favorite chair on the hotel porch at Saratoga would be pointed out to the curious. Yes'm, that there's the very chair Commodore Van Derbilt used to sit in. But he wasn't afraid of that day's dawning. Not he! He'd simply fight to hold it off as long as he could — because it was his way to fight. If a thing was worth havin' it was worth keepin'. And life had been so rich, so full of experience. He hated to think of letting it slip through his fingers, those long, bony fingers, bristling with faded yellow hairs, which had seldom relaxed their clutch upon anything.

Thinking on the subject, and with his young wife and Dr. Deems ready to spur his inward scrutiny, he became mildly religious. He didn't go to church, as did eighty per cent of Americans in that churchgoing era, but he liked to hear and participate in religious discussions at home. His manners were less brusque, his speech less rough. He was more careful of himself than in the days of his heedless vitality, adjusting his routine to comply with Dr. Linsley's advice. Rising early, he'd walk around the block to his office in Fourth Street, run through his mail, receive callers and settle pending questions. At eleven he'd go to the stable, examine his trotters and discuss their needs with the hostlers. Then home to midday dinner. After dinner perhaps a nap, but sooner or later, if the weather was pleasant, a drive, handling the ribbons himself. At least half his evenings were spent at home, but whether home or out he played whist. It was his one relaxation. Of books he knew nothing at all, except for the dog-eared copy of *Pilgrim's Progress*, which his wife had given him. Pictures he regarded with indifference. Polite chit-chat bored him.

More than ever he was an institution, disliked and envied by some, admired and respected by others. His authority was legendary. He was reputed to be more powerful than was actually the case. Gruffly discourteous to those from whom he withheld his friendship, gruffly jovial with those he accepted. When Chauncey M. Depew, a young lawyer he had employed on the New York Central's legal work, was offered a nomination for governor, Corneel rapped at him curtly: "Stick to railroads, young man. Railroads are the career for young men. Ye'll never git anywhere in politics. Don't be a damn fool." Depew accepted the advice, and never had cause to regret it.

His simplicity was what impressed people most. He didn't put on any lugs. He made little or no attempt to reform his uncouth, illiterate speech, and criticisms of it by his wife or children only aroused his anger. He was, in all things, absolutely natural, without self-consciousness. Whatever he did, he did because it seemed best to him. Whatever he thought, he was inclined to say. It was the same in his business. One room, sparsely furnished, sufficed for his transactions; for staff he had Lambert Wardell and a boy. He would receive anyone who called there, but for long-winded or footless callers he had no patience. Git to the p'int, Mister. What? What? You said that before. All right, all right. I understand. No, I cain't talk to ye any longer. I'm a busy man. Good mornin'.

Sir Henry Holland, Queen Victoria's surgeon, was taken to call on him by Thurlow Weed. After the introductory remarks Sir Henry surveyed the bare Fourth Street office, and said:

"I should like, if you will permit me, sir, to see your bureaus of affairs."

"What bureaus?" asked Corneel, puzzled — bureaus, to him, were articles of bedroom furniture.

"Your departments of business," explained Holland. "Where do you conduct your affairs?"

"There," answered Corneel, pointing to the office boy sitting at a plain table at the opposite end of the room.

Mr. Weed intervened with a laugh.

"The rest is in the Commodore's head," he said. "But come, Commodore, pull out your business drawer for Sir Henry. Show him your materials for work."

Corneel complied, smiling slightly, and Sir Henry looked over his shoulder at a checkbook and a box of cigars.

He was never much of a hand at keeping elaborate

books or records. Many transactions he carried in his memory, which was efficient in all matters of detail. Correspondence, especially, he abhorred. He refused to read a letter over a page in length, and his form of answering a communication was to toss it to Wardell with a brief direction: "Tell the damn fool I wanted money from him, not soft soap, Lambert. And don't ye wrap it up too purty, neither." But he could, if occasion required, compose a very terse, well-expressed letter; his note to Morgan and Garrison declaring war over the Nicaragua Transit is a classic of its kind. Nobody was a surer judge of men than he; he read faces as a scholar reads books, and with the same speculative enthusiasm.

It is odd that Weed and Holland happened to see a checkbook in his desk, for one of his marked idiosyncrasies was a custom of writing checks on half-sheets of plain paper; his banks were all used to this form, and were instructed to honor nothing else. There is a story of a man who came to him for a loan of $27,000 to swing a rational proposition. Corneel had every intention of granting the loan, but the man was inclined to take his case for granted, and Corneel resolved to toll him on a mite.

"See here, Commodore," exclaimed the would-be borrower. "It's only $27,000."

"That's a heap of money, $27,000," rejoined Corneel doubtfully.

"Nonsense, all you have to do is write me out a check for it."

"Think so?"

"Of course! Here's a blank check. I'll fill it in, and you sign."

"Well, well, it does seem easy, don't it?" assented Corneel, scratching a bold "Cornelius Van Derbilt" at the bottom of the proffered check.

The man burst in upon him next day, aggrieved and irate.

"The bank won't pay your check, Commodore. They say it ain't good."

"What check?" inquired Corneel, a twinkle in his ordinarily frosty eyes.

"Why, that check for $27,000 you —"

"Humph," grunted Corneel. "Thought ye said all I had to do was write a check to git ye that money?"

"Yes — I know — That's true, but —"

"'Tain't so easy as ye figgered, hey? Here, try this."

And he scrawled an order to pay $27,000 on one of the little half-sheets of paper always ready on his desk.

The stories told about him were innumerable and largely apocryphal. He was represented as stingy, mean-spirited, deceitful. Any of these indictments could be proven technically, yet he was not the man they would indicate him to be. His disposition to shave personal expenditures was merely a relic of the earlier years when he sacrificed his own and Sophia's health and the comfort of their children to amass the capital he required to establish himself. There is nothing funny in his answer to Dr. Linsley's prescription of a pint of champagne a day for his dyspepsy: "Oh, no, doctor, I cain't afford champagne! Won't sody-water do?" That was the instinctive reaction of a mind bred in the traditions of poverty and self-denial. Money, to Corneel, didn't connote luxury; it was power, a means to an end. It mustn't be abused or wasted.

Mean-spirited? Deceitful? Corneel's history presents fewer openings for such aspersions than almost any American's of the period which saw capital slowly working toward a position of arrogant authority in national affairs. There was nothing mean-spirited in his conceptions of financial or industrial coups. Invariably, he adopted the broad viewpoint. And he was certainly not deceitful as were Drew and Gould. He didn't trap opponents by circulating fake tips or welch on his commitments when he was caught short. Not a lovable man. Not a great-hearted man. A man who trampled ruthlessly upon all opposition, who had no spark of chivalry. But a man whose ambition was to build up, not to tear down. According to his own standards, an honorable man. And always, a fighter: fighting for steamboats, fighting for railroads, fighting for life.

V

He aged rapidly after eighty. The responsibilities of that dreadful year '73 sapped reserves which might have carried him further. He lay down oftener, was seen less frequently on the Park roads and trotting tracks. But he was never acquiescent. His battered, craggy head was lifted more proudly than ever. He remained assertive and confident. If he looked back over his shoulder at the Shadow there was nothing furtive in his manner. He recognized it — and refused to bow to it. His chief concern was over his family's reception of his will. Again and again he spoke of this.

"Dan'l," he'd say to his son-in-law, Daniel Allen, Ethelinda's husband, "there's goin' to be hell to pay when I die."

And to Billy, savagely admonitory:

"Bill, I'm leavin' ye close to $90,000,000."

"Yes, father," answered Billy, neither affirmatively nor inquisitively.

"Know what it means?"

"Yes, father."

"The devil ye do! What ye think the others are agoin' to say?"

"What can they say, father?"

"Wisht I knew," Corneel admitted, almost wistfully. "There'll only be 'bout $15,000,000 to divide among the lot of 'em. I jest hitched a new codicil on

for your boy, Neeley. He'll git five millions. A good boy
— credit to the name."

"I'm glad you think so, father."

Corneel ruminated a moment.

"Main thing is to keep up the name, Bill," he continued. "I've made it stand for something. Now, you
and Neeley and the rest have got to keep it goin'.
Keep the money together, hey? Keep the Central our
road."

"Yes, father."

"Wisht I knew what the gals 'd do," reflected Corneel. "And there's that no-account feller that disgraces
my name."

"I don't see as any of them could do anything
troublesome, father," said Billy in his flat, unemotional
voice.

"Huh, ye never kin tell. Ye got a great responsibility
on ye, Bill. I want ye to carry out that will faithfully."

"You can rely on me, father."

"Keep the money together. Keep up the name,
hey?"

"Yes, father."

If Corneel had been able to foresee the future of
those millions would he have acted differently? If he
had been able to read the black headlines and columns
of spiteful family gossip and bickering that attended the
Vanderbilt Will Trial a couple of years later would he
have added other codicils besides the one registering
his pride in the grandson who bore his name? If he
had seen the dispersion of his millions as the family
increased in numbers would he have recognized the

futility of attempting to erect a financial dynasty of principalities and dukedoms under one imperial authority? My guess is that he wouldn't have altered his purpose. He'd no more bow to posterity than he would to the Shadow.

VI

On May 10, 1876, Corneel was taken suddenly, desperately, ill. The news spread rapidly downtown; it was reported that he was dying, and men laid their heads together and speculated on what would happen in the market. A. T. Stewart and the second John Jacob Astor had died recently, and the Commodore's passing would remove from the stage within the space of a few months the three richest men in the country. There was a vague, premonitory flicker of apprehension in the day's trading.

Newsboys ran through the streets, shouting the tidings. The shrill yelp — "Commodore Van Derbilt dyin'! Old fy-nanseer very ill!" — rose from the sidewalk beneath the window of his room, and he cursed irascibly as he groaned with pain. Faithful Dr. Linsley worked over him, and other physicians assisted. His will-power reacted savagely against the inroads of the digestive upset; in the night he rallied, and by morning was out of danger. Sitting up in bed, he heard the doorbell ring downstairs, and demanded who it was. They told him a newspaper reporter had called to inquire after him.

"I'll answer the wuthless rascal," he roared, and for all their restraining efforts, got himself out of bed and staggered to the balustrade of the stairs.

"Come to see me, young feller? Well, here I am. I'm Commodore Van Derbilt, and I ain't dyin'. The doctor says I'm 'bout well. But if I was dyin' I'd have strength enough to knock all this abuse down your lyin' throat and give the undertaker another job."

His very belligerence pulled him up to convalescence; but he continued too weak to travel, and the summer heat of New York undermined his strength. On August 3, he had a relapse, and for some minutes it was thought that he was dead; but again he rallied, dragging himself by strength of will from under the nimbus of the Shadow. Organically, he had gone to pieces; his heart was affected; his digestion was almost paralyzed. Still, he fought on. He *wouldn't* die! And he didn't.

The cool weather of fall revived him. He sat up, received company, made pretense of following market operations, was eager to hear of his railroads. But with the first touch of winter he began to sink, and this time he knew he had reached the end of his resources. All the ferocious energy, the last remnants of that seemingly inexhaustible well of vitality which had carried him through hardships sufficient to kill a dozen ordinary men, had been expended. The Shadow hung over him now, close; sometimes it was as if a cool breath touched his neck or blew upon his eyelids. He was surprised to discover that he didn't mind its nearness; he was curious as to what might lie behind it. His thoughts, drifting aimlessly back and forth across the vista of his memories, turned to those who had preceded him.

Religion, as his wife and Dr. Deems taught it, had weaned him finally from spiritualism. He was boyishly ashamed of the credence he had placed in cabinet spooks, but — Well, mebbe he hadn't really spoke to Ma. Then ag'in mebbe he had. He was aware, these last days, of unseen presences behind the faces that hovered around his pillow. He had a feeling of comfort, of willingness; for the first time in his life he succumbed to a lassitude that was grateful to his gaunt limbs. If he hadn't spoke to Ma, would he speak to her presently, when — when — He remembered, as with a little jerk, Sophia's worn features. Wherever Ma was he guessed Sophia'd be. And George. Ma'd see to that. Matter of fact, she'd see to him, too. No use worryin' — worritin', Ma used to say. Folks laughed at ye if ye talked thataway nowadays — laughed at him when they thought he wasn't watchin'. But it didn't hurt. Jest seemed kind of funny, now. Nothin' hurt — or mattered.

Christmas came, Christmas of '76, and messages of greeting poured into Washington Place. It had been an eventful year, the centenary of freedom. Men were doing strange things with this force they called electricity. Some people said it would supplant steam as a motive power. Corneel had asked about it, but when the men who studied it admitted they didn't know what it was, he was inclined to scepticism. However, it was interesting. He was glad to have lived into such interesting times. He noticed, in the excitement of the holidays, that the Shadow seemed to have lifted slightly, and for a day or so he felt light-hearted; but then he realized his foolishness, and chuckled, in his quiet, grim way, to himself. Joke was on him, b'God. Hold on, he mustn't cuss. Jesus was his friend, Deems said. Frank believed it, too. Call on Jesus, they said.

Jesus was better 'n spooks. Sounded damn' reasonable. But he mustn't cuss. 'Twasn't fittin', Frank said. A smart woman. Took a sight of managin', she did.

New Year's Day followed Christmas, and Corneel had a thrill of satisfaction. He'd lasted into another year, anyhow. Born in 1794, and here it was 1877! From the periauger to steam — and electricity. Billy said they was talkin' over wires. What 'd they be doin' next? Lying wakeful at night, he'd speculate. He recalled New York as he had known it, the sleepy, red-brick town, huddled around the Battery, with farms stretching up to Harlem. And look at it, now! Huh, anything could happen.

On January 3, he was so well that he sat up, and talked to his callers, but after he returned to bed that night he felt queer. Frank came hastily, Billy and the gals and their husbands. Linsley was there, and three or four more doctors. Deems entered toward morning, quiet-footed, deferential. The clergyman talked to Mrs. Crawford, Frank's mother, standing by the bedfoot, and Corneel beckoned to them weakly.

"Sing," he whispered. "Hymn."

Mrs. Crawford raised her voice, and one by one the rest joined in. "Come, ye Sinners, poor and needy," they sang, and when he signed for more, "Nearer, My God, to Thee" and "Show Pity, Lord." He asked Dr. Deems to pray, listening avidly as the words fell from the clergyman's lips.

"That's a good prayer," he murmured.

His fingers groped out, and fastened upon Deems's hand.

"I'll never give up trust in Jesus," he quavered. "How could I let that go?"

The Shadow settled over him like a blanket, cool, soothing, pleasantly restful. Rest, that was what he needed. A feller got so damned tired.

INDEX

338 INDEX

COSIMO is an innovative publisher of books and publications that inspire, inform and engage readers worldwide. Our titles are drawn from a range of subjects including health, business, philosophy, history, science and sacred texts. We specialize in using print-on-demand technology (POD), making it possible to publish books for both general and specialized audiences and to keep books in print indefinitely. With POD technology new titles can reach their audiences faster and more efficiently than with traditional publishing.

> ➤ **Permanent Availability:** Our books & publications never go out-of-print.

> ➤ **Global Availability:** Our books are always available online at popular retailers and can be ordered from your favorite local bookstore.

COSIMO CLASSICS brings to life unique, rare, out-of-print classics representing subjects as diverse as *Alternative Health, Business and Economics, Eastern Philosophy, Personal Growth, Mythology, Philosophy, Sacred Texts, Science, Spirituality* and much more!

COSIMO-on-DEMAND publishes your books, publications and reports. If you are an Author, part of an Organization, or a Benefactor with a publishing project and would like to bring books back into print, publish new books fast and effectively, would like your publications, books, training guides, and conference reports to be made available to your members and wider audiences around the world, we can assist you with your publishing needs.

Visit our website at www.cosimobooks.com to learn more about Cosimo, browse our catalog, take part in surveys or campaigns, and sign-up for our newsletter.

And if you wish please drop us a line at info@cosimobooks.com. We look forward to hearing from you.

CPSIA information can be obtained at www.ICGtesting.com
Printed in the USA
LVOW081531190112

264655LV00001B/95/A